Lonesome Cowgirls
and Honky-Tonk Angels

Lonesome Cowgirls and Honky-Tonk Angels

The Women of Barn Dance Radio

Kristine M. McCusker

University of Illinois Press
Urbana and Chicago

Music in American Life / *A list of books in the series appears at the end of this book.*

Library of Congress Cataloging-in-Publication Data

McCusker, Kristine M.
Lonesome cowgirls and honky-tonk angels : the women
of barn dance radio / Kristine M. McCusker.
p. cm. – (Music in American life)
Includes bibliographical references (p.   ) and index.
ISBN-13: 978-0-252-03316-2 (cloth : alk. paper)
ISBN-10: 0-252-03316-7 (cloth : alk. paper)
ISBN-13: 978-0-252-07524-7 (pbk. : alk. paper)
ISBN-10: 0-252-07524-2 (pbk. : alk. paper)
1. Women country musicians–United States.
2. Country music–History and criticism.
3. Radio and music–United States.
I. Title.
ML3524.M347   2008
781.642082'0973–dc22   2007035937

For Larry

and in loving memory

of Bob McCusker

Contents

Illustrations follow page 102

Acknowledgments

When asked how I chose this topic, I usually tell this story: growing up in suburban San Francisco in the late 1960s, it was our family tradition that each night, my mother, Nancy, would bathe my sisters and me while my dad, Bob, entertained us with his guitar. We would then spend the evening singing old folk songs (some of which appear in this text) and contemporary favorites. What began as a family gathering later became my newest hobby; music lessons, especially voice lessons, filled my time during elementary, junior high, and high school. We also started an amateur band called Bob and the Girls, which we later renamed the Non-Nuclear Family Singers once we added my husband and step-brother. The first solo album my dad and I recorded was done my first semester of graduate school and was appropriately titled *Songs My Father Sang Me in the Bathtub*. For these memories and for the path they set me on, I thank my mom and dad.

The training I received in graduate school turned what was once bath-time fun into professional research I am quite proud of. At the University of Kansas, I want to thank Bill Tuttle and Angel Kwolek-Folland, who suggested this topic to me. I also want to thank dear friends at KU, especially Brian Dirck, who heard more than they wanted to about early country music radio. At Indiana University, I thank Steven M. Stowe and Wendy Gamber, who were first-rate advisors, and John Bodnar for his terrific evaluation of the original research. Thank you, too, to Indiana's graduate office for its support of the initial research.

Archivists at the following places made my task in writing this book much easier: the Franklin and Eleanor Roosevelt Institute, the Country Music Hall of Fame, the Marr Sound Archives, the State Historical Society of Wisconsin, the Museum of Broadcast Communication, the Southern Folklife Collection at the University of North Carolina, the Nashville Public Library, the National Broadcasting Corporation, Mary Dean Wolfe (who gave me access to her late husband Charles's papers), and the Bayer Corporation, which allowed me free access to the Miles Laboratories Papers. The Roosevelt Institute was all the more helpful because of its financial assistance. I must thank, above all, Harry Rice at the Southern Appalachian Archives and Brenda Colladay at the Grand Ole Opry for their kindness, for their knowledge of their collections, and for their willingness to support my research. I gratefully acknowledge *American Studies, Southern Folklore,* the University Press of Mississippi, and the University Press of Kentucky for their willingness to let me publish in this book portions of articles written for them.

Ann Lair Henderson and Lily May Ledford's granddaughter Carri Norris both graciously spoke to me about their families. Rose Lee Maphis was a gem to interview. She spoke candidly for six hours, sang to me, and then taught me to make that most southern of drinks, sweet tea. Mary Ann Cateforis gave me *National Barn Dance* items from her parents' collection and Eunice Puzzo recalled her first trip to the *National Barn Dance* for me. Judy McCulloh lived up to her gracious reputation while Laurie Matheson proved to be an outstanding replacement. I am particularly thankful for Laurie's ability to turn manuscripts around so quickly and for being supportive of her authors. This is also a much-improved manuscript thanks to the book's reviewers, but I am especially grateful to Ellen Wright, who made this book a much more readable one.

Other colleagues have been supportive of me and my research. They include Diane Pecknold, Michael Bertrand, and the other authors associated with *A Boy Named Sue* as well as the scholars who are regulars at the International Country Music Conference, so ably run each year by James Akenson and the late Charles Wolfe. Participants at other conferences, especially the Berkshire Conference on the History of Women, were also helpful.

This book is the sixth book either published or under contract that was supported in substantial ways by my colleagues in the MTSU Women's Work Group. It bears, especially, the mark of Mary Hoffschwelle's keen eye. The former chair of MTSU's history department, Thad Smith, was a true gentleman, always able to find money even in a scarce funding environment to complete this project. I want to thank other friends and colleagues who have made this a better manuscript including John Dougan, Sally LeCroix, Jeanmarie Martin, and Cheryl Floyd. I love teaching at Middle Tennessee State University because of the smart, kind students, both undergraduate and graduate, whom I am honored to teach each semester. I thank, too, Middle Tennessee State's graduate office for its meaningful support of my work since I have been a professor here.

I am surrounded by a group of women who lift me up when I am down and who revel in my successes with me. This book is a good one because they make me a better person. They are Sherri Barbee (and family), Andrea Broxton, Pidge Cash, Beth Cateforis (and David and Alex), Sally Palmer (and family), Ellen Garrison, Jan Schneider, Jane Smith, and the grande dame of them all, Jo Wintker. Christina Madl made me look good even at my worst. I wish Sarah Broxton, Bob and Virginia Clirehue, Shelli Griffiths, and, most especially, Violet Bradbury and Doris McCusker could have lived long enough to see this book come to fruition as an example of their faith in me.

My daughters, Katie Lou McCusker and Grace Puzzo, make me laugh and love harder than any two people have the right to. They also could not have cared less about this project, which made home a sanctuary for me. My husband, Larry Puzzo, has done everything but actually write the words that appear here: he did more than his share of parenting, cleaned, cooked, copied in archives, copyedited page proofs, and helped with the multiple other tasks associated with finishing this book. It has been a hell of a ride, my love, and I am glad you have been on it with me.

Finally, one of my proudest moments was reading an early version of these acknowledgments to my dad (as he was dying from lung cancer) and my stepmom Cindy (who cared so well for my dad during his final illness). Like any good Irish Catholic storyteller, my dad taught me how to tell a good story, whether it was through music or the written or spoken word. I hope this book is lasting evidence that those lessons took. Thanks, Dad.

INTRODUCTION

Women, the Barn Dance Radio Genre,
and the Roots of the Country and
Western Music Industry

"I think the most distasteful thing of all," Kentuckian Lily May
Ledford wrote in her autobiography, "was learning to make work of my
music."[1] But make work of it she did, portraying the "banjo pickin' girl"
on barn dance radio programs in Chicago, Cincinnati, and Renfro Valley,
Kentucky, from 1936 to 1957. Selling her traditional music was distasteful to Ledford because she believed in its inherent authenticity. But she
learned that the mountain values she portrayed on stage provided an
image of stability for her fans in an otherwise chaotic, terrifying world.
She also learned that radio work was a good job in tough economic times.
It was for these reasons that, in making work of her music, Ledford wrote,
"I enjoyed it much of the time tho." Indeed, she enjoyed it so much the
epitaph on her grave reads "banjo pickin' girl."[2]

Making work of her music may have been distasteful, but Lily May
Ledford eventually became so popular that she played for British royalty
and with musical luminaries like Woody Guthrie and Burl Ives. And it was
barn dance radio—a genre based on a rural ritual, the Saturday night
dance party—that made her popular. In turn, she and her female peers
helped shape one of the most important radio genres, the forerunner
of the commercial country and western industry, not only in terms of

its structure but also its form and content. On these new stages in the 1920s, 1930s, and 1940s, Ledford and her female peers sold barn dances as remnants of an authentic past: their music was a work of vernacular (common, traditional) art kept safe and secure by the generations of Southern mountain and Western women who had preceded them. They promised stability and comfort in an era when both seemed lacking, and they were wildly successful. During the dark and gloomy Great Depression or the terrifying days of a world war, a banjo pickin' girl who sang old English ballads and who had a deceptively simple picking style called clawhammer proclaimed that a safe and secure world was just around the corner. It was these performances—rendered in old theatrical tricks made modern by the radio—that brought an obscure group of radio programs out of the margins and tied them together into a national business, out of which the modern country and western music industry later emerged.

In this study, I examine the lives of seven women whose hard work and musical talent helped define and then spread barn dance radio nationwide. Some were stars, some were not, but all lived and transformed their performances in response to barn dance radio's potential and limits. New sources (the John Lair and Bradley Kincaid Papers, the Bayer Archives, the Franklin and Eleanor Roosevelt Papers, the Sarah Colley Cannon interview tapes, and the NBC Papers); new scholarship, particularly women's history and radio studies; and a pretty good story have certainly dictated which women appear here, but each woman's biography illuminates certain common themes that a focus on the men of country music does not. The argument here breaks away from common assumptions that country and western music's women were important only in forging a place for themselves in a male-dominated industry. Instead, I highlight themes that stress women's essential roles in creating the barn dance radio genre and, later, the modern country and western industry, indeed, how their characters helped build the genre and then helped it transform in response to historical trends. In no way am I suggesting that women should supplant men in country music histories; instead, I suggest more balance and a modern scholarly assessment should be part of country and western music's larger narrative.

What are these common themes? First, barn dance radio inherited vaudeville's assumption that women needed to be onstage and in the audience in order for shows to be successful. Performers, broadcasters, advertisers, and audiences then wielded female images—especially the mountain woman and cowgirl—to mark important changes on stage.

These images did not necessarily promote a working-class rusticity on stage; in fact, female performers expose a substantial middle-class influence on the air, one that was far more dominant than scholars have credited.[3] Moreover, this book suggests that we do not know who listened to barn dances because broadcasters themselves did not know. They responded to that lack of knowledge by incorporating their own assumptions regarding women onto the stage.

A second theme is the way rural imagery and performances provided cover for what were remarkably modern business practices. Even as they sold themselves as relics from the past, radio women prominently displayed advertising, a desire to control consumer behavior, and other decidedly up-to-date business tactics designed to entertain contemporary audiences and entice them to spend scarce dollars. The cowgirls and sentimental mothers portrayed on the radio may have seemed old-timey and homespun, but they were remarkably modern. Third, women's performances of old-time music (as many called it) served multiple purposes beyond building a new music industry. For some eager to rejuvenate a national culture undermined (they thought) by 1920s commercial media (such as jazz), barn dance radio's women promoted a more wholesome and moral national culture. For others, especially Franklin Delano Roosevelt and the American military, women helped create a unifying national identity that readied diverse groups of Americans to fight World War II. Fourth, performers walked a minefield between portraying rural images on stage and the modern business routines that supported them. This is what made musical work in part so distasteful to Lily May Ledford. Some performers were able to devise ingenious practices to manage that minefield, however. One woman might create multiple characters that catered to every taste and whim. Others changed with the times, recognizing that a skilled worker was a flexible one who learned new music for new radio friends on stage and off.

After a description of the roots of barn dance radio in vaudeville, "local color" writers, and new technology, seven women—Jeanne Muenich, Lulu Belle Wiseman, the Girls of the Golden West, Lily May Ledford, Sarah Colley Cannon (better known as Minnie Pearl), and Rose Lee Maphis—appear in a loose chronology that exhibits these common themes. The "Coda" features country and western music star Loretta Lynn and the ways her career built on her barn dance predecessors' successes and mistakes. This "collective biography" approach is, in some ways, awkward since these women, like all historical subjects, did not live their lives in names and dates. Given the overlap in the subjects' lives, the chronology also seems to start over in each chapter; Lily May Ledford's performance for the king and queen of England in June 1939, is essential to understanding barn dance stars' importance to constructing American national identity in the prewar era, but she was born in 1917 and therefore her story starts there. This collective biography approach will seem familiar to those who have read other country music studies in which multiple biographical snippets are used to plug a larger idea.[4] Those snippets have been effective because country music is about the real lives of real people, and songs and musical innovations need those real people to sing them. My approach is different in that I systematically examine only one or two women's lives in each chapter to see how their experiences reflect larger, evolving trends on stage.

As much as possible, I have allowed the women to speak for themselves, to introduce their lives and tell their stories because their words have either been erased from country music history or have been claimed as feminist (in other words, odd, rare, not normal) by previous scholars.[5] I want readers to hear them sing and speak in order to rectify this glaring problem, but using their words also makes this an awkward history at points. Jeanne Muenich's words do not exist, and I have had to use other women's experiences to fill out an otherwise invisible story. In other instances, the words show the foibles of their creator. Broadcaster John Lair, for example, typed his own scripts, and his poor typing skills are apparent throughout. His use of a constructed Southern dialect in those scripts may also hamper easy comprehension.

This study is also different from studies of country and western women like Mary Bufwack and Robert Oermann's *Finding Her Voice,* an encyclopedic work that first appeared in 1993.[6] The authors' focus was appropriate for the time since there was little or no work at that point on women in the industry. Who, they asked, were the women who sang country music? I ask a different question now: why were those women on stage and what was their effect on radio and, later, in the country and western industry? Answering this question requires me to use the tools of various scholarly trades. From history, which evaluates changes in culture and media over time, I explore the events, feelings, and motivations that caused Americans to listen to certain kinds of music. From ethnomusicology, which examines the ways that people make music as a social group, I describe how music was made from instrumental choices, lyrics, and stage performances and then presented to an audience that history had made eager to hear it. Where historical trend meets musical production, I argue, is a process out of which emerged a revolution in taste and desire in the interwar period.

To highlight the interaction between a performer and her audience, between history and music, audience reaction has been woven into the narrative as much as possible to see how this revolution affected what people listened to and why. What made banjo pickin' girls special and important was their explicit interaction with their audience and their interpretation of its fears, dreams, and wishes. Barn dance radio's listeners were all but on stage when Lily May Ledford made work of her music. That interaction had a significant effect on the listeners, on radio during years of dynamic change, and on American culture in the 1920s, 1930s and 1940s.

"Family Songs of Surpassing Sweetness"

Vaudeville, Appalachia,
Technology, and the Emergence
of Barn Dance Radio

Let me begin this tale by describing three remarkable women who gave different kinds of performances, each important to the development of barn dance radio. The incomparable Sarah Bernhardt is the seemingly odd first example. The legendary French actress came to America for the first time in 1880 and performed dramatic plays in cities across the nation, playing at what one historian called "highbrow affairs."[1] Her financial success meant more tours, and by 1912, Bernhardt began performing on more middlebrow stages (like vaudeville) where she earned $7,000 per week and where her audience (when she visited Kansas City) included a young Harry Truman.[2] Her popularity and passionate excesses were so famous that young girls like Sarah Colley (later known as Minnie Pearl) dreamed of their own passionate excesses on stage, of being able to "out-Bernhardt Bernhardt," as Colley recalled.[3]

While Sarah Bernhardt became both a household name and a career model for young girls, Tennessean Emma Bell Miles used her "local color" writing to scratch out a living from the Appalachian mountains. At once a connoisseur of Appalachian culture and its prisoner, Miles used commonly held assumptions about the mountain South—that it was a pure pristine area, unaffected by time or industry—to sell articles about indigenous music, poetry, and paintings of local plants and animals.[4] The money she earned contributed substantially to her family's fragile economy but did not save her: she died in 1919 from tuberculosis at age forty.

Emma Bell Miles lived a short, hard life in the Appalachian mountains. Grace Wilson, on the other hand, lived an easier one, parlaying her early vaudeville experience into a long-lived career on a new technology— the radio—that repackaged fading theatrical techniques (and artists) for sale.[5] A former vaudevillian who was called "The Girl with a Million Friends," Wilson began appearing in 1924 on Chicago radio station WLS's Saturday night barn dance.[6] Her million friends, however, did not make Wilson the star of the program. It was her compatriot, Bradley Kincaid, "The Kentucky Mountain Boy with his Houn' Dog Guitar," who fans fawned over because he was able to take the practices Wilson and others transported to the stage in the 1920s and meld them with Miles's idealized descriptions of the mountain South for a popular audience.

As these three stories demonstrate, women were considered not only appropriate for the stage (defined broadly here) but even necessary, although their performances were defined in specific ways and circumscribed by the expectations of audience and management alike. Specifically, vaudeville defined which female characters were appropriate for the stage, local-color writers provided a vague chronology and a geographic region, and radio determined how the combination of the two would sound to listeners. Some of this story will be familiar to country music scholars, but here are incorporated new insights from vaudeville and radio scholars who have (separately) examined women's important influence on stage performance and transformations in technology. With these insights, I will describe the foundations of what would become the barn dance radio genre and later, the country and western industry.

❖ ❖ ❖

Barn dance radio built its reputation on familiarity, and nothing was more familiar to audiences than theatrical tricks dating back to Sarah Bernhardt and before. Bernhardt came to America just as theater was evolving from regional, working-class venues that were immigrant-friendly and predominately male into a national theatrical network with a heterogeneous audience. On her first American tour in 1880 and on subsequent tours, Bernhardt performed in that evolving theater world, one that exhibited new rules for performers, new locations, and, especially, new audiences who desired to be entertained. Her presence (and that of other women) was essential to making theater a viable art form and financially successful entertainment for the masses.

Theater had been the province of urban working-class men, and the rowdy performances by actors and audiences alike gave it a reputation for salacious and infamous behavior. Elite and middle-class Americans avoided theaters, choosing to stay home or to attend highbrow events like the symphony. But as the Industrial Revolution gave Americans more time for leisure in the late nineteenth century, theater entrepreneurs applied a kind of assembly-line mentality (a fixture of new industrial processes) to the stage, especially in their push for new customers. To counter old assumptions about theaters and their immorality, wrote historian M. Allison Kibler, entrepreneurs feminized them by putting women, Victorian symbols of respectability, on stage and in the audience to promise no untoward behavior would occur in their presence—or so entrepreneurs thought. Producers thus secured talent like Bernhardt to entice middle-class women into theaters, a decided difference from the early nineteenth century when those audience members would have been assumed to be prostitutes.[7] Those efforts eventually gave rise to a "national system of entertainment," one that presented similar entertainment to audiences in large and small theaters, and in big cities and small towns. Small rural towns like Marquette, Kansas (population 600), had their own "opera houses" where traveling vaudeville troupes appeared in shows they had performed in larger venues like Nashville, Tennessee's Ryman Theater. Audiences willingly paid from ten cents to two dollars for a ticket to see from two to six shows per day.[8] The national system had other consequences, too, namely making acting a viable profession. In 1870, 2,000 women declared their profession to be acting; in 1890, 10,000 made the same claim, constituting about 40 percent of all actors. By 1920, women like Sarah Bernhardt numbered nearly 20,000 nationwide.[9]

Women's presence may have helped secure a theater's respectability, but their presence also allowed diverse cultural tensions to be described, discussed, and then diffused (sometimes) on stage. In the late nineteenth and early twentieth centuries, many of those tensions were about the women themselves. Would actresses act demure like their middle-class counterparts, reflecting contemporary desire for women to be moral stewards of the home (and by extension, the theater), or would they demand spectators look at them? Would they focus on uplifting their audience or exhibit their bodies for audience titillation, possibly degrading them in the process? Or would they make fun of both? What would relationships between men and women be in an era when actresses like Bernhardt had stable, independent incomes?

These questions faced audiences in all theaters, including road shows, musical comedy, and legitimate theater, but they were particularly apparent on the most popular stage, vaudeville. Vaudeville was a new kind of theater that emphasized an eclectic content, and it was that eclecticism that made it possible to perform diverse issues. Each show included multiple fast-paced acts that mingled on stage before a star performer appeared. A typical show might include a dog act, a Swiss yodeler, a comedy team, a Hawaiian guitar act, a "singing baseball pitcher and a miniature drama," according to one 1921 program.[10] These were all acts that relied on visual cues to entertain their audiences; visual oddities like clarinet-playing Siamese twins were especially prominent on stage. All shows were centered on a "name" act, famous people like Bernhardt who had a unique personality or act that made their popularity the draw for the entire program.[11] Sarah Bernhardt's special talent, wrote historian Susan Glenn, was that she "aimed not only to attract but also to seduce her audiences. Body language and gesture contributed to that effect. Her smoldering gazes, her 'serpentine' undulations, her ability to arrange her slim figure into a curving 'spiral,' even her unusual habit of smiling on stage, made a Bernhardt performance into an erotically charged event. Writing in 1892, a New York critic captured this aspect of her stage persona when he claimed that 'Bernhardt's skill lies in portraying the abandonment of animal passion—the idiosyncrasies, the hysteria, the caprices, and the tragic denouements of illicit love.'"[12] For middle-class Americans who believed that passion was immoral and rigid control a sign of moral authority, Bernhardt's passionate performances must have been a sight to behold, a spectacle that allowed them to relax their severe demeanor, if only for a moment and in the darkness of a theater.[13]

Eclecticism meant not only an array of acts, but also a variety of characters. Stock characters like the comedienne, the sentimental mother, or the cowgirl provoked laughter, tears, and feelings of nobility, sometimes in the same act. Comediennes were especially popular in the fast-paced world of vaudeville, and many used their bodies—usually considered old or ugly, a joke in a world that praised the seductive allure of a Bernhardt—as a way to mock both themselves and Bernhardt. Performers like Sophie Tucker and Marie Dressler touted their ugliness and size (both were considered large women) as appropriate models of femininity, all with a wink and smile at audiences since they knew they parodied conventional womanhood. This caused audiences to laugh because the actresses preceding them had already established what a "real" woman was. By acting as parodies of womanhood, many assumed that comediennes eschewed conventional female roles, making them men. Vaudeville comedienne Kate Elinore suffered from this assumption. As historian M. Allison Kibler argued, "Kate Elinore's characters depict a woman's power to disrupt hierarchies . . . As opposed to the civilizing woman, the female clown rejects the feminine role, often triumphing over the femininity, class status, and acculturation associated with the civilizing woman."[14] Playing an Irish working-class mother, Elinore poked fun at the limited roles assigned to women, but her comedic role prompted some in her audience to accuse her of literally being a man.

The working-class drone, the fat woman, and the immigrant were common comedic characters, but another popular character was the rube, a rural migrant who, like the immigrant, made people laugh because of her inability to fit into an urban setting. In cities especially, rubes became a joke because their country ways seemed naive to the supposedly more modern and capable audiences. Elviry Weaver was one popular rube character who played stages with "The Weaver Brothers and Elviry" as "vaudeville hillbillies."[15] She later toured the country with her troupe of "Home Folks," which included future barn dance star Margaret Lillie, who performed as A'nt Idy on the Renfro Valley Barn Dance in the late 1930s and 1940s. The specifics of Elviry's act are gone, but it seems she evoked that rube naïveté on stage, performing for those who worried their own rural naïveté made them something to laugh at. In her hands, the stage became a place to diffuse those tensions and assure her audiences that no one was as incapable as she.

Comediennes might make audiences laugh, but the sentimental singer made them sob. Built on a common musical icon ethnomusicologists call the "sentimental mother," the sentimental singer referred to that Victorian idol, the deified mother who was the mistress of the home and the moral guide for men, a key character in moralizing the stage.[16] She was also part of a musical tradition called the "elegiac tradition," where a song or poem dramatized the writer's grief at the death of a loved one; in the hands of vaudevillians, the beloved icon came to personify children's separation from their mothers. When a female sentimental singer stood on stage, her intention was to provoke tears, to sing about some motherly act so that her audiences could recall the sacrifices of their own mothers for their children. Tragic consequences often accompanied mothers in songs like "I'll Be All Smiles Tonite," "Letter Edged in Black," or "Dear Mother, I'll Come Home Again."[17] In "Letter Edged in Black," the errant child receives a letter with news of the mother's death and her forgiveness of the child's misdeeds even as she draws her last breath:

> I was standing by my window yesterday morning,
> Without a thought of worry or of care,
> When I saw the postman coming down the pathway,
> With such a happy smile and jaunty air.
>
> Oh, he rang the bell and whistled while he waited,
> And then he said Good morning to you Jack,
> But he little knew the sorrow he had brought me,
> When he handed me a letter edged in black.
>
> Then with trembling hand I took the letter from him,
> I broke the seal and this is what it said.
> Come home my boy your poor father wants you
> Come home my boy, your mother's dead.
>
> O your Mother's words the last she ever uttered
> Were, Tell my boy I want him to come back!
> My eyes are blurred, my poor old heart is breaking,
> While I'm writing you this letter edged in black.[18]

Sentimental mothers may have invoked sadness, but audiences also demanded heroism and nobility, which was supplied by cowgirls who were pretty good at calf-roping and rifle work, too. Two prominent actresses, Annie Oakley's gun-toting antics and Mommie Gray's steadying hand, promised that nobility still existed in a mythic frontier world. Oakley worked with "Buffalo Bill's Wild West Show," a vaudeville Western show, and programs touted her riflework as "the pioneer of civilization, for it has gone hand in hand with the axe that cleared the forest, and with the family Bible and school book."[19] Gray followed in Oakley's theatrical footsteps (or boot steps) onto vaudeville stages. The daughter of a Kansas rancher, Mommie Gray and her husband Otto worked the vaudeville circuit as trick ropers and singers from 1924 to 1936. At once the skilled cowgirl and the sentimental mother, Mommie was the star attraction in the couple's act, singing famous nineteenth-century sentimental ballads such as "Bury Me on the Lone Prairie" and "Your Mother Still Prays for You, Jack" as well as doing rope tricks.[20]

Vaudeville's focus initially was on women's steadying moral hand (or at least a parody of it if the performer was a comedienne), and physical attractiveness counted, but only in implicit ways. When Broadway revues challenged vaudeville's popularity in the 1920s and 1930s, beauty became something more: a theatrical commodity and a skill. As historian Susan Glenn wrote, "something called 'beauty' was practically a form of talent, an aspect of feminine presence as highly prized as any other quality a woman might bring to the stage."[21] The work of producers like Florenz Ziegfeld, the Ziegfeld Follies and other Broadway revues rewarded what Glenn called the "Tired Business Man" (the middle-class man worn out from his day in the corporate world), displaying for him "nationally advertised legs": the exposure of women's bodies for viewing and consumption.[22] Long lines of scantily clad chorus girls stood onstage, displayed within opulent scenes and surrounded by consumer goods that made the viewer believe the women, too, were for sale—a reward, if you will, for a hard day's work. Ziegfeld became an expert in theatrical beauty, describing scientifically what a beautiful "girl" looked like, using rational figures to make beauty a rational commodity. The perfect girl was, he reported, "Height—Five feet five and a half inches. Weight—One hundred Twenty Five pounds. Foot size—five."[23] Broadway revues were still popular in the 1930s and traveled to various venues around the country, for example, Mrs. Florenz Ziegfeld's presentation of the "Ziegfeld Follies Glorifying the American Girl with Fanny Brice and Willie and Eugene Howard" at Nashville's Ryman Theater (future home of the *Grand Ole Opry*) in the mid-1930s.[24] Ziegfeld imitators came to Nashville, too. In classic Broadway revue style, Earl Carroll brought his "Earl Carroll Vanities" to the Ryman in the 1930s and showcased eight beautiful women "acquired by" Carroll. And like Ziegfeld, he touted himself as a kind of expert in beauty. The perfect girl in Carroll's show was five foot, seven and a half inches; she weighed 125 pounds, had thirty-five-inch hips, a twenty-five-inch waist, and appropriate measurements for ankles, thighs, bust, and wrists as well.[25] His measurements suggested, like Ziegfeld, that beauty was quantifiable, not some elusive, indefineable factor.

❧ ❧ ❧

These theatrical traditions—a belief in a national theater that required women both as moral characters and as something pretty to consume—formed the core of the barn dance radio genre. With the exception of the cowgirl (and then only generally), these traditions remained geographically and chronologically rootless, with little or no reference to a specific place or time. Local-color writers provided the time and place. Writers discovered Appalachia, or at least began to consider it a "strange land and peculiar people" in the late nineteenth century.[26] In what was more of an intellectual movement among middle-class writers and reformers, Appalachia's residents and their folkways became fodder for that ambivalent middle class made anxious by the changes wrought by the Industrial Revolution. Some were concerned by Appalachia's "otherness," its supposed backwardness in an age of progress as well as its potential drag on America's advancement toward a new, more civilized nation using the wheels of industrialization. That otherness distressed those especially influenced by the new science of eugenics, which attempted to turn cultural difference into biological fact. In the case of Appalachia, believers feared that mountaineers were weak links in the American race and needed to be reformed through missionary work to make the entire nation stronger. Popular culture would broadcast these views—first in movies, then on the radio—as the immoral hillbilly who was unable to read, hypersexual, unable to keep from fighting, and unable to refrain from alcohol.[27]

Others called Appalachians "contemporary ancestors" or the "folk," and lauded their supposed isolation from industrial manufacturing. Contemporary ancestors kept modern technology from corrupting Appalachia's music and other cultural material, considered remnants from America's colonial past.[28] The "folk" lived "primitive," preindustrial lives, and scholars romantically envisioned them, according to scholar Jane S. Becker, as flourishing "in simple societies not dominated by industrial organization and production; in such worlds, communications were presumably personal and informal, the community took care of its members, human and spiritual values reigned, and beauty and value lay in carefully crafting from raw goods the material necessities of everyday domestic life."[29] Contemporary ancestors promised that pure, unadulterated ideals of family and community from colonial times, of tradition itself, continued to exist. Their purity and community spirit seemed a counterpoint to the sterility and artifice of a modern industrial culture based not on family values but on consumption and greed. Folk scholars, typically Northern, envisioned Appalachia as a repository of all that was good and true and honest about being American in general.[30] What was lacking in Appalachian culture would simply be provided through the modernization of the region via education or industry.[31]

Raised by strict Presbyterian educators, Emma Bell Miles was an example of this new perception of Appalachia. Born in 1879, she moved to the mountains above Chattanooga, Tennessee, in 1890 for her health. Her parents and doctor believed that the mountain environment and its isolation from unhealthy urban factors would resolve whatever chronic illnesses she suffered. The move simultaneously allowed her missionary parents—whose beliefs were a mixture of both eugenics and folk thought—to minister to the region's mountain children, who seemed like "ignorant, primitive folk."[32] While they worked, Emma explored the natural surroundings of her new environment since ill health kept her from school (although it did not hinder her explorations of her new home). Although she later matriculated at the St. Louis School of Art, homesickness and distaste for city life eventually drove her back to Appalachia and to her future husband, Frank Miles, whom she married in 1901.[33]

Frank's constant unemployment forced Emma to exploit her talents as a writer and artist as his inability to hold a job, multiple pregnancies (pregnant seven times, she gave birth to five children including twins), and illness continued to wrap the family in poverty. Wealthy benefactresses paid for her services as a lecturer, but publishing provided a steadier income, and her first poem appeared in *Harper's Monthly* in March 1904.[34] In her published work, she acted as an intermediary between those who desired to know more about mountaineers and the mountaineers themselves, an educated expert who could describe what she considered the "true" nature of the mountains and the folk who lived there. Whether her audience desired to see Appalachia as an isolated region in need of biological elevation or as an example of a truer, more patriotic past, her work was their access point. But as an intermediary, she romanticized the region, erasing from it some, though not all, of the hardships she knew intimately. Why she erased those problems (especially the poverty and illness she knew well) is unclear; however, early twentieth-century media required material that uplifted readers, not discomfited them, and it may have been in that vein that she eliminated anything problematic.

In Miles's hands, Appalachian music and other folk material proved a core part of the mountain's natural landscape as much as any tree or flower. Her poem "The Banjo and the Loom," published in August 1907 in *Century,* linked two core Appalachian folk metaphors together in one poem:

> THUMP-chug-a-tinkle-tang, tump-a-tinkle tine!
> Listen at the banjo and the loom;
> Banjo keeps a-pickin' in the shadow o' the vine,

> Batten keeps a-thuddin' th'ough the room.
> Cabin in the sunshine—*chug-a-plunk-a-pling!*
> Mocker in the sarvice-bush—listen at him sing!
> "Possum up a 'simmon-tree," hear the music ring
> Out across the meadows all in bloom![35]

Apparent in this poem is the dialect that Miles assigned to her mountain protagonists, marking them as odd and different, typical of many local-color writers. That unique dialect also suggested that unique words and phrasings were rendered as they had been when the original settlers came south. In the same poem, the loom responds to the banjo in that vernacular:

> Says the loom to the banjo: "Thump-a, chunk-a-choo!
> *You* lazy, good-for nothin' scamp!
> My head's a-swimmin' with the work I've got to do,
> My back's a-th'obbin with a cramp.
> Goin' up Cripple Creek, layin' in the shade,
> Waitin' for the money that the old man made—
> Nary hill o' taters hoed, and your ax has laid
> More 'n a week a-rustin' in the damp![36]

Dialect marked these anthropomorphized objects as mountain entities, but Miles also marked them as male and female, giving each qualities associated with fictionalized mountain men and women. In the above example, the male banjo avoids work while the female loom bemoans his laziness. This was typical of Miles, who used music and musical instruments to characterize gendered divisions in labor and experience in Appalachia, a division where her frustration with her husband's inability to work colored her writing and where she brushed off some of the mountain romanticism. In other work, Miles called string band and square dance music men's music since they were fast-paced, public music that appeared to be recent additions to Appalachian repertoires. Ballads were women's music since they were slower, softer (hence, feminine), and tragic. They were also far older, a clear survival from the original migrants to the Southern mountains. Miles wrote with not a little bitterness that "the man bears his occasional days of pain with fortitude such as a brave lad might display, but he never learns the meaning of resignation. The woman belongs to the race, to the *old people*. He is a part of the *young nation*. His first songs are yodels. Then he learns dance tunes, and songs of hunting and fighting and drinking, and couplets of terse, quaint fun. It is over the loom and the knitting that old ballads are dreamily, endlessly crooned [by women]."[37]

As part of a nation of old people, women's music was impervious to change, thanks to their work as oral historians and skilled musicians. Preservation of early Appalachian music was a woman's familial responsibility, and maintaining oral libraries of songs from the past were as important to her day as raising her children. She crooned those songs softly as she worked, using skills that were as timeless as the music itself. Miles wrote, "The mother is crooning over her work, some old ballad of an eerie sadness and the indefinable charm of unlooked-for minor endings, something she learned as a child from a grandmother whose grandmother again brought it from Ireland or Scotland. As she bends above the loom, sending the shuttle back and forth, her voice goes on softly, interrupted by the thump of the batten."[38]

Appalachian music was also a "potential source of a 'native' American art music, more reflective of the national spirit" than other American folk music, for example, Native American or cowboy music.[39] Miles assumed that mountain music had been transported to colonial United States by white migrants from Britain, Ireland, and Scotland, and scoffed at "negro themes" and "aboriginal Indian music" when they were cited by others as sources of "real" American music.[40] "Negro" and "Indian" sources also tainted the racial purity of America's foundational music, at least in her eyes. The belief that mountain music was more reflective of an American national spirit drew notice from others, especially English folk song expert Cecil Sharp and his assistant Maud Karpeles, who envisioned Appalachian music not as quaint folklore but as an important element in American national identity during World War I.[41] Their *English Folk Songs from the Southern Appalachians* identified British music still extant in the Southern mountains and claimed mountaineers were "conservators of the essential culture of America," according to historian Henry Shapiro.[42] Certainly Miles imagined mountain music this way, too, but it took an outside expert with Sharp's international reputation to move Appalachian music and culture from a marginal problem or archaic oddity to a mainstream treasure. More importantly, his identification of British survivals in the Southern mountains strengthened American support of the British during World War I, since our indigenous culture seemed to be linked intrinsically with theirs. Sharp's research would not, however, completely eclipse eugenicists' assumptions, and the divide between eugenicists and folk scholars would manifest itself as a divide between hillbilly music and mountain music on the radio.

❖ ❖ ❖

Vaudeville determined who would appear on barn dance radio while local-color writers proposed a place and time. Radio provided the technical means to transform these two ideas into a new system of national entertainment. Unlike television, which would build on radio's innovative practices, radio started from scratch, evolving from small stations scattered about the nation into large centralized networks (the National Broadcasting Corporation, for one) with specific business practices and advertisements to pay the bills. Those small radio stations first began cropping up in 1923 and 1924, growing out of what had been a hobby for young boys, and were self-promotion tools used by small companies to hawk their wares. WNAX in Yankton, South Dakota, was representative of many of these first stations: it was started by the Gurney Seed and Feed Company's owner in order to sell more seed to local farmers.[43] Large corporations invested in radio too, using it to boost their bottom line. The Sears, Roebuck Company in Chicago, which quickly became a major broadcasting center, "began broadcasting uncertain where radio was going but eager to dive into the new technology," according to radio historian Susan Smulyan.[44] Sponsored by Sears's nonprofit Agricultural Foundation, early WLS broadcasts were as geared toward Midwestern farmers as they were toward city residents. George Biggar recalled, "Traditional country dances and toe-tickling harmonica-guitar medleys were interspersed with heart songs and popular sweet and novelty numbers which brought nostalgic memories of hay-rides and country 'sociables' to thousands. It is doubtful if southern folk songs or cowboy ballads were sung, as very few midwesterners of that day were familiar with them."[45] Whether the sponsoring company was Sears or the Gurney Seed and Feed Company, radio was not a financial end unto itself: all financial rewards would come from increased publicity for the station owner's business, not from ad revenues paid by outside organizations.

Because of the scattered and local nature of radio stations, early programs reflected local tastes. In urban areas like Chicago, Dallas, Nashville, Detroit, and Atlanta, broadcasters reached out to the new migrant audiences that had moved to the big city during and after World War I. Industrialists transformed their production facilities to military output and then to the mass production of consumer goods such as the automobile. That transformation required a workforce willing to work long hours on assembly lines, and rural Southerners and Midwesterners flocked to those jobs. Between World War I and 1970, millions of

Americans (both black and white) from the rural South migrated to the job-rich areas of the urban South, North, and West.[46] They followed "social highways" established by friends and family to industrial centers, which beckoned with promises of opportunity and of riches no longer available at home.[47] By 1930, 54,000 former Tennesseans, 206,000 former Kentuckians, and 130,000 former West Virginians lived in the industrial areas of Ohio alone.[48] In Chicago, the black population increased by 248 percent between 1910 and 1920.[49] But it was not just Southerners who moved in the interwar era; thousands of rural dwellers moved from the Midwest and West to the big city, too, creating heterogeneous populations on the assembly line and in homogeneous enclaves around their places of work.[50]

The riches migrants sought proved elusive in new environments, however, where job competition was intense between whites, blacks, and immigrants. Locals scorned white newcomers with derogatory labels such as hillbilly or "foreigner," and migrants suffered a deep sense of longing for home.[51] They turned to bars called honky-tonks, to local churches, and eventually to the radio in their search for familiar social situations where they were welcome neighbors, not oddities. They especially liked a program called the barn dance, which was based on a rural tradition, the Saturday night dance party. The first singers sounded like home to rural migrants (whether Southern or Midwestern) because their untrained voices and simple musical accompaniments evoked farms and family.[52] It was no accident, then, that the first barn dance programs appeared on WFAA in Dallas (1923), WLS in Chicago (1924), WSB in Atlanta (mid-1920s), and WSM in Nashville (1925), all cities with new migrant populations.[53]

Even though they may have sounded like home, that familiarity was based as much on the common theatrical forms that broadcasters used rather than on a strict replication of a rural barn dance. Broadcasters were remarkably derivative in the 1920s as they experimented with different kinds of theater on the air, and migrants at first heard relatively eclectic programs, much like vaudeville shows. Broadcasters and performers had to transform theater's visual techniques onto radio's audio stages, and acts that used words and sound were needed on the air, not those that used sight gags, facial ticks, arm gestures, and other kinds of visual display. Dog acts were out, but certain singing and comedy acts, performers found, were in, especially when they catered to the listening needs of their migrant audiences. Sarah Bernhardt's passionate excesses were out because microphones forced performers to stand still and sing quietly, unlike vaudeville stages where a loud voice and movement were key. Finally, because broadcasters and performers quailed at beaming radio waves directly into private homes, considered sacred, sacrosanct places, they hired expert vaudevillians like Grace Wilson, who knew how to act like a theatrical production's moral steward.

In search of a winning combination, broadcasters seemed to have welcomed all comers, although no scripts were written down until the 1930s, so this is difficult to confirm. One author did note that anyone who could "sing, whistle, play a musical instrument, or even breathe heavily" appeared on the air.[54] When Chicago station WLS ran out of material, for example, it broadcast from the Hotel Sherman Inn where the Maurie Sherman Orchestra was playing. WLS's desire to find professional performers caused them to hire former vaudevillian Grace Wilson, who had been on stage from the age of four and who had appeared on her first radio program in Elgin, Illinois, in 1922.[55] George Biggar, WLS's farm and market director in the 1920s, remembered Wilson as "a versatile singer of sentimental songs from vaudeville." She was a skilled theatrical performer who had traveled, like many vaudevillians, to large and small cities and performed nightly for strangers, presenting herself as the neighbor next door. She said, "I'm not a glamour girl and haven't tried to be. I'm a homey person and like people—just 'Grace Wilson, your old friend and neighbor,' singing the songs everyone likes to hear. . . . My whole heart goes into every song I sing and every word I speak. Nothing makes me happier than the kind letters from listeners and to know that my efforts have given joy to others."[56] Some listeners claimed to have heard her from the very first. One listener, Mrs. Jean Warner, tracked Wilson's career for fourteen years (her letter to WLS was dated 1936), recording in a notebook the 3,500 performances of 796 different songs Wilson had done.[57] It was that consistency and her neighborliness that led to her moniker, "The Girl with a Million Friends."

Looking backward, historians have located performances on WLS (as well as on other radio programs such as the *Grand Ole Opry*) as the beginnings of the barn dance craze. But at the time, there was no sense that Wilson and others were starting what came to be a standardized genre known for its packaging of Southern and Western performers. WLS manager Edgar Bill recalled, "We started WLS with a large variety of entertainment programs. We would try anything once to see what our listeners thought about it. We had religious programs and services on Sunday. We featured high-brow music one night; dance bands on another; then programs featuring large choruses. Other nights, we'd have variety or might have a radio play."[58] Broadcasters did focus on local mores and tastes. Nothing points this out better than the contrast between Grace Wilson's performances on Chicago radio of sentimental favorites and former vaudevillian Uncle Dave Macon's tenure on WSM's *Grand Ole Opry* in Nashville. Reflecting Tennessee mores, where an earthier persona was more appropriate, Macon played the working-class man who could sing, drink, and play simultaneously on the air, all in a "natural" manner. "Natural men" reminisced about farms and cows, where bodily functions and alcohol (Macon always brought his "medicine bag" of sipping whiskey with him on stage) were talked about openly. One broadcast executive, after meeting Uncle Dave Macon, said, "I have never met a more natural man in my life. He prays at the right time and he cusses at the right time and his jokes are as cute as the dickens."[59] Another author wrote, "'Uncle Dave' confessed to some embarrassment in being transplanted from a home far back in the country to the stage without a big wood fireplace in which to expectorate and throw things."[60] The emphasis on his earthy character made Macon seem more like the mountain hillbilly rather than a solid, upstanding mountaineer, at least in these first years.

The influence of black musicians on white ones was another local issue Opry performers were willing to acknowledge, albeit in a superficial way, by including black harmonica player DeFord K. Bailey in the cast.[61] Granted, broadcasters only allowed Bailey on the air late at night, but fans like Missourian Nelda Underwood were willing to wake up late (her father typically shook her awake at 11:30 P.M. on Saturday nights) to hear Bailey's harmonica.[62] But if local mores allowed a black man on stage, they also tended to preclude the appearance of women because of Southern prescriptions against their "public work" (work outside of the farm or home). The rare woman did perform with her family—for example, Uncle Jimmy Thompson was accompanied by his niece, Eva Thompson Jones—but Southern prescriptions seemed to have barred solo women like Grace Wilson from the Opry.[63]

The Opry was "a good-natured riot" to Southerners, rife with hillbillies who were natural, earthy men with good Christian morals.[64] To others, Macon's performances were a sign of cultural regression, particularly in their willingness to cross racial boundaries and their references to alcohol. Radio hillbillies, to middle-class eyes, had transformed sacred folk tunes into soiled objects for purchase; sin and gin (or in the case of Dave Macon, sippin' whiskey) were cause for alarm, not a hoedown in the hayloft. In contrast to Uncle Dave, Grace Wilson's colleague Bradley Kincaid was one of those middle-class Americans who believed that folk tunes were sacred and should not be used for commercial purposes.

Wilson may have been "The Girl with a Million Friends," but Kincaid was the artist with 100,000 fan letters. His popularity—indicated by that fantastic amount of mail—helped him bring Emma Miles's image of Southern music on stage in order to educate audiences in appropriate morals.

Not all who migrated to urban areas were working-class Southerners in search of a job. College graduates also moved. Bradley Kincaid was a Berea College (Kentucky) graduate who moved to Chicago to attend the Y.M.C.A. College in 1926.[65] When he first secured work on the WLS *National Barn Dance,* Americans still listened to battery-operated receiving sets (my great-grandfather would bring in the battery from the family's Model T for an especially good radio broadcast); by 1927 when Kincaid's popularity began to build, radios switched over to the easier-to-use and more accessible all-electric receivers.[66] Thus, more Americans began buying radios and tuning in to hear Kincaid, who billed himself as the "Kentucky Mountain Boy with his Houn' Dog Guitar." He sold himself as an expert on "old-time" music, as folk music was initially called on the air, with his Kentucky mountain upbringing a device to claim for himself a role as expert on Appalachian music. Part of that claim was rooted in Kincaid's memories of his mother's musical ability:

> my mother, she went farther back [than his father]. She sang the old English ballads. I learned a lot of ballads from her, like "Fair Ellender," "The Two Sisters" and any number of English ballads. I sang these as a kid. I didn't sing much in church. Course I sang in Sunday School class, but I didn't do solos or anything like that. My mother never did show too much musical ability, though she used to—in a very lamentable voice—sing some of the old blood curdlers to me, and my hair would stand straight up on my head.[67]

His success in "contributing to the wholesomeness of WLS," as a peer later wrote him, eventually caused WLS broadcasters to search for musicians who could replicate Kincaid's success.[68]

Kincaid's act was reminiscent of the reformer impulse implicit in local-color writers' work, but no longer was Appalachia the place to be saved. Now it promised to save America from the moral decay of cities as well as the Jazz Age and its decadent symbols: the jazz baby, the flapper, and hillbillies like Uncle Dave Macon. Kincaid was the genuine mountaineer who tried (unsuccessfully, he eventually decided) to supplant these immoral icons with the stalwart, simple mountain man and woman. And like Miles, in his portrayal Kincaid erased some (though not all) of the problems he knew existed in the mountains.

Kincaid began his career claiming he was an expert who could transport mountain music and values to the radio. He dedicated his third songbook to "his" mountain people to promote his authority:

> To all the Mountain Folks . . .
> Your Paths are My Paths . . .
> Your songs are My Songs . . .
> With great gladness that this is so,
> I dedicate this book to you . . .
> My Own People . . .[69]

His expertise was also indicated by his clothing: Kincaid avoided any outfit that evoked a hillbilly mountaineer (overalls, for example), favoring a suit, a necktie, and horn-rimmed glasses that suggested a professor.

Kincaid then endowed mountaineers with a variety of morals and values he wished his listeners to learn. His mountaineers withstood hardship without complaining, respected God and all that was sacred, were patriotic, and worked hard. Their core values were not temporary, rooted as they were in a challenging past. He used what he considered uplifting instruments on stage: the guitar, considered by some Southerners an elite instrument, the dulcimer (a woman's instrument), and the banjo, which many Americans considered a quintessentially Southern instrument. He eschewed fiddles, which he associated with hillbilly music. He wrote,

> These mountain ballads are songs that grew out of the life and experiences of hardy Scotch, Irish, German, English and Dutch natives, who came to America because they desired freedom and the right to worship according to their own desires. They are the people who braved the unknown forests, established their crude huts and feared no one save the God whom they devoutly worshiped. It was around the hearthstones of these poor, though proud settlers that these songs were born. They are not songs that were written for commercial purposes—they were never written, but were handed down by word of mouth . . . The early mountaineer knew nothing of the piano, but used the guitar, the banjo or the dulcimer for accompaniment to his songs.[70]

The mountain man was a stalwart in this image, a noble, stolid, "rugged" patriarch who adhered to the principles of patriotism. Calling him a "warrior-farmer," Kincaid claimed pioneer men wrenched the land from "savage" Indians and then established the basics of a democratic government. He told listeners, "Not only did the Mountain men take the first steps towards definite and independent self-government, but they did much to make it possible for millions of others to enjoy the kind of freedom which they themselves had tried." The mountain man's life was a stable one, fixed in a colonial past, and he did not react to the whims of the Jazz Age. According to Kincaid, the mountaineer "doesn't bother his brains about 'Trial Marriages,' or 'Companionate Marriage,' or 'Birth Control,' or certain other social questions which seem to be driving some minds towards the brink of the social precipice. To him marriage means mating for life; a home is a place for rearing children; and his responsibility as a father is more precious than any other honor that can come to him."[71]

The mountain man's steady, reliable companion—and the featured symbol in Kincaid's cultural work—was the Southern mother, an icon that dominated Kincaid's addresses and songbooks. His mountain woman was a traditional mother who followed a long line of successful parents. She reared her offspring to be "stalwart, dependable children," and she "sacrificed herself to the altar of motherhood that the best in her blood and her family ideals may be perpetuated, and that her country may enjoy the benefits of her parental love and pride."[72] Because she had inherited her parenting skills from the past, she did not worry about things that modern (read: Northern or urban) women worried about like "family budgeting," "careers outside the home," "diets for people who are reducing," or "professional advice about childbearing and child-rearing." While her sacrifices for the national good were crucial, so, too, was the mountain mother's artistry. Kincaid accentuated the mountain woman's ability to make specially crafted household goods that had been, he said, "woven by hand on ancient looms made by pioneer hands of long ago. Some of these articles bear evidence of rare skill and artistic taste in the women who make them."[73] Ancient treasures included family songs of "surpassing sweetness" that had been brought "by early settlers across the sea." Mountain women loved to "sing these old ballads and songs while they are doing the housework. It drives away lonesomeness. They sing as naturally as the wood thrush sings, and for very much the same reason."[74]

Mountain men and women helped Kincaid excise the hillbilly from WLS's stage. In Kincaid's eyes, hillbillies vulgarized "an ancient cultural treasure," scholar David Whisnant wrote.[75] The hillbilly was not an earthy drinking buddy from back home; he was an illiterate, ignorant drunk whose loose morals allowed him to sell sacred folk music. Significantly, Kincaid associated hillbilly songs and singers with icons of the industrial era, particularly railroad gangs and lumber camps, assuming, of course, that mountain ballads had existed before railroads and lumbermen built America's industrial economy. Kincaid wrote in a songbook, "There is a practice among recording companies, and those who are inclined to speak slightingly of the mountain songs, to call them Hilly Billy songs. When they say Hilly Billy songs they generally mean bum songs and jail songs such as are often sung in lumber camps and among railroad gangs. Such songs are not characteristic of mountain songs, and I hope that with this brief explanation you will come to distinguish between these fine old folk songs of the mountains, and the so-called Hilly Billy songs."[76] Worse yet, hillbilly singers, according to Kincaid, "sing thru their noses."[77]

Kincaid offered mountain images for sale on the air at the same time as he used them as standards of behavior for his listeners, but from the first, he encountered a critical problem that would frustrate broadcasters (and scholars) in the years to come: who listened to him on the radio? Were listeners working class or middle class? Urban or rural? How many tuned in and to what program? Kincaid turned early to the fan mail he received, if not to answer these questions, to at least acknowledge there was a listening audience and elicit more mail. And those letters became an early way to ascertain why some listeners tuned in as writers wrote to describe a favorite song he sang, to proclaim him their favorite performer, or to purchase one of his songbooks.

Kincaid used innovative techniques, unique to the radio, to entice his listeners to write. Whereas in the late 1920s he referred to them as "the invisible audience," by 1932 he addressed listeners in more informal tones, using the informal "you" and emphasizing that friendly connection. He treated his listeners like family, hoping that relationship, however it was imagined by fans, might prompt them to write. He told the audience one night, "When I sing for you on the air, I always visualize you, a family group, sitting around the table or the radio, listening and commenting on my program. Some of you have written in and said that I seem to be talking right to you, and I am. If I did not feel your presence, though you be a thousand miles away, the radio would be cold and unresponsive to me, and I in turn would sound the same way to you."[78]

One might think listeners responding to this familial link would have written back about Jazz Age immoralities or their troubles in the emergent Great Depression, but the letters are notably silent. The only exception was those who wrote Kincaid looking for work in the songwriting field, perhaps as a way to stave off the Depression's economic woes. Where the increasingly troubled times did manifest themselves was listeners' veneration of Kincaid's lack of pretense, part of an evolving belief that 1920s elitism and artificiality had caused the Great Depression. Referencing the mountain man who was not pretentious, listener Ethel Ater wrote him after a personal appearance that "we thought you a very fine cultured young gentleman. You know what we mean, all real, no false make believes."[79] Other fan letters reprimanded him for not upholding the image of "all real." Angered by a Kincaid appearance where he wore overalls rather than his customary suit, listener Emma Riley Akeman questioned whether he had made his mountain mother proud by wearing hillbilly togs. Mrs. Kincaid, according to Akeman, sat:

> till the wee hours of the morning, with tears of being over tired, mingled with the thread she knit the socks that your dad wore, no doubt, and spun the yarn for the thread, made the trousers, with her tired and over worked fingers, that prayed before she went to bed for help and strength that she might rear her son to the highest plains in the wor ld [sic] of whom she may rightfully be proud, and see that smile thru those tears as she lovingly came to see her child tuck in bed? Ah [And] how her heart aked when she saw from some heavenly place her strugles personified?[80]

In the case of Akeman's diatribe, the mountain mother crooning to her babes as she wove homespun became the mother wounded by her son's easy willingness to ignore her sacrifices and tears to put on low-class overalls.

Whether they liked him or not, the sheer amount of fan mail he received (most of which has disappeared) proved that Kincaid had successfully translated an old image of Appalachian South into one for sale over the radio. In a given year, Kincaid supposedly "pulled," or received 100,000 letters, probably an apocryphal number used to tout his success. His songbook sales (books that included lyrics, musical accompaniments, and pictures of his Kentucky home) also showed broadcasters how popular he was. One songbook sold 250,000 copies, and another, released in 1928 and titled "Favorite Mountain Ballads and Old-Time Songs," went through six printings by July 1929.

Bradley Kincaid was the unexpected outcome of the three stories that began this chapter. From Sarah Bernhardt's vaudeville days came theatrical practices and character types as well as assumptions that women be on stage and in the audience to control any untoward behavior. From Emma Bell Miles came local colorists' assumptions that the Appalachian mountains were an isolated place that had preserved a unique culture that might reform mainstream American culture. From Grace Wilson and other early radio performers came the translation of vaudeville techniques for a new medium based on sound, not visual cues. Kincaid melded these three stories into a commercially successful stage persona that provided broadcasters still searching for clear and coherent radio programming new characters on which to build the barn dance radio genre.

"Bury Me beneath the Willow"

Jeanne Muenich, Linda Parker, and the Appearance of Southern Female Characters on Barn Dance Stages

My heart is sad and I am lonely
Thinking of the one I love
I know that I shall never more see him
till we meet in heaven above
Then bury me beneath the willow.

—Karl and Harty, *Karl and Harty with the
Cumberland Ridge Runners*

On the *National Barn Dance,* its new "girl" singer Linda Parker was the quintessential wholesome performer. She was born in Kentucky and, like many in her audience, had migrated to the industrial areas around Chicago. But Linda was special; her knowledge of old Southern ballads from Kentucky as well as "the plaintive note, so typical of mountain music," WLS Chicago's fan magazine, *Stand By!* observed in 1934, made the Southern mountain woman come to life.[1] Indeed, she had learned to sing "just as her mother and grandmother sang, artlessly, but from the heart," and her repertoire included traditional ballads such as "I'll Be All

Smiles Tonite" and her signature song, "Bury Me beneath the Willow," a folk song popularized by the Carter Family.[2] Linda's sentimental music did more than refer to the past; it tamed a world out of control. As one listener wrote,

> There is something poignantly appealing about Linda's songs . . . something that takes us away from the cares of mundane strife and the daily chores of the big city . . . something that sweeps the smoke and the heat, or intense cold away . . . the worries and the cares of the day when Linda begins to sing her songs in her own sweet, inimitable way.
>
> Linda Parker mirrors fresh breezes . . . mountain peaks . . . tall timber . . . rushing streams. She brings this refreshing and soothing essence into our tiny living room. We always listen to her with nostalgia in our hearts.[3]

When Parker died from peritonitis in August 1935 (she was twenty-three years old), the *National Barn Dance* cast and its audience were devastated by her tragic death, and letters of condolence poured into the station. One listener wrote, "It is with deep regret and sorrow that I write this letter concerning that beautiful little sunbonnet girl, Linda Parker, my favorite feminine performer."[4] Another listener wrote, "Her sweet songs and beautiful character shall always live in loving memory of her."[5] Her manager, John Lair, told audiences, "'Bury Me Beneath the Willow' was the last song she sang that dreary pain-racked afternoon before she went to the hospital and was, consequently, the last song she ever sang."[6] Therefore, he announced, it was a fitting tribute that Parker had been buried beneath a willow, which wept continuously over her early death.[7]

Linda Parker, a character performed by actress Jeanne Muenich (1912–35), appeared on the *National Barn Dance* beginning in January 1932. And this admittedly obscure singer had an impact far beyond what her short, tragic life might suggest: she was the first solo Southern female image that combined vaudeville, ideas about Appalachia, and radio technology. Muenich and her manager, John Lair, determined what costuming a mountain woman would use on stage, what her musical sound would be, and what stage plays would give the character shape and form. In short, they took various elements from live theater and transformed them for audio use on the radio. Using these tactics, Muenich and Lair then integrated the Parker character into the show's new format and sense of purpose. They succeeded in making a character with little substance in the material world—but who seemed to be stable and traditional in the *National Barn Dance*'s fictive one—that became a powerful archetype that could be reinvented over time. In the early 1930s, before the *National Barn Dance* was a national show, Linda Parker, "the Little Sunbonnet Girl," became an image that promised a kind of therapy for Chicago and other Midwestern listeners. And she proved so powerful (particularly in the hands of others) that current country music stars still reckon with her.

There were discrepancies between the stage character and the woman who played her, although it has been difficult to reconstruct Muenich's life because she hid behind the character so well. What is clear is she was born in Indiana, not Kentucky (one need not be a real Southern woman to play the character in January 1932); may have been a juvenile delinquent; was probably singing in nightclubs when broadcaster John Lair discovered her; and, most grievously, does not have a gravestone guarded by a weeping willow. Otherwise, only rumor and innuendo concerning her life remain.[8] To tell this story, then, of women's early solo work on the *National Barn Dance*'s stage, it is necessary to use the words of others to fill in the gaps left by Muenich's early death.

❖ ❖ ❖

Folklorists, at least those practicing in the 1930s, thought that music and other folklore were more than simply entertainment; they also served practical purposes. Those "functionalists" (as those folklorists were called) would have approved of the *National Barn Dance*'s two practical goals as it began to build its popularity using folk music in the early 1930s.[9] Whether the program realized those goals explicitly is beside the point, although Kincaid's use of folk music to teach his audience good morals may have cued listeners that music had other uses beyond mere entertainment. What is the point is that regional radio not only became a new stage to display cultural anxieties (as vaudeville had been), but it used folk music to provide solutions, too. In the hands of producer John Lair, who imagined himself a student of American folklore and who began writing shows in 1930 that catered to his audience's anxieties about moving to a new city and about the evolving Great Depression, folk music and other material provided solace to his listeners, material where Linda Parker seemed a perfectly natural part of the stage. The stage, once again, became a place where various tensions could be described, discussed (at least implicitly), and then diffused.

As a local program, the *National Barn Dance*'s first goal was to mediate between the area's new migrants and old residents in the four-state region surrounding Chicago, its main audience between 1930 and 1933.[10] Vaudeville's diversity served the program well in this regard, but where its diversity once emphasized different acts and people (the sentimental mother, dog acts, comedians, and ethnic humor), it now emphasized place over person, all mingled together on stage just as they might be on a Chicago assembly line. On barn dance radio in these early years, stage shows served as tools to integrate like-minded migrants, forging a new "imagined community" that welcomed some Midwestern and Southern migrants but excluded others.[11] In that almost exclusively white community, some ethnic whites—German, Swedish, or Irish—stood on stage next to Southern and Midwestern characters and were displayed prominently to realize relationships based on common experiences and a common love of music.[12] WLS bands now included the Maple City Four (a reference to La Porte, Indiana); the Prairie Ramblers; the Georgia Wildcats, all of whom performed alongside Olaf Yonson; Christine, the Swiss Miss; and Irish tenor Bill O'Connor, all representing immigrant groups that had migrated in the late nineteenth century to Chicago. The music they played did not necessarily refer to their supposed home place (one program listed the Maple City Four "in Songs, Chatter and Washboard Band Novelties"), but that did not matter since a band's most stable element was its name (repertoires could change on a whim, but if a band wanted a fan to remember it, the name had to stay stable).[13] Grace Wilson, "The Girl with a Million Friends," still performed, but she faded to a supporting role rather than a featured act.

Kentuckian John Lair (1894–1985) secured his first job on the *National Barn Dance* in 1930 in this era of migrant performers.[14] Born near Bradley Kincaid in Mount Vernon, Kentucky, Lair grew up believing that his boyhood differed little from previous generations, that the values of hard work and neighborliness he learned had been inherited intact from his ancestors. But he was disturbed by the changes industrialization had wrought during his adulthood and used radio to educate his audience in old-time values as well as to entertain them. By 1930, Lair had replaced Kincaid, who had left for a National Broadcasting Corporation (NBC) network program in New York, and was a part-time producer of regional programming (he also worked as an insurance executive). He would be responsible for adding many Southerners to WLS's stage, among them some of the most popular performers on barn dance radio, including Red Foley, Lulu Belle Wiseman, and Lily May Ledford.

Lair helped WLS render invisible some of those who were part of Chicago's ethnically and racially diverse landscape—typically blacks and Jews, odd choices since much of WLS's music had black roots, and Jews were key contributors to vaudeville's development. On the radio, they were absent unless portrayed passively or represented as powerless. In Lair's Civil War show, broadcast in either 1930 or 1931, blacks were passive bystanders to the war, empty-headed, grinning fools (not unlike minstrel stereotypes) who would rather play the banjo than direct their future. According to surviving scripts, he told audiences, "Slave labor was makin a lot of money fer people in the South—also a lot of trouble between the North an South. The slaves theirselves didn't take much part in the racket. They wuz busy gittin all the enjoyment out of life that they knowed how to. They druther set an lissen to the banjer as worry their heads off about what was gonna become of em. An you can't blame em much, when this was the kind of banjer pickin they was listenin to."[15] While this quote suggests Lair was no racial liberal, he did at times acknowledge the black roots of folk songs, most likely in his quest to portray a true Southern atmosphere where blacks represented a kind of authenticity. Lair portrayed them only as originators of folk music rather than as current singers as the Opry did. As people closer to their supposedly more animalistic origins, as contemporary racial thought purported them to be, African Americans' naturalness and supposed lack of development helped Lair sell his music as more real and genuine, free from the taint of the modern world. This model of black passivity or invisibility (and white power in its face) worked in WLS's favor in the early 1930s, when network radio created a mainstream culture that favored white American music exclusively and erased blacks from their air except when they were minstrel-like caricatures.[16]

The *National Barn Dance*'s second goal was to respond to the Great Depression, which began to seriously affect Chicago's economy in 1930 and 1931. Those days proved to be dark ones as Americans faced unemployment, starvation, environmental disasters, and an inadequate response by federal, state, and local governments and private charities to the catastrophe. The Depression hit durable goods industries especially hard, and steel-making and auto manufacturing cities like Chicago suffered higher unemployment rates than elsewhere. While unemployment rates hovered around 25 percent nationally, 50 percent of Chicago's workforce was unemployed and one-third of the remaining workforce was underemployed.[17] Relief funds were quickly exhausted, and elites feared a bloody revolution instigated by the unemployed that might uproot them from their privileged place.

Because the Depression hit durable goods industries (considered men's work) hardest, more men were unemployed than women. Women were segregated into service jobs (for example, waitressing or clerking in department stores), secretarial work, and light industry jobs like wiring radio sets rather than into heavy industrial jobs like auto manufacturing.[18] Women's higher employment rates caused substantial tension within Chicago families as women's economic stability boosted their power within the family at the expense of men's. As historian Margaret McFadden wrote, "Because millions of un- or under-employed men were unable to be productive and to support their families (both crucial aspects of male identity), the depression helped cause a widespread crisis of masculinity and a related crisis of male authority in the family. Many men's self-images and sense of authority over their wives and children derived from their economic roles as providers; thus they experienced their inability to provide adequate family support as a failure of masculinity."[19] As one Chicago woman, who remained employed when her husband was not, said, "You know, who make the money [*sic*], he is the boss."[20] Here WLS's second goal becomes clear. At the moment when women were gaining economic power in Depression-era Chicago, Southern women began appearing on radio shows—first as symbols, then as live performers—in ways that promised a stable set of patriarchal gender relations just as they (supposedly) had always been. Men were in charge, the authority figures in their mountain families, while women remained the supportive mothers who cared for the home and the children. Their roles on the *National Barn Dance* seemed firm, unlike those outside the studio.

The main male authority was John Lair, and his success came from his ability to sell himself as an expert on folk music. He was not some crass businessman out to make money. Like Emma Miles, he was a mediator with a mission: in his case, it was to preserve old-time music from commercialism and use it to affirm his version of appropriate gender roles. His duties at WLS reflected his patriarchal role. He wrote a fan magazine column that featured a music exchange (listeners wrote in searching for cherished songs from other listeners), and he regularly appeared on shows with his "trusty" notebook of old-time music that dated as early as 1673.[21] In one show, WLS announced, "John Lair of WLS, authority on American folk music and legends of the hill country, will be heard as narrator, giving continuity to the weekly rural community gatherings and presenting origins and histories of many of the songs included in the broadcasts. The original Renfro Valley homestead, scene of the series, is still standing. It was built by Lair's great aunt."[22]

An old-time community of male singers provided a stable foundation for Lair's role as an expert, beginning in 1930. He organized groups of talented musicians and then created scenarios featuring folk music, games, and rituals from his Kentucky home (although he also acknowledged music and other cultural material from other regions, especially the West). His first band was (literally) from Kentucky: the Cumberland Ridge Runners included Hartford Connecticut Taylor and Karl Davis (later known as the duo Karl and Harty) as well as Doc Hopkins, who performed on Lair's *Aladdin Mantle Lamp Shows* (a regional barn dance show) in 1930. Other members eventually included fiddler Slim Miller and Red Foley, the most popular singer to emerge from the Ridge Runners.

In the gendered tradition of vaudeville, a sentimental manhood was almost as significant as a sentimental motherhood (although no one could evoke tears the way Mother could), especially if a song's protagonist died and Mother was somehow present as an emblem of mourning or sorrow. On the radio, traditional men like the Ridge Runners sang songs of missing Mother or a dog, and many tearjerkers (for example, "Letter Edged in Black") were plucked from vaudeville stages to be sung on the *National Barn Dance*.[23] But in Lair's hands, sentimental men were boys who had left their family and traveled far from home. In reference to band members' own migrations to Chicago, Lair told his audiences, "When we wuz goin over it [the song "Back to Old Smoky Mountains"] while ago back ther in a back room gittin ready to come on the air it jest struck us all in a heap how dogonned homesick we wuz. We got to talkin old times over an we jest decided all at once to throw away the program we'd bin workin on an com out here an kinda relieve our feelins some by tellin everybody about it."[24] In a similar vein, Lair described the song "Home on the Range" as a memorial to Texan Charlie Rutledge, who had "left his Mother alone back in Texas an hadn't seen her in three years, so he wuz gettin anxious to go back home fer a little visit." Of course, in true sentimental fashion, Rutledge was tragically killed before he could make that visit.[25]

The Ridge Runners also performed music that fit WLS's first goal of dramatizing familiar social situations so that those Southern migrants in the audience might reconcile their migrant, urban present with their rural past. Migrants might not be able to bob for apples or attend a candy pull in downtown Chicago, but they could listen to musicians sing about those rural games on the air and hear plays where the performers pretended to play and sing just like in the old days. Lair's shows catered to a broader audience, however: to anyone who found contemporary life shallow, depressing, or unfamiliar. Whether a listener was a migrant, was frightened by the Depression, or was just an everyday listener, she found respite when she tuned in to Lair's old-time shows. References to "good old-fashioned parlors" and "play parties" showcased wholesome, clean fun for any listener who desired to live in Lair's traditional world.[26] Shows thus became aural refuges for both urban and rural people where Lair wielded nostalgic themes to comfort his listeners. Schoolhouses and gingham dresses played an important part in these nostalgic images:

> An there's the little ole log school house—Red Bud—where we usta go to school, an all them good old days comes back to us an standin' there lookin at the ole tumbledown schoolhouse seems like we kin see shadders flittin around through the moonlight that looks like us when we wuz kids, an all the kids we usta go to school with—why there they are, plain as day, with ther little ole gingham dresses an sun bonnets an straw hats an homemade overalls—an there's the teacher, Uncle Bill Davis that usta walk five miles acrost the mountain evr day to try to pound a little sense into our heads. Uncle Bill an a lot of the boys an girls we usta know kin never visit the place as anything but shadders now, but there tonight jest as plain as they wuz long time ago.[27]

Reminiscent of Kincaid's pioneers, Lair's community always appeared in the past, never the present, at least for his urban listeners (rural listeners may have lived a life similar to the one presented on stage). And like Emma Bell Miles, his community tended to be devoid of anything that might make a listener uncomfortable (poverty, alcohol, or the impact of industrialization on the Southern mountains). Unsure of who exactly tuned in, Lair and other broadcasters tended to chose the least controversial material possible, which reflected their own beliefs and ideas. The past the Ridge Runners staged was a Kentucky one, filled with "a breed of of [*sic*] men an wimmin fit to carry on their heritage of hard work an tribulation," Lair told listeners.[28] In some ways, Lair's shows were not as romanticized as Kincaid's were. "Wimmin," Lair said on one show, "are walkin 20 miles with a baby in their arms to git a head of cabbage to feed their starvin' brood on."[29] But he echoed Kincaid's assertion that those hardships produced strong, capable, hardworking "wimmin" and men whose values could, if imitated, save the nation from its current crises. Other character-building hardships included encounters with nature and "savages" who threatened pioneering ways: "The wolves howled along their trail the indun always had a fire ready to torture their flesh er destroy their home. New-made graves dotted the clearins around the cabins, but the survivors kept grimly on."[30] By emphasizing the hardships and fortitude of early mountaineers who built a nation by staving off wolves and "savages," Lair announced to his audience that those values still existed.

Indeed, this was another place where WLS implicitly addressed the Great Depression. With the exception of a fundraiser for a soup kitchen in November 1930 (which occurred before the real devastation was apparent), WLS and Lair did not mention the Great Depression at all, at least in surviving documents.[31] This most likely occurred because radio was intended as an escape from reality, not a reminder of the economic chaos evolving outside the studio (although this fiction was unevenly maintained when Franklin Roosevelt broadcast his Fireside Chats on the same network). Reminders of pioneers were examples of survival in a difficult time, not unlike the emergent economic downturn; in the case of the Great Depression, Americans came to believe that the only wolves and savages about were the businessmen and politicians they saw as at fault for the calamity. Since American pioneers had suffered and endured difficult times in the past, it was no great leap to think Chicagoans could endure in the present. After all, as Lair suggested, they came from good pioneering stock.[32]

But the Cumberland Ridge Runners did not only provide models of long-suffering pioneers. Pioneers were a counter to modernity as well. Lair and the Ridge Runners, no matter how much a part of Chicago's urban landscape, kept honest, true values even when challenged by immoral modern technology, at least the way they told it on stage. Movie theaters were one such threat: "Country people wouldn't believe it fer a long time [that a movie theater had arrived in town] an after they did, an got kinda used to it, a lot of them never would have nothin to do with em. My Daddy was never inside of one in his life and I ginerally had to keep it kinda quiet if I went to em much."[33] Lair also challenged modern secularism, telling his listeners, "The People livin in small towns an in the country git the most out of Chrismus. They still spell it CHRISTmus—not Xmas—they aint took Christ out of their Chrismus."[34]

Lair also imagined many in his audience to be homesick or depressed Southerners like him, and catered to their common Southern prejudices, especially those against women and public work (work outside the home), which had most likely limited the number of women on the Opry's stage. This kept women from being more than an unnamed symbol and a musical reminder of the past, at least in 1930 and 1931.[35] Vaudeville's sentimental mother figure came to represent, in Lair's hands, white migrants' real separations from their homes and families. Lair updated her to a distinctly Southern idol by portraying her as the mother left at the rural, Southern homestead while her children migrated—geographically, to new places and mentally, to new modern times.[36] An icon that had not been regionally specific was now armed with a Southern past, and that allowed Lair to create a broad character that many in his audience found familiar and attractive while tying her to his shows' themes of nostalgia, homesickness, and refuge.

The sentimental mother icon began to appear in scripts Lair wrote for regional shows just as Americans began to lose their jobs to the Great Depression. In a remarkably intuitive step, Lair responded to the chaos by claiming the sentimental mother was the traditional mountain mother who was constant and incorruptible, even when the outside world changed rapidly. That made the music she preserved equally pure, unadulterated, and uncommercial even when it was sung on the radio.[37] In one script, Lair wrote, "It was the women who really kept them [Old English and Scottish ballads] alive—the men didn't seemt o [*sic*] find much time for such things . . . but I used to listen by the hour to my great-grandmother and grandmother reciting some of those old ballads in a sing-song voice."[38] He touted these women as the keepers of the past, the true curators of traditional music who remained stable, secure, and firmly in their traditional place in a chaotic world. And, in keeping with the desire to solve as well as present cultural anxieties on stage, the sentimental mother would help listeners as their own circumstances changed since she was intended to be both a salve and an image of stasis for the region's troubled residents.

This saintly doyenne tended to be a passive icon who was rarely more than a memory or a reminder of one's home or responsibilities. Lair's Civil War commemorative show contained a typical early reference to women. Discussing the controversies that preceded the war, Lair said, "Nobody could talk about anything but the war and its attendant heartaches," but, he continued, "It's always the wimmin that shed them [tears] in times like this and mighty few wimmin either North or South was made outa that kinda stuff. Northern mothesrs [mothers] sent their sons with aprayer fer their return an Southern Mothers done the same. Motherhood aint m ch diffrunt, no matter which side of the line they're on."[39] Later, it was her name that dying soldiers cried out as they writhed in pain on battle-fields. Lair attempted to recreate those battlefields, interspersing his comments with music to bolster the image in listeners' imaginations: "Thousands of dyin boys cryin out in their last precious minnits fer Mother, like this boy [Bob and Mack sing "Break the News to Mother"]. An Mother heard. Don't think she didn't. No matter how fer apart they were. Here's a song about one Mother who knew her boy would never come whistlin up the lane agin never smell the honeysuckle coverin the old palin' fence around the yard, never see another sunset acrost the pasture field ner sing around the farm with the joy of livin."[40] "Break the News to Mother" reinforced the assumption that women were sanctified mothers whom young men, whether from the North or South, fought to protect.

On other shows, Lair used this musical trope to acknowledge that many rural migrants found it difficult to return home because they liked their urban environments. Whereas cold water and the reliance on oil lamps had been common parts of rural life, modern conveniences such as running water and electric lights made these formerly trivial matters unendurable. Thus migrants may have strayed from home to avoid those hardships and the ensuing guilt. Other migrants may have feared that home was not what it used to be. Mother, in these instances, represented the old traditional life of hardship and sacrifice. Lair reminded his audiences that a migrant had to remain responsible to her memory: "Maybe the old place aint the same no more; maybe there's a Stone Neath the Maple Tree at yore old home an Mother aint there to greet you, but aint they somebody there you owe somethin to?"[41] Listeners could, of course, fulfill their responsibilities by buying the sponsor's product, an Aladdin Lamp, and sending it to the home folks.

If the sentimental mother made sporadic appearances on Lair's early WLS shows, she was a prominent and common figure in the music he wrote. "Take Me Back to Renfro Valley," a song about one person's desire to return home, included the line, "Mother sang in Renfro Valley."[42] Another song, "One Step More," described one person's desire to leave earth for heaven so that heavy burdens could be unloaded. Lair devoted the third refrain to the narrator seeing his sainted mother:

> Mother's long been over Yonder;
> She'll be waiting for me too;
> She'll be Oh! so glad to see me—
> Proud to know that I've pulled through.
> She will be the first to greet me
> When I enter Heaven's door.
> Oh, I'll soon be with you, Mother,
> For it's only one step more.[43]

He wrote other music, of course, to fit his show's many moods; but as long as nostalgia as an emotional release and a calming mechanism dominated, so, too, did the sentimental mother.

Why John Lair hired Jeanne Muenich is unclear. Perhaps he overcame his own objections to women and public work by hiring a Midwesterner, rather than a Southerner, to play the sentimental mother. Perhaps he came up against radio's implicit sale of itself as the embodiment of everyday life rather than a fantasy constructed and commercialized for its listeners' pleasure. The lack of women in his stage shows would thus have been glaring. Perhaps the old icons were too passive. Whatever the case, the woman he found to play Linda Parker was born Genevieve Muenich in Covington, Indiana. Her family migrated to Hammond, Indiana, and she found work performing on local radio stations and in nightclubs after she was expelled from high school for being an "incorrigible youth."[44] Lair discovered her, he later told an interviewer, when she came to WLS to do an advertisement for her nightclub act. By hiring her away from the nightclub, Lair suggested he had saved her from the immoral life she was leading there. Thus he implied WLS's wholesome stage rehabilitated not only listeners but performers.[45]

In keeping with the radio world's evolving practices, he transformed the sentimental mother figure to meet radio's professional requirements when he hired Muenich. Two demands were most pressing. The first was a technological one: microphones required a singer with a voice that was not too nasal or boisterous, since microphones were subject to feedback from shrill noises. Someone with a soft, melodic voice, who crooned as popular singers Bing Crosby or Rudy Vallee did, was more appropriate for a miked performance. The shift to a crooning style made singers like Uncle Dave Macon seem "forced, corny, and distinctly old-fashioned," noted one scholar.[46] Microphones loved Jeanne Muenich's melodic alto voice as she sang softly and sweetly songs like "I'll Be All Smiles Tonite," and microphones gave this song and others more life and depth since crooning sounded more feminine and motherly than older Macon-like styles.

The second demand emerged as radio inherited from its theatrical predecessors their celebration of youth and beauty. A pretty young woman, not an old mother weary from her mothering, was required since, thanks to Broadway revues, her beauty was a skill and a commodity to be sold. The popularity of movies in the 1920s reinforced that theatrical tradition as Hollywood movie stars used their physical features, especially their faces, to sell themselves, a nod toward what historian Kathy Peiss called the "rising commercial value of the human face."[47] Visuals became even more important at WLS when, in March 1932, the *National Barn Dance* moved to the 1,200-seat Eighth Street Theater in Chicago. Over the next twenty-five years, 2,617,000 people paid to see the barn dance's Saturday night shows.[48] Broadcasters broadened that visual pleasure to an aural one for radio audiences who tuned in on Saturday nights, intending comments such as "Right pretty girls they have in them thar hills" as a verbal cue for listeners to imagine their own versions of pretty and beautiful.[49] This demand required Lair to put onstage not his Southern elderly mother worn by her hard work but a young woman he called the Little Sunbonnet Girl, who wore "little ole gingham dresses an sunbonnets."[50] Blond, slender with an aquiline nose, Jeanne Muenich fit the physical requirements of the character.[51] And, because pretty women came to be required, barn dance broadcasters began requesting evaluations of women's appearance, sometimes via photos, before considering them for a job. Booking agent W. M. Ellsworth, writing John Lair well after these values had been established, had several potential performers for Lair to audition in June 1942, one of whom was "nice looking" and another who "makes a nice appearance."[52]

Once they were hired, broadcasters continued the Broadway revue's custom of describing pretty women in scientific ways, implying that women's music and women's bodies were both available for purchase on the air. This attitude manifested itself in WLS's fan magazine, *Stand By!* which rationalized beauty by using numbers to codify it. Although Parker died before she could be featured in station fan magazines (only her obituary appeared there), other female performers were described by appearance and measurement. *Stand By!* described Eileen Jensen (part of the sister team Winnie, Lou, and Sally) as a "great big, little girl, just five feet tall, and she weighs 110 pounds. She has waist-length light brown hair and a roguish look that is attributed partly to laughing blue eyes and partly to a pert turned up nose."[53] Her sister, Helen, suffered the same treatment from *Stand By!:* "Helen is a little girl, five feet, two inches tall and weighing 112 pounds. She has dark gray eyes, brown hair highlighted with auburn, a wide smile and a hearty laugh."[54]

Comediennes were the exception to the industry-wide standard that women be young and attractive. Once again, vaudeville assumptions influenced Lair and others. Women who were old, ugly, rural, or obese were considered physical oddities and therefore appropriate to laugh at. They were funny because they defied physical or social conventions for women as defined in the measurements that appeared in fan magazines. Six-foot-four Beth Cremer, who performed as Little Eller on the Renfro Valley Barn Dance and who was more than a foot taller than Eileen and Helen Jensen, contradicted notions that women were diminutive—and therefore dependent—while their male counterparts were tall and physical—and therefore independent. Lair paired Cremer with fictitious boyfriend "Shorty" Hobbs, who was literally short, about five feet tall.[55] Jokes on the show revolved around the discrepancy in Cremer's and Hobbs' heights and the supposed change in gender roles it represented. This was displayed on a later barn dance show where performers gathered autumn leaves to decorate an old schoolhouse. Performers spoke these lines:

> Roland: Girls is too lazy to do that much walkin' nowadays, Mr. Lair. They druther jest set here in the schoolhouse an' wait fer us to bring the stuff to 'em—all but Eller. She went with Shorty.
> Homer: Shorty an' Eller gethered more leaves than anybody, Mister Ler. Eller would hold Shorty up to where he could break off them purtiest big limbs an' he didn't have to take time to climb the tree like the rest of us boys had to do. (CAST LAUGH)[56]

Because the cast and audience expected Hobbs to fulfill the masculine role and Cremer the female one, when each's height caused them to reverse their roles, it was funny.

Once he had hired her, Lair and Muenich then reworked her physical image through costuming to fit Lair's Kentucky mountains style and cue the public, through what historian Jacquelyn Dowd Hall called the "language of dress," that Muenich was a mountain resident.[57] The mountain mother wore homespun, a material woven by her on ancient looms. But the modern sentimental mother used calico or gingham material instead, since homespun was not available in Chicago. Nor was it attractive and probably a little too earthy for Chicago listeners who wanted pleasing images, not ugly ones. Other items accompanied Muenich's dress, including a sunbonnet (with the strings hanging loose, the hat was a possible reference to the West as well as the South), makeup, and a dulcimer (claimed as a woman's mountain instrument by Bradley Kincaid in the 1920s), which she never seems to have played. In some photos, she also wore pearls and high heels, which put her squarely within contemporary standards for beauty and style. Pearls and high heels, after all, were unsuitable when one worked in a field or slopped the hogs, but were perfectly appropriate for a walk down Michigan Avenue in Chicago. Her limited adoption of contemporary styles suggested that migrants might separate themselves from their rural past and embrace at least some of their urban present.

A performer's most important choice was her name because it told audiences what kind of performance to expect. Names chosen in the

1930s typically referred to a specific place to acknowledge migration, and no reference to an ethnic background was allowed. It was clear what kind of performer Patsy Montana (born Ruby Blevins) was because her last name was a Western state and her name cued audiences to expect a Western song from her. When their birth names did not fit a character or an act, women assumed a new moniker. In some cases, they changed their names themselves, as Sarah Colley Cannon chose Minnie Pearl. More commonly, a manager or station producer changed a performer's name. In Muenich's case, Lair experimented with various names including Piney Linville, Dulcie Lewis, Linda Parker, Linda Marshall, and Linda plus fifteen other last names, finally coming back to Linda Parker.[58] Because stage personas could change in response to historical trends, name changes could also occur many times over. Doris Schetrompf was Rose of the Mountains, then Rose Maphis, and finally, Rose Lee Maphis.[59]

Industry insiders called some acts "a real name act," because the name had commercial value to broadcasters and sponsors.[60] But the money-making potential of names (a leftover from vaudeville days when big-name stars like Sarah Bernhardt drew crowds because of name recognition) caused performers to guard names ferociously, since they were one of the few viable commodities they had. As musician Clayton McMichen told Lair much later in 1948, after these practices had become commonplace, "us hillbillies as a rule don't have nothing but our names."[61] Some performers knew that, in some cases, they did not legally own the name; a manager, an advertising agency, or a sponsor could own or lease them. The Mantle Lamp Company controlled the Cumberland Ridge Runner name as long as the company sponsored its regional programs, and contracts with the Mantle Lamp Company required that "the Artists will broadcast no programmes under the name of Cumberland Ridge Runners/Renfro Valley Boys over so-called chain broadcasting systems."[62]

Jeanne Muenich, of course, left no record of her feelings regarding her name change, but other performers' reactions suggest the conflict it may have engendered because of the implications for a performer's identity. Rose Lee Maphis loved her name because she felt her birth name did not suit her stage character, and she was more than willing to become the person she portrayed on stage.[63] On the other hand, Cincinnati barn dance performer Judy Perkins did not like that a program director changed her name. In Perkins's case, she not only felt a loss of identity but a loss of control. "My birth name is Evelyn Kyser," she said, which the director thought was a poor stage name, "So he renamed me and I hated it. But you know when you're young like that and you're trying to get started in a business, you think other people know better than you do."[64] Even though she hated it, she kept her new name and told an interviewer, "The reason why I never changed my name again was that every place I ever went to work after I began my career I worked with people who'd known me before so it wasn't easy to drop the name once you start building an audience and build a community with people so I never did change it."[65]

Women not only needed new names, they also needed new life histories to match the perfect, moral past broadcasters sold on stage. If the stories about Jeanne Muenich and her stint as a juvenile delinquent are true, then she was a prime candidate for a new life history. No longer was she an incorrigible youth from Indiana; she was now from Covington, Kentucky, a former Southerner who had migrated with her family to industrial Hammond, Indiana.

Because the Little Sunbonnet Girl was a musical image as much as a cultural icon, an appropriate repertoire was important since Parker was supposed to put her knowledge of old Southern ballads from Kentucky to good use. She needed songs such as "Meet Mother in the Sky" and "Some Mother's Boy" that emphasized her motherly duties but were still familiar and well within the weepy vaudeville tradition of sentimental songs.[66] In some cases, she took music like one of her signature songs, "I'll Be All Smiles Tonite," straight from the vaudeville stage. Lair wrote other songs to fit the sentimental feel he produced on stage, for example, "Mother's Old Sunbonnet," which described Parker's desire for God to care well for her mother:

There's a faded old sunbonnet
On a peg behind the door.
It's the one my sainted Mother used to wear.
Till one day she hung it up and
Never took it down no more
And since that day we've left it hanging there.

Oh, God be good to Mother.
Wherever she may be!
Please grant her rest and comfort over there.
And keep her just the same sweet smiling angel,
She always seemed to me.
In that old sun bonnet that she use to wear.[67]

When Muenich sang this song, she was the dutiful daughter who wished her mother a restful place in heaven. But, wearing her own sunbonnet, she also seemed to be that mother, at least one whose future would be sacrifice and toil for her children. In either case, the intention was to make the audience cry or mourn, something expected of someone who had just left home.

The sound of her voice reinforced the words she sang. Her lush, soft, melodic voice fit microphone technology, and her evocative sound made her singing seem an intimate performance targeted at each listener, a kind of lullaby to her radio children.[68] Fan publications linked her singing to her mother's, and John Lair later reported, "If Linda had any one favorite song I believe it was 'Babes in the Woods.' She used to tell me that she had always loved it and remembered that as a child she was always moved to tears when her mother sang it to her."[69] Motherly music and motherly sounds reinforced Depression-weakened assumptions that women's roles were primarily motherly ones, not ones where they asserted their economic independence. Indeed, as she stood on stage, there was never a suggestion that Muenich earned her living by performing these songs, just that she soothed her radio children with her sweet singing.

Because radio inherited old theatrical assumptions that only immoral women appeared on stage, broadcasters made women's presence a virtuous possibility by pairing them with stage chaperones such as a male backup band or an older woman. The Cumberland Ridge Runners served that purpose for Jeanne Muenich. Other women such as Rose Maphis and Lily May Ledford sang with all-girl groups (Ledford also used former vaudevillian Margaret Lillie) to ensure their onstage virtue. Fictitious (or real) boyfriends or husbands were useful, too, such as when Lulu Belle used fictitious boyfriend Red Foley, nicknamed "Burrhead" on stage, until she married *National Barn Dance* banjoist Scott Wiseman, who also served as her stage chaperone (although married women who appeared on stage were less of a threat).

The Ridge Runners might have been her chaperones, but Muenich helped them, too, since her sexuality could be used to sell all-male bands. "Right pretty" women became a standard component for all-male bands who searched for "girl singers" to add to their acts, whether it was the Ridge Runners, Roy Acuff's Smokey Mountain Boys (with Rachel Veach), or Bob Wills and his Texas Playboys (an unnamed female singer is pictured with the troupe in an early 1940s photograph).[70] The Ridge Runners played up Parker's appearances with them, billing themselves as "The Cumberland Ridge Runners with Linda Parker."[71] But women also performed their femininity as they had done when making vaudeville a respectable place for customers. Muenich's moral womanhood (secured by her claims to motherliness) promised that the show was respectable; no immoral behavior would occur as long as she was around to control the musicians.

Invoking a cabin in the Kentucky hills surrounded by nature's blessings was the final step in remaking Jeanne Muenich for radio. On her first show in February 1932, Lair asked his listeners to "shut yer eyes an imagine you kin see a little ole grey log cabin settin back aways frum the bend of a lazy, windin river . . . an a long cool front porch runnin the full length of it with mornin glories an honeysuckle climbin around on it . . . An up on the porch . . . sets a little ole girl in a gingham dress, with a sunbonnet slung over her shoulder, settin there an strummin away on a two dollar gittar an singin a million dollar song. Got the picture? Well, hold it—an lissen to this!"[72] Then, according to surviving script material, a costumed, made-up Muenich stepped up to the mike and sang "I'll Be All Smiles Tonite," with the Cumberland Ridge Runners playing backup. Afterwards, Lair told listeners that Parker had moved "all the way up here to WLS to make music with her old buddies, the Cumberland Ridge Runners."[73] He impishly added, "an if you make it real nice I won't tell em about yore red hair an the freckle on yer nose an all that."[74] Finally, in recognition of listeners' important contribution to the airwaves, he said, "But it's yore air we're puttin these here programs on an YOU'RE the one that's gonna say whether we keep her up here or not."[75]

Other shows repeated the context that made the character Linda Parker possible. Jeanne Muenich could change everything, but without a backdrop, music, or fictional scenarios, Linda the character was meaningless. The *Play Party Frolic,* the *Hamlin Wizard Hour,* and the *Coon Creek Social,* all regionally broadcast shows to the four-state region around WLS, replicated the themes that Lair had displayed on that first show with Linda Parker. The *Hamlin Wizard Hour,* broadcast on February 24, 1934, was a typical show that the announcer touted as "an imaginary trip down to a cabin in the Renfro Valley of Old Kentucky, there to hear these mountain folks in their weekly gethering—laughing, chatting playing fiddle tunes and singing the songs that they love."[76] These "getherings," Lair told the audience, had taken place since 1796 and were slow to change because "these Renfro Valley folks, when they know somethin's good they're mighty slow about changin."[77] One of those traditional folks, of course, was Lindy Parker, "frum up on Parker's Creek."[78]

The character Muenich played—Linda Parker—appeared on all shows, but Muenich played other parts, too, sometimes simultaneously. One night, Jeanne Muenich, playing Linda Parker, participated in a fictitious mountain wedding on stage. She spoke the lines for a character named Maggie, saying, "Why must you men always hanker to hear of wars and killins? It's my weddin night. Less have a song of sweethearts in love."[79] On a January 1935 *Coon Creek Social* show, she played an older woman named Aint [Aunt] Viney who was married to an old "codger" named Uncle Doody. Yelling at him as a long married woman and veteran mother might, Parker spoke these lines: "Yer mighty right I wont, you ole Swamp Owl. Ef I let you have yore way you'd have them great big, lollipin, sorry boys trackin mud in an outa my house all the time, an eatin up all the cold vittles on the place."[80]

In other shows, her character was used to display—and then dispel—through comedic means conservative Southern prescriptions against music and musicians, views that migrants may have carried with them to the big city. Fiddles, banjos (nicknamed the "devil's box"), and other instruments carried a bad image among churchgoing folk in the South who thought music making frivolous and therefore immoral. It also bore a bad name because of its links to dancing, alcohol imbibing, and other illicit behavior. Aint Viney's visit with her mother highlighted these prescriptions and then rendered them harmless on that same January 1935 *Coon Creek Social*. Both women were portrayed as being against fiddle playing, and Slim Miller, playing Uncle Doody, first told the announcer (Lair), "I reckin I haint gonn be no help to the boys tonight a-tall. That there wuz the old lady's mammy that come in with us. She's worse agin [against] my fiddlin than Viney is, an I didn't dast to even bring hit along tonight."[81] But Aint Viney (Parker) quickly contradicted her husband's assumption that she was against fiddle playing in a way that was worthy of a comic character, not a sentimental one. In response to Lair's question about what Uncle Doody would play on the fiddle, she said, "What's th'use in astin that, Cal? You know hit's gonna be Free Little Bird er Turkey Buzzard one er tother—them two's all he knows. (laff) Efen he'd learn him a new tune ever now an then I wouldn't keer so much fer him playin the fiddle, but aginst a body hears them two pieces over an over every day fer nigh onto forty year they git mighty tarsome."[82] In this case, conservative prescriptions became something to laugh at in Parker's hands, since her problem was not immoral fiddle playing (or women on stage), but Uncle Doody's limited musical ability, thereby transforming the problem from a moral one to an issue of bad musicianship, a travesty on the *National Barn Dance*.

Lair wrote scripts in dialect to remind Muenich (and other performers) to speak as a fictional Southerner, not as a Midwesterner. Language in this case marked her as different, unique, and rural, and, tellingly, the words differed from those spoken by other performers on the show. The language also referred to local-color writers who had portrayed mountaineers as speaking a vernacular speech different from mainstream English in magazine articles and books. Parker was thus a malleable and contingent character that depended on the language and contexts scripts provided since they determined the specific outline and form of her various stage performances. Even so, marriage and motherhood remained a constant in her act as the *Play Party Frolic's* Mother's Day show in 1932 displayed. John Lair announced,

> An now, folks, before we break up the party we want to take no-tice of this bein the eve of a speshil occasion—a mighty speshil occasion—an dedica a number to Mothers—not the "Mothers old an Gray" etc, you' hear hundreds of songs *to* them an *about* them tonight an tomorrow—but to the mothers who carry the world on their tired shoulders, the workers, the mothers on the farms an the plantations, the backwoods an the prairies, the mothers that wear the badge of sacrificin Motherhood everwhere—a faded old sunbonnet—to your sunbonnet Mother and the memory we dedi-cate this song. Lindy![83]

Then Linda Parker stepped to the microphone and sang "Faded Old Sunbonnet," a song about mothers, sunbonnets, and their unending sacrifices.

Muenich was so successful performing Linda Parker that listeners wrote to thank her for her performances. Listener W. Demont Wright wrote barn dance broadcasters in February 1934 that when Linda Parker sang "I'll Be All Smiles Tonite," he knew he was truly listening to old-time music. He remembered, "That is a song my mother sang when I was a boy (I am now 54) and if I remember correctly, it was an old song then, one she knew when she was a girl."[84] Wright was so taken with Parker's sing-ing that he asked broadcasters to "kindly convey to her my appreciation and enjoyment while she was singing this old, old song."[85] The letters of condolence that began this chapter echoed these sentiments. Yet not all listeners enjoyed the changes that had evolved during Lair's tenure, and some writers wished that Grace Wilson and her heart songs would come back. An anonymous writer wrote, "People are certainly fed up on 'The Cumberland Ridge Runners.' One can scarcely tune in between 6 & 12 unless you hear them . . . Lindy Parker is an 'agony.'"[86]

Muenich's death in 1935 fit well with her character because the mother's sacrifice on earth could only be rewarded in heaven. Her performance of songs such as "Meet Mother in the Sky" were explicit reminders that only by dying would the song's main character find her peace, but as in any good weepy song, her children would mourn her death until they, too, died. Muenich's death thus made Linda Parker more popular since the tragic component in her character was now obvious.

Lair used her death to sponsor a new regional program called *Bunk House and Cabin Songs,* an affirmation of the commercial potential of Parker's death. The *Bunk House and Cabin Songs* show was a regionally broadcast program that promised to bring "the good old-time songs of long ago frum hill an plain, frum cabin an bunkhouse—the songs yer daddies and mammies grew up with."[87] The sponsor in this case was the Lair compilation, *100 WLS Barn Dance Favorites,* a songbook that included a picture of Parker and the words to her signature songs, "Bury Me beneath the Willow" and "Take Me Back to Renfro Valley." Lair dedicated the book to Parker (not Muenich) and touted its memorial qualities to those who had an extra fifty cents to spend (sixty cents if you were Canadian). "It's a dandy," he said, "an then there's a nice big picture of Little Linda Parker, to whose memory the book is dedicated."[88]

Moreover, because Linda Parker was a mask that could easily be donned by others, she did not really die. A case in point was the *Bunk House and Cabin Songs* show, which staged a memorial for Muenich on her birthday in January 1936, where other female performers sang Parker's signature songs, and, for a brief moment, became Linda Parker. As the Girls of the Golden West sang "I'll Be All Smiles Tonite," Lair reminded the audience that Parker was "always 'All Smiles' around her friends and the boys and girls she worked with, always ready for fun and laughter."[89] When Patsy Montana sang "Take Me Back to Renfro Valley," Lair told listeners to "remember Our Little Sunbonnet Girl—when she was young an' eager for life . . . instead of thinking of her racked with the pain an' torture of those last despairin' days before she left us."[90] Lair then announced that although they could not send birthday cards to Linda, he gave out her mother's address on the air so listeners could send cards to her mother. Mrs. Muenich later reported she received hundreds of letters, cards, and poems.[91]

Jeanne Muenich and John Lair operated in new territory when they developed the Linda Parker character between 1932 and 1935, a character that still appears on country music stages today. Costuming, name changes, and script material combined to create the character. It then met the *National Barn Dance*'s two new purposes: to mingle the diverse migrants who tuned in to a new imagined community mediated by WLS, and to create a female character that bespoke consistency and stability in an era where economics promised nothing but chaos and masculine crisis. The consequences were significant for Muenich, however, as the character became so all-encompassing that little remains of Jeanne Muenich's own hopes and dreams except her desire to perform on barn dance radio.

3

"Hey, Hey, Hey, the Hayloft Gang Is Here"

Lulu Belle Wiseman and the
Emergence of the Professional
Radio Barn Dance

If Fed Up doesn't like Lulu Belle's type of music, why in the heck
don't they tune in on some grand opera program and leave us
simple folks to enjoy the type of program we appreciate?

—C. L. Finley, Heath, Illinois

Criticizing barn dance performer Lulu Belle Wiseman was more
than a critique of her singing, at least according to listener C. L. Finley.
It was yet another attempt to supplant "simple" values and mountain
ballads with modern conventions and grand operas. Lulu Belle represented those simple values: she was "clear and plain and, well, not so
highfalutin'," one listener wrote.[1] Another listener acknowledged Lulu
Belle's ability to fend off the challenges of the modern world when she

wrote, "There is so much tragedy in human life, most folks seek in radio a way of escape."[2] It made no difference to listeners that they heard Lulu Belle's simple kind of music on a quintessentially modern invention, the radio. It mattered only that she pledged stability and security while the world around them devolved into chaos.

Which grand opera did C. L. Finley dislike? Was it the opera program from a local Chicago hotel that WLS used as a filler? Or was it an oblique reference to fears that elites (represented musically by references to opera) were taking over WLS in another attack perpetrated by those who were to blame for the Great Depression? Or was it a charge against WLS's new professional atmosphere that made Lulu Belle's widespread popularity possible? What is clear is that while Finley saw Lulu Belle (1913–99) as a counter to grand operas on the air, broadcasters saw her as big business, albeit dressed in mountain homespun, by 1934 and 1935. A comedic version of Linda Parker, Lulu Belle helped WLS widen its appeal from its regional audience to a national, heterogeneous one (just as women had legitimated and broadened national appeal for the theater) by using WLS's new business practices and advertising machinery. In turn, daunted by the now mass audience that tuned into the *National Barn Dance,* performers and broadcasters confronted a core problem when evaluating letters like Finley's: what exactly had angered Finley? How did it affect his or her desire to spend money on sponsors' goods? WLS responded to that uncertainty by hypothesizing a bland, homogeneous version of its listeners, one that focused on the performer (thereby reinforcing her popularity) rather than a unique focus on the listener's class, background, race, or income potential. Still, listener desires managed to seep through the heavily edited letters that appeared, courtesy of WLS's new advertising machinery.

Where once a folk image like Linda Parker served regional needs, now that icon, spruced up with bubble gum and high-top shoes, provided therapy for a national audience seeking stability in an uncertain world. This chapter, then, examines how barn dance radio's professionalization and its relationship with its listeners as well as Wiseman's ability to play the sentimental mother helped forge her phenomenal success: in 1936, she was ranked fifth in popularity nationwide, lagging only behind male entertainers such as Jack Benny and Eddie Cantor. Her success (as well as that of WLS) was verified by Depression-era radio scholars who found that barn dance radio (called "old-time favorites" in their studies) ranked number one among listeners nationwide.[3] That popularity helped the genre expand, and by 1939 old-time favorites were broadcast on some 500 shows nationwide, many of which mimicked the *National Barn Dance*'s standards, formats, and performances. But who tuned in to the *National Barn Dance* and to those other 500 shows and what they bought remained invisible even as broadcasters and performers attempted to rationalize radio programming in order to make apparent that customer base. Only fans' love of Lulu Belle, her ability to invoke mountain streams, and her ability to avoid grand operas were visible.

❧ ❧ ❧

Lulu Belle's rise to stardom started innocently enough, and, in fact, part of her charm was her rather inauspicious beginnings. John Lair hired Lulu Belle (née Myrtle Cooper) seven months after he hired Jeanne Muenich in 1932 most likely because as a rural Southerner, Lulu Belle had a greater authenticity in his mind. But, of course, certain elements of her background had to be erased before Lulu Belle could appear on stage. Born to a convicted moonshiner's family in North Carolina, her father forced them to move constantly.[4] Later, the family settled in Elizabethton, Tennessee, and Lulu Belle worked in the hosiery mills that would become famous for a female hosiery worker strike in 1929 (there is no evidence that she participated, although she was still there in 1929).[5] Her father was jailed for running moonshine in Elizabethton, escaped from jail, and quickly moved the family to Evanston, Illinois, to avoid further prosecution. Once there, Wiseman worked as a maid, a dime store employee, and nursemaid, and earned extra money playing guitar and singing at chamber of commerce–type gatherings.

Wiseman's start at WLS is part of her legendary rise to barn dance stardom because it made her seem more homespun, ordinary, and therefore, genuine. Like many who made the transition from live performance to the radio, she had difficulty adjusting to microphones. She recalled, "I had never sung on a microphone before. I was accustomed to singing in the high school auditoriums and other places where there were no microphones, and to be heard you had to project. So when I sang as loudly on the microphone in Studio A there at WLS as I had been doing on stage, I just about blasted them out of the control room."[6] She failed that first audition but practiced for two weeks and then auditioned again, this time earning a spot on the WLS *Smile Awhile* program. Then she became a Lair protégée and underwent a transformation similar to Jeanne Muenich's. He changed her name from Myrtle to Lulu Belle, and had her study vaudeville rube Elviry Weaver's act. Lulu Belle said,

I'll tell you who I think John Lair patterned me after: Elvira Weaver,
of the Weaver Brothers and Elviry. I know he did, because he had
Daddy and me go down to the State-Lake Theatre where they were
playing. And she was real feisty. I think that's what he wanted me
to do. Well, I know he did. And so I did it insofar as I could, but
she was older and knew more about what she was doing; I was
young and ignorant. But as far as the *costume* went, that was from
her—even the high-top shoes. It would have had to have rubbed
off, since they sent me down to see her. Daddy and I went down to
see their show. Somewhere in between there, there was time for
Mom to make a dress for me to wear. John kind of explained what
he wanted with the high-top shoes, the way Elviry dressed, and
Mom had a chance to make a dress by hand for me to wear, that
first dress on the Barn Dance.[7]

Her new costume included handmade calico dresses with exaggerated
ruffles (a "Mother Hubbard" style, she recalled), high-top shoes (rather
than high heels like Jeanne Muenich wore), and extensions in her hair
she called "rats." Other props (called by theater insiders "trademarks"
since they were associated solely with Lulu Belle) consisted of a hope
chest filled with bubble gum, sandwiches, and grapes that she offered
to peel for audience members during shows.[8]

When Lulu Belle initially went on the air, she was part rube comedienne
and part sentimental mother, but packaged with a youthfulness and exu-
berance that was all her own. Station documents told listeners that Lulu
Belle had learned her craft at "her mother's knee," and her "mountain
girlhood" included a substantial education in "the old songs of the hills
which had been sung in the mountains for well over a century. They had
been handed down from one generation to another, with occasional new
verses added."[9] She later moved to Chicago and was the "belle of the
barn dance."[10] Lair paired her with Cumberland Ridge Runner Red Foley
(called "Burrhead" on the air) as her fictitious boyfriend to provide her
the chaperone she needed on stage, and, simultaneously, make her a migrant like those in her audience. She remembered, "They introduced me
on the Barn Dance as Red Foley's long lost girlfriend from down around
Berea, Kentucky, where he was from. They told the listeners I had heard
him singing on the Barn Dance and had decided that I wanted to come
up and sing on the radio, too."[11]

Perched on hay bales, the two sang duets like John Lair's composition,
"Hi Rinktum Inktum Doodee," a novelty song with lyrics similar to a folk

ballad in its focus on marriage, but with a twist that made it a parody of that music.[12] They sang:

> Will you marry me, my pretty little miss,
> Will you marry me, good-looking?
> I'll marry you but I'll not do
> Yore washin' an yore cookin'

> Then I wont have you, my pretty little miss,
> I wont have you, my dear-o.
> Well, they aint nobody asked you to,
> You yaller-headed skeercrow![13]

Lulu Belle may have been a peppy, flirtatious version of the sentimental mother (albeit one who refused to wash and cook), but her character exposed some tensions inherent in the mountain woman character and in the rube vaudevillian. The mountain woman could be dissatisfied with married life and the poverty associated with it; in rube comedienne Elviry Weaver's act, her popularity and economic independence suggested that single life, too, was preferable to married life. That independence appeared early in Lulu Belle's repertoire selections. Her choice of Sara and Maybelle Carter's song "Single Girl, Married Girl" portrayed a married singer who desires to be a single girl again because her responsibilities as a mother are expensive and exhausting:

> Single girl, single girl she's going dressed so fine
> Oh, she's dressed so fine
> Married girl, married girl she wears just any kind
> Oh, she wears just any kind

> Single girl, single girl she goes to the store and buys
> Oh, she goes to the store and buys
> Married girl, married girl she rocks the cradle and cries
> Oh, she rocks the cradle and cries

> Single girl, single girl she's going where she please
> Oh, she's going where she please
> Married girl, married girl, a baby on her knees
> Oh, a baby on her knees.[14]

The song (which earned substantial royalties for the Carter Family, much to Sara Carter's surprise) was a direct refutation of the sentimental mother. Mothering was not a noble profession capable of rejuvenating a nation but one that drained a woman of her youth, spirit, and money. And, in fact, the song may have been popular with those women in Lulu Belle's audience who had become more economically independent during the Great Depression, the same women Linda Parker was supposed to erase.

These two core elements—sentimental mother and independent rube—were essential to Lulu Belle's superstar status, but her marriage in 1934 to performer Scotty Wiseman (they were called "The Hayloft Sweethearts") and her well-publicized pregnancies made the sentimental mother even more popular. Scotty was a friend of Bascom Lamar Lunsford (best known as the originator of an Asheville, North Carolina, folk festival in 1928), who graduated from Fairmont (West Virginia) Teachers College thinking he would teach. Instead he performed on WLS, singing Appalachian folksongs and playing banjo as a solo act until he married Lulu Belle.[15] He studied Bradley Kincaid's act and later told an interviewer, "Bradley had a great influence on me and is largely responsible for my decision to make a career in music instead of teaching."[16] On stage, the Hayloft Sweethearts performed a kind of comic "battle of the sexes," perhaps modeled on the comedy patter of former vaudevillians George Burns and Gracie Allen who were making their own name on the radio. They stayed together during the tense atmosphere of the Great Depression, an example of a good marriage that survived even when the wife was financially independent.[17] It helped, of course, that Scotty seemed the calm patriarch ready to clamp down on Lulu Belle's antics if she was too mischievous.

The best example of their marriage's stability was the birth of their two children—Linda Lou in 1935, Scotty in 1938—who were clearly welcomed to the Wiseman family in an era when infants represented an additional financial hardship rather than a joyous occasion. Indeed, some listeners may have welcomed the opportunity to exult a new child in WLS's fantasy world when a new child in their own homes would have provoked tears and recriminations. More importantly, children made the sentimental mother concrete. Broadcasters highlighted the connection with the deceased Linda Parker when Lulu Belle's daughter was born: *Stand By!* fan columnist Marjorie Gibson reported, "Linda Lou [Wiseman] was named for the Little Sunbonnet Girl, Linda Parker, also for Scotty's sister, whose name is Linda."[18] It was Lulu Belle's first pregnancy that she thought gave her the coveted *Radio Digest* title "Radio Queen" in 1936, an award voted on by listeners nationwide.[19] In a bold acknowledgment of the reason she won the award, Lulu Belle told her listeners that she "was a-crawlin' around on the floor with Linda Lou" when she was initially told about the award.[20]

Children and a good marriage may have been key to her popularity, but no one outside of Chicago would have heard of Lulu Belle if it had not been for new radio practices that made barn dance popular nationally, a kind of programming that other shows wanted to emulate. Whether it was the new fan documents that promoted her, ties with national networks, or the addition of sponsors, Lulu Belle's star status and the financial rewards that came with it were made possible by this new reality.[21] Yet Lulu Belle's mountain persona that proved so attractive masked profound tensions as broadcasters and sponsors jockeyed for control over the stage, performers, and listeners using new practices, formats, and themes that were often at odds with the genre's wholesome or musical image. A real clash of cultures appeared, smoothed over for audiences who heard only sweet songs from Lulu Belle.

The federal government provided WLS the first impetus to change how it did business. A new regulatory agency, the Federal Radio Commission (the FRC, which later became the Federal Communications Commission) began to manage the airwaves in 1927 because of concerns with "bandwith overcrowding" (meaning multiple stations using the same frequency at the same time). But scholar Derek Vaillant argued that the FRC was biased against independent stations who wanted to retain their local character and toward a network model that was a "market-driven model in which heavily capitalized, centralized producers should supply a national market with programs created for mass appeal."[22] WLS's new arrangements, Program Director George Biggar remembered, were handed down in 1930 when the FRC ordered changes in its time-sharing arrangements, changes that put the spotlight on the *National Barn Dance*. He recalled, "In 1930, following the Federal Radio Commission and court hearings in Washington, WLS was ordered to share 87-kilocycles frequency equally with WENR, Chicago. The time-sharing arrangement gave WLS all Saturday night to midnight and all weekday time from early morning sign-on until 3:30 P.M. This made the *National Barn Dance,* from 7:00 to midnight, easily the dominant program on WLS—the climax of every week's schedule."[23] WLS gave up time in order to become part of the centralized business model, one that would boost its popularity. With this more structured time came a need for better performers during daytime and Saturday night hours, and WLS (now owned by the *Prairie Farmer* magazine) began to secure that talent by offering small weekly salaries. Biggar remembered that appearing on these daytime programs gave the performers "almost daily exposure to build them up."

WLS's sharing agreement was only the first catalyst. In the Depression's severe economic times, radio networks in general emerged as a viable commercial alternative to print media. The networks had emerged in the late 1920s (the National Broadcasting Corporation [NBC] and the Columbia Broadcasting Service [CBS]) that linked up stations from around the country under one umbrella network. Stations had the option then to play shows produced in New York or Chicago, or to find their own entertainment, which had become increasingly expensive as radio programs competed for the best performers. This and other money problems caused broadcasters to decide paid sponsorship would serve as radio's economic base, turning WLS from an act of goodwill (as it had been when Sears owned it) to a financial force in and of itself.

Radio corporations enticed sponsors to buy radio time by touting the effects of on-air advertising on sales in an era when print advertising seemed less effective. While total advertising expenditures for companies nationwide declined 25 percent from 1928 to 1934, NBC claimed, expenditures for radio advertising had increased by 416 percent, likely an inflated figure that NBC used to promote its services.[24] Companies like Miles Laboratories, the maker of Alka Seltzer, found that NBC's claim of successful sales over the air was correct. Miles Laboratories endorsed a one-hour portion of the *National Barn Dance,* beginning in January 1933, which was then broadcast over NBC's national network on Saturday nights. Miles Laboratories quickly extended its contract when sales of Alka Seltzer increased by $1.2 million in 1933 alone; the partnership lasted until 1946.[25] Miles accountants, who were not generally known to be effusive, stated in their 1936 annual report that the *National Barn Dance* "was primarily responsible for the wonderful increase in Alka-Seltzer sales."[26] Because it produced the desired results (increased sales), Miles increased the amount it paid the *National Barn Dance* from approximately $120,000 in 1933 to $766,000 in 1936.[27] While not the first *National Barn Dance* radio sponsor (Aladdin Mantle Lamp is the earliest recorded contractual agreement between a corporation and the program), Alka Seltzer's payments allowed the program to expand its roster of musicians from thirty cast members to forty-five. Some of the *National Barn Dance*'s most famous performers were hired to fill out its roster, including the Girls of the Golden West, Louise Massey and the Westerners, Clayton McMichen and the Georgia Wildcats, Patsy Montana, the Hoosier Hot Shots, Scott Wiseman, and former vaudevillian Pat Barrett, who performed as Uncle Ezra.[28] Lulu Belle's pay increased steadily thanks to Miles Laboratories, who paid her $200 per week, a figure surpassed only by Uncle Ezra, who made $800 per week.[29]

The show also began featuring star acts backed by small bands of lesser known musicians in order to attract listeners, just as theater owners had done with Sarah Bernhardt and other name acts. Now called a "unit period," the *National Barn Dance* broke its broadcast from 7:00 P.M. to midnight into half-hour segments. Each unit period, as Program Director George C. Biggar recalled, was then built around a star act, with three or more acts supporting the star as she or he performed.[30] By the end of the night, approximately twenty units had performed, mostly to regional audiences with the exception of the portion sponsored by Alka Seltzer and featured on NBC. Lulu Belle was served well under this new system as she became the feature attraction of the *Keystone Barn Dance Party* (sponsored by Keystone Steel and Wire Company) on the 8:30 P.M. segment of the Saturday evening barn dance.[31]

Alongside those performers, only certain products were successfully advertised on the air: goods that mimicked the mountain woman's and man's ability to soothe listeners' ills tended to do well. Medicinal products such as Alka Seltzer, Pinex Cough Syrup, and Hamlin's Wizard Oil (a muscle relaxant) were thus common products sold on the air. All promised to cure listeners of aches, pains, and stress associated with tough times. Tobacco products, tractors, and inexpensive consumer items like Aladdin Lamps and Keystone Wire also appeared on the air since they could be sold as making life easier in difficult times (they also fit the program's rural atmosphere). Ads, then, reinforced the therapeutic qualities of both the barn dance and the products sold. Alka Seltzer ads told listeners that ills such as colds, stress, and upset stomachs could be cured by listening to the barn dance—and by buying some Alka Seltzer. A 1936 WLS *National Barn Dance* program told audiences that performers were just "home folks" who strove "to lighten your cares by bringing you wholesome fun and entertainment."[32] "Get Well, Keep Well," said an ad for Alka Seltzer, poised beneath a group picture of the *National Barn Dance* cast.[33] Another Alka Seltzer program said, "It's a regular thing for the WLS artists to use ALKA-SELTZER to get relief from everyday aches and pains. 'Arkie' says its [*sic*] fine for headaches. Bill Vickland says it's great for sour stomach and acid indigestion. The Maple City Four says it's wonderful after a long session of the barn dance show."[34] In this case, it was the sponsor who soothed performers so they could sing for their audiences.

Because they paid for shows, advertisers began demanding a say in what broadcasters and musicians performed, all set out in a legal contract, another addition to radio programs. Aladdin Lamps and WLS broadcaster

John Lair contractually agreed in December 1930 that Aladdin would sponsor Lair's bands, the Cumberland Ridge Runners and the Renfro Valley Boys, for a salary of $100 per week. In return for salary considerations, the company reserved the right to "be the sole judges of the suitability and acceptability of the programmes broadcast by the Artists."[35] To judge suitability, sponsors wanted to see a written script before a show aired and demanded changes if they deemed it unacceptable. Sponsors feared barn dance comedians the most because they tended to ad lib instead of sticking to the script. While *National Barn Dance* comedians had a reputation for being "as a whole pretty clean" (no overtly offensive material), Miles executives still bristled at ad-libbed jokes. In 1934, one joke in particular caused executives to dash off telegrams of complaint. A comedian (it is unclear which one) said,

> The straight-man asks: "Do you know how to milk a cow?"
> Answer: "Yes, let her drink Alka-Seltzer, sit on a stool and drain
> the crankcase."[36]

Although connections between cows, laxatives, and Alka Seltzer were acceptable for rural folk accustomed to an earthy humor, companies considered the inferences objectionable. More importantly, comedians ad-libbed the joke, which frightened sponsors who wanted to control comedic behavior on stage. Thus, while all performers now had to clear their material with the sponsors, jokesters bore the brunt of network interference. By 1938, WLS comedian Pat Buttram could describe in *Stand By!* how program directors and sponsors censured comic material (as well as his discomfort with it). He wrote,

> After the comedian has assembled enough gags, or jokes, to fill a 15-minute program, his work still isn't over. He can always depend on some of his best jokes being marked out by the program director, or the advertising agency, or by the sponsor himself. This is done for various reasons. Some jokes are against station policies. Some, the advertising agency doesn't consider. And I have even had a joke taken out because the name used in it was the same as that of the sponsor's sister. Although most of the censoring is done for the best, there is nothing that makes a comedian feel worse than the cutting and changing of his script.[37]

Network executives tended to act as the sponsor's agent when censuring material and issued "continuity changes," or demands, when jokes were considered in "poor taste."[38] No continuity changes (beyond the complaint telegram regarding Alka Seltzer) exist for the *National Barn Dance,* and indeed, they may not have been a part of its successful relationship with Alka Seltzer. But by the postwar era, continuity changes were relatively common. The *Grand Ole Opry* was constantly under the network's watchful eyes once it went on its national roster in 1939. A March 27, 1947, continuity change deleted the following joke from (most likely) *Grand Ole Opry* star Whitey Ford, the Duke of Paducah's repertoire: "I'll never forget the April Fools day party we had last year. It's imprinted in my memory. And that ain't all. Somebody pushed me backwards, and I sat down on the hot kitchen stove and that was the seat of my troubles."[39] Most of the offending jokes, rendered in typical earthy, barn dance fashion, referred to body parts, sexual situations, or cross-dressing that might prompt listeners to turn the radio off.

Other stage behavior also began to disappear, especially drinking alcohol, and props such as jugs and stills disappeared from all barn dance stages (they were infamous props at the *Grand Ole Opry* and on North Carolina's *Crazy Water Crystals* show), names of bands changed (the Cumberland Ridge Runners and the Prairie Ramblers eased out the Fruit Jar Drinkers, another reference to drinking), and repertoires excised songs with any reference to alcohol. Where once Okeh Record executive Ralph Peer could record a simulated corn-shucking party where, historian Pamela Grundy said, "loud slurps of corn liquor played as prominent a role as musical performance," radio broadcasters now banned any mention.[40] Some songs, including Lulu Belle's popular recording of "Mountain Dew," which referred to alcohol, were also censored. Lulu Belle remembered, "You weren't allowed to sing anything about liquor, or cigarettes, or divorce, or anything that sounded the least bit shady or crude."[41] Another target when a program went on a national network was black performers. While the only African Americans on the *National Barn Dance* continued to be symbols, not actual performers, the *Grand Ole Opry* no longer touted virtuosity over race and fired harmonica player DeFord Bailey in 1940, just after it began appearing on NBC.[42] Black-faced minstrels remained, such as the black-face comedy act Jamup and Honey, which was still popular, but the acts decreased in popularity as the genre expanded its reach (or perhaps they were cut so liberal white or black consumers would not be offended).[43] As scholar Derek Vaillant found for other radio stations, though the presence of minstrels had dwindled, they still "encoded the airwaves as a domain of white pleasure and power produced at the literal and figurative expense of racialized African Americans."[44]

Even though Lulu Belle and others avoided taboo subjects to keep the sponsor and network executives happy, broadcasters and advertisers still squabbled over how performers would appear on stage. John Lair later encountered problems with advertiser Freeman Keyes when he produced the *Renfro Valley Barn Dance* in Kentucky just before World War II began. Keyes wrote Lair, "I am not putting myself up as a critic nor do I intend to tell you how to run your business, but unless you get some things into your shows that are different from other hillbilly shows on the air you are definitely not going to draw an audience over on the Blue (NBC) Network. I heard five hillbilly shows Saturday night and you could have changed the names of the talent and the sponsoring products and not known the difference."[45] Many times, Keyes's directives opposed Lair's musical repertoire and instrumentation (typically fiddles, banjos, guitars, and the occasional piano). Keyes once told Lair that his show needed an accordion and, in another instance, told him the sponsor wanted an electric guitar added to the *Renfro Valley Barn Dance,* which countered the genre's exclusive use of acoustic instruments.[46] John Lair pleaded with Keyes to loosen up, to let performers like Whitey Ford ad lib on his programs so Keyes's "copy writers wont be tempted to dream up a lot of fancy and unnatural situations that only take up time and strain the imagination of our bulk of listeners."[47]

Show formats seemed to have kept sponsors happy because they were intended to control maverick performers while providing listeners the comfort of a ritual—the expectation that certain singers, musicians, and jokes would appear on each show. The *National Barn Dance*'s format became the national standard for other shows (like the *Grand Ole Opry*) that modeled themselves on the Hayloft Gang's performances in hopes they might emulate its popularity. The *National Barn Dance* always opened with the same song, "Hey, Hey, Hey, the Hayloft Gang Is Here," which was then followed by Master of Ceremonies Joe Kelly's greeting, "How's mother and dad and the whole family?"[48] Listeners then expected at least one musical performance or a skit from each cast member within each unit period. Broadcasters mixed regular cast members with visiting musicians so that listeners' desire for familiarity could be balanced with their desire for new songs and jokes. In every show, too, listeners heard at least one square dance segment, which signaled an advertisement for the show's sponsor.[49]

The changes worked, as the *National Barn Dance* was ranked in the top ten of all radio programs in 1937 and 1938 by the *New York Times.*[50] Yet even as broadcasters and advertisers attempted to rationalize radio and make it more financially successful, the most difficult task remained: determining who the customer was and what material was most likely to prompt fans to spend money on a product. Audience surveys became a tool to evaluate fans and their willingness to spend money on products. In a 1937 survey long hidden in the Miles Laboratories' Archives, surveyors measured the *National Barn Dance*'s audience in cities and towns across the nation, described its knowledge of Alka Seltzer, and determined some of its likes and dislikes. Surveyors found that the program had a national audience that was middle or lower middle class (described as small business owners, postal workers, and school teachers). They also found that the proportion of listeners went up as the size of the city went down and that New York City residents hated the program. Surveyors reported fans "said it was a clean show, fine music and good singing" and that "they liked hill-billy girls," too.[51] Most importantly, surveyors found listeners bought Alka Seltzer after hearing about it on the *National Barn Dance*. Surveyors reported, "The great majority of respondents of the rural populations of the entire Central area praise the Dr. Miles Laboratories for giving them such enjoyable radio programs."[52]

But in a world where an "intangible product" (music and jokes) was sold, surveys did not satisfy broadcasters or sponsors since the results tended to reflect surveyors' attitudes, rather than give a true picture of listeners.[53] The biggest problem was the lack of substance in surveys: which parts of a show did a listener like? Which parts had been offensive? Unable to answer these questions, broadcasters tended to integrate their own assumptions about wholesome and clean entertainment rather than a specific listener's desires. Moreover, if radio was to educate listeners in moral and ethical standards, as Bradley Kincaid had done, listener desires could have been irrelevant. Finally, surveys could not reinforce the *National Barn Dance*'s commercial success, and letters continued to be broadcasters' best tool to evaluate its audience and reinforce the show's popularity. They turned to new publicity methods to elicit as much mail as possible. WLS's new owner, *Prairie Farmer* magazine, used its presses to produce a *Family Album,* a picture album of performers, broadcast executives, and other employees, which was available every November from 1929 to 1956, and which provided even more advertising for both the station and for the *Prairie Farmer.* WLS's fan magazine, *Stand By!* was another publication used to promote performers and establish the outlines of their characters. Lulu Belle graced its cover at least twice. But for editors, *Stand By!*'s second page, called "The Listeners' Mike," was probably the most important page in the book. Here, editors published snippets of fan mail received throughout the week, heavily edited (only the rare letter was printed in its entirety, and no letters appeared with spelling and grammar mistakes unless it proved useful) and with a clear intent: to create a homogeneous listener community that loved WLS (little hate mail was published unless it helped sell a show or a performer). The bland general listener was important, not the specific information included in the letters. That homogeneous listening community may have also helped elicit more mail: fans may have felt the urge to write because it seemed all were welcomed, not an exclusive few.

The original impetus to write came from a variety of sources. Some wrote to praise Lulu Belle or another performer; others criticized a performer or letter writer. Still others wrote to connect with listeners who shared similar interests.[54] But the main reason listeners wrote was to announce themselves as part of a fan community. Published letters were remarkably self-referential. Mildred Madrinovich, Milwaukee, Wisconsin, responded to another letter when she wrote, "As Mrs. Mullins of Oleny, Illinois, says, 'I drop everything when I hear Arkie sing'—well that goes for me, too, for I drop everything when Georgie [performer Georgie Goebel] comes on the air."[55] Part of the self-referential quality came from listeners' presumption that radio tied together friends from distant places, and writers in *Stand By!* regularly referred to performers and each other as "radio friends." Mrs. R. M. Kirby had just moved to Detroit, Michigan, and wrote, "But I appreciate my Stand By [*sic*] just that much more since that is the only way I have of getting the news of our radio friends and keeping up to date with the programs. I especially miss Lulu Belle and Scotty's early morning program."[56]

A set of rules helped cultivate that self-referential community, rules that "Fed Up," the letter writer that elicited C. L. Finley's outrage at the beginning of this chapter, abrogated when he or she criticized Lulu Belle Wiseman. Letter writers insisted that fellow writers act respectfully and policed each other's behavior via fan mail. Maretta Terrill of Ridgeway, Ohio, wrote to remind her radio friends of that etiquette: "When I read letters such as the criticisms of Lily May's playing and of Lulu Belle, I wonder if those people would walk up to a guest in their home and speak to them in the same way they write about the guests who visit their home via radio. One is just as rude as the other. If you don't like a visitor, you don't invite him back. If you don't like the radio guests, learn the hour he or she is on and leave the radio off."[57] Mrs. Myra Bowers of Covington, Indiana, agreed with Terrill, writing, "So praise loudly and criticize softly. If he or she is doing his or her best, there's no harm in patting them on the back."[58]

Writers were not the only ones required to behave properly; editors, too, were held accountable for their mistakes. Fans prided themselves on their knowledge of performers (birth dates, members of their musical troupe, and names of family members, for example) and wrote in when the editors were incorrect. Edith Lamb of Kingman, Indiana, was one fan who wrote in to correct editors who mislabeled a published photograph.[59] But fans also took broadcasters to task for letting Lulu Belle perform out of character, ironically the character that had been established using *Stand By!* One writer, S. E. J. from Sturgis, Michigan, believed that Lulu Belle was a natural singer who countered modern artifice: "When Lulu Belle and Scotty sing, we can understand everything they say. And that is more than we can say of a lot of so-called singers. Some call it classic, some call it modern, but I don't call it singing at all. So as long as Lulu Belle and Scotty continue to sing in their natural voices, they will have plenty of admirers."[60] But when Lulu Belle tried new routines, fans wrote in outrage, particularly when her character did not police the boundaries between mountain music and other kinds of music considered elite, modern, or jazz (typically used to suggest some racial intermingling). Dorothy Sheldon wrote from Cherry Valley, Illinois, in 1937,

> After reading two letters in Stand By which made me feel very badly, I want to put in a word on the other side. Please don't let Lulu Belle sing any more popular songs. Anybody can sing jazz but there is only one Lulu Belle and if you spoil her, you'll never find anyone to take her place.
>
> When I heard her sing "The Love Bug" that Saturday night, I thought it was going to be her own old song by the same name. When I found out otherwise, I was so bitterly disappointed that I sat down and cried, especially as we didn't hear her again before her vacation.
>
> We don't want any more jazz. We want Lulu Belle and the old songs that are hers alone and that nobody can sing so well. They stand for Lulu Belle to those who really love her and we don't want her made over to be like everybody else.[61]

Here, jazz represented the interracial mingling of whites and blacks, which Lulu Belle hinted at when she sang jazz. Having accepted, at least implicitly, that mountain music was white music in WLS's professional world and therefore, a moral counter to jazz (thanks to Bradley Kincaid), listeners reminded her and her producers to police racial boundaries, not mix them up.

As suggested in these letters, performers neutralized the racial mixing associated with modern times (represented by references to jazz), a particular concern for Depression-era listeners who believed these modern ways had caused the economic catastrophe. Like broadcasters who believed it was a "God-given instrument," listeners believed that radio, especially its microphones, could discern between a genuine act and an artificial one.[62] As Allan Mawby, Grand Rapids, Michigan, wrote, "Remember you cannot deceive the 'mike.'"[63] That genuineness elicited equally genuine emotion from listeners and when they wrote, they described performers in emotional terms as an almost antidote to the Depression. Dorothy Sheldon's letter certainly implied this with Lulu Belle, but other performers were also proclaimed the real thing. When Cumberland Ridge Runner Red Foley sang "Echoes of My Plantation Home," Mrs. Ethel Price pronounced it "perfect. Red is a real interpreter of human emotions and I cry when he sings 'Mother's Old Sunbonnet.'"[64] Listener Kathleen Whiting wrote to say how much she waited to hear "the delightful bass voice of Rocky Racherbaumer. . . . When he sings, the worries and cares of the day seem to vanish," she added.[65]

Yet listeners also expressed some of the tensions that radio attempted to hide. One main tension centered on that performed authenticity: was the performer a genuine, kind human being or was she a fake only out to make money by singing mountain tunes and jazz? How could listeners tell the difference when radio programs could be broadcast from miles away? Radio's lack of visual cues (the main way most Americans determined character) reinforced that discomfort since it relied on aural cues. *Stand By!* and the *Family Albums,* with their heavy emphasis on photographs, were probably published in part to assuage this fear.[66] Writers also went to local concerts and then wrote to the Listeners' Mike, reassuring fellow radio friends that performers were not false, pretentious cheats. None reported on Lulu Belle (although listeners did use the Listeners' Mike to drum up support for her Radio Queen title), but Mrs. John F. A. in Gifford, Illinois, wrote, "Just let me add a word of praise for your wonderful entertainers. We saw Ramblin' Red and his crowd at Crystal Spring Park and we surely did enjoy it. Red and Eva were grand. The Girls of the Golden West are sure good, and Miss Pauline and her dancing can't be beat. As for Uncle Tom Corwine, we sure thought he was the most lovable old man. His imitations and good humor are to be envied by all." In case other readers missed the point, the writer then said, "Any of the gang are welcome at a chicken dinner any time and all the time at our house."[67]

There was rarely other information in published letters regarding a listener's background, at least in the portions editors published, unless it helped the station build goodwill. Typically, a letter listed a name (or a pseudonym in the case of "Fed Up") and the place from where the letter writer wrote, if that was available. Some social information did appear like migrant status, age, or a crippling health condition; WLS printed a number of letters from shut-ins since they gave the impression that WLS was providing a public service, not just entertainment. Age appeared when it would elicit the "oh-how-cute" response from other readers, and only in instances when a child identified his or her age. Spelling and grammar in these instances were printed without the usual corrections. Marilyn June C., Chicago, wrote Hotan Tonka (a WLS performer),

> Ime so soree yor in the hospital.
> Ime haf pas six years old and ime a red hed and i have got long cerls and i have got freculs wher the sun kist my nose. I have seen you at wls lots of times and you lookt like a indeum are.[68]

The air of outrage generated by "Fed Up" then was a consequence of editorial attempts at creating a homogeneous body of listeners where behavior, not social information, counted. The initial letter was printed in the December 1936 issue, just after Lulu Belle had been named Radio Queen. "Fed Up on L. B." wrote, "You give me a pain in the neck the way you praise Lulu Belle. The way you act, you'd think she was the only person on the air. How foolish those singers at your station, who know something about singing must feel when they hear her sing all the time and forever the mention of her name being praised. I know this won't be published because, of course, anything that wasn't praising her wouldn't be."[69] The response was instantaneous and vehement since the letter seemed an attack on all writers and their love of Lulu Belle. One writer called the initial missive "that disgusting letter about Lulu Belle"; another "boiled up" after reading it.[70] Mrs. Maybelle Harvey, of Saginaw, Michigan, sniffed, "Lulu Belle may not be an opera star but she gives more pleasure and happiness to people than anyone else on the radio."[71] In almost every letter, writers believed criticism of Lulu Belle was automatically a criticism of those who loved her. In shaping the conversations between listeners on the pages of the Listeners' Mike to reinforce the popularity of Lulu Belle and other performers, one consequence seems to have been that the writers intertwined their identities with the performer: fans had invested emotionally in performers as they determined who was and was not a genuine performer, so much so that an attack on the performer seemed an attack on them and their own values. One writer said, "The millions of people who love Lulu Belle made her queen and I don't think her loyal subjects would be very well pleased if they couldn't hear her as often as possible."[72]

Editors, ever eager to foment irritation in the name of more mail, also printed letters from listeners who agreed with Fed Up although they did note that in the deluge of mail that followed, many letters gave "some sound advice on turning the dial if he didn't like Lulu Belle."[73] Intriguingly, all letters in support of Fed Up were printed with only the writers' initials listed, maybe so no rabid Lulu Belle fan would attack them when they said (as U. C. Y. in Pine Ridge, South Dakota, wrote), "I am more than fed up on Lulu Belle although we only get the Barn Dance but that is almost too much. We do not hear much of anything but you folks praising Lulu Belle and her singing. This is like giving candy to a baby and the rest have to stand back and watch her eat it."[74]

To some listeners, Lulu Belle was the cheap performer who relished the attention lavished on her; to others, she seemed to stave off the challenges (like grand operas and jazz) of the modern era. What was hidden in the controversies over Lulu Belle and her listeners was the *National Barn Dance*'s new professional structure that made hearing her possible. Sponsors paid for her performances; broadcasters provided formats and censured her material; mentors like John Lair showed her how to perform on stage. Thus, that relationship between those fans who disliked Lulu Belle and those fans who adored her (a number that seems to have vastly outnumbered her detractors), though contentious, was big business for the *National Barn Dance* as it became one of the most popular programs in the country.

4

"WILL THERE BE ANY YODELERS IN HEAVEN?"

The Girls of the Golden West
and Selling the Stage

Will there be any yodelers in Heaven?
That is what I'd like to know.
There can't be any wrong
in just singing a song and [yodel]
Will there be any yodelers in Heaven? [yodel]
In the heavens above, will they sing the songs we love?
While they yodel . . .

—Girls of the Golden West

In the early mornings over Cincinnati's WLW, the soothing sounds of yodelers filled the airwaves. The Pine Mountain Merrymakers (the Girls of the Golden West and Red Foley) greeted their listeners each day in 1937 and 1938 with their theme song, "When I hear that mountain call, my thoughts begin to stray back to old Pine Mountain where I spent my happy day."[1] Announcer Whitey Ford then called out over the air, "Good morning friends and howdy neighbors. How's everybody this morning?" before introducing the next tune. The Girls of the Golden West might then sing their signature song, "Will There Be Any Yodelers in Heaven?" Mingled in with the entertainment were ads for wholesome Pinex Cough Syrup; the Girls and Foley hummed softly and sweetly in the background as an announcer promised relief not just for sore throats and coughs, but for listeners' Depression-depleted wallets (Pinex was "the most economical cough remedy because it's concentrated!" according to those ads).[2] The Pine Mountain Merrymakers then yodeled their theme song once again before Ford signed off, promising listeners that they would "never say goodbye but so long til tomorrow."[3]

Lulu Belle Wiseman proved sentimental mothers were big business, but in the broadening of the genre from a handful of shows in the 1920s and early 1930s to more than 500 by 1939, new performers like the Girls of the Golden West used their special talents to popularize their barn dance stage. The Girls, Milly (1913–93) and Dolly (1915–67), sang about their Western home, their cattle drives, and their love affairs with their horses. They were particularly known for their cowgirl yodels—a soft, crooning sound rather than the trick yodeling or blue yodels typical of their predecessors—that invoked a mythic Western past, free from the modern burdens of the Great Depression and New Deal.

The Girls are part of another story, too, where radio executives, performers, advertisers, and Wharton School of Business professors attempted to rationalize consumer behavior as radio changed how sponsors sold their products and as the Great Depression limited consumers' ability to spend. Executives called that rationalization "scientific advertising," and women working within barn dance radio's professional structure were particularly adept at using its practices since their behavior on stage seemed decidedly uncommercial. The Girls' unique abilities display the subtle mechanisms used by advertisers on the air, especially by women. In fact, their yodeling mimicked one of those rational practices, an old advertising technique called the soft sell, reinvented as a musical form. Based on its popular music counterpart, crooning, yodeling approximated "the one to one relationship between salesman and prospect," as one historian wrote, but hid its commercial properties behind its rural referents.[4] That allowed yodelers to erase the line between ad and entertainment, saleswoman and customer, so that an entire show became an ad for (in this instance) Pinex. And the warm feelings engendered by the program prompted consumers to buy the sponsor's product in order to recreate those feelings. While Lulu Belle represented the new professional structure that made her popular then, the Girls of the Golden West serve as an exemplar of the genre's advertising content that made the barn dance genre so lucrative, and therefore, so appealing to broadcasters across the country.

Because how a program sounded was critical in the age of scientific advertising, broadcasters recorded shows for advertisers so they could hear how their products were sold on the air. Called transcriptions, performers had no problem providing them because they allowed performers to be in two places at once: appearing live all around the country and on recorded programs every morning on the radio. These transcriptions have never been used in a published work before, and they provide the evidence for this chapter. The problem, of course, is describing musical sound using the written word since the Girls' emotionality and Whitey Ford's warm voice cannot be conveyed. Given these limitations, however, I have tried to have the Girls sing, instead of speak, to this reading audience as much as possible.

⁂ ⁂ ⁂

While station documents told listeners that Mildred and Dorothy Goad were born to good Western parents in Muleshoe, Texas, their real biography was not quite so colorful.[5] In an interview from the 1970s, Milly Goad McCluskey described their working-class, Midwestern background and its influence on the Girls' development as musicians. She told interviewer Charles Wolfe that she and her sister were born near Mt. Carmel, Illinois, and it was their mother (a postmistress) who nurtured their incipient talents, teaching Dolly to play guitar and both girls to sing. In Milly's eyes, that familial influence proved their authenticity because she was able to insist their talent was natural and unaffected, a step toward claiming an authentic stage presence. As she recalled, "It's a God-given talent and I just have a natural ear for harmony."[6]

Barn dance broadcasters discovered the Girls' talent early: Milly was seventeen and Dolly fifteen when they landed their first job in 1930 on St. Louis' WIL. They later moved across town to KMOX, and then worked on border radio station XER ("The Sunshine Station Between the Nations").[7] WLS hired them in May 1933 to fill out its roster of Western singers, which by then included Gene Autry (with whom they performed) and, later, Patsy Montana (whom they discovered).[8] Their popularity earned them a spot on entertainer Rudy Vallee's show in New York City as well as their own fifteen-minute program broadcast from New York. Their work with Vallee was particularly important since he was considered the King of the Crooners and one of the most popular radio stars in the country in the late 1920s and early 1930s. From him they learned that crooning was, as scholar Allison McCracken wrote, a "homogenizing synthesis of American music, as it combined the intense romanticism of the Victorian ballad with the amorality of the urban novelty song and the emotionalism and sensuality of jazz music."[9] Their yodels were thus influenced by mainstream singers like Vallee rather than Southern stars like "Blue Yodeler" Jimmie Rodgers, and were designed to evoke a more romantic, emotional feel rather than a blues feel as Rodgers did.

Their recording career began in 1933, but records, as Milly admitted, were merely a sideline that never garnered them much money (approximately one-half cent per record sold). Moreover, the Great Depression cut record sales back significantly, and most performers knew the real money was to be made on the radio. Back at WLS by 1936, they joined John Lair's Pine Mountain Merrymakers program and followed Lair to WLW in Cincinnati ("The Nation's Station") in 1937 when he started the Renfro Valley Barn Dance. They were never Lair protégées as Jeanne Muenich or Lulu Belle Wiseman were because Lair had only a passing interest in Western acts, which waned as he built his Renfro Valley vacation complex in Kentucky and moved the radio program there in 1939.[10]

Like Gene Autry, who began his career on WLS in 1930, the Girls' popularity stemmed from their transformation of venerated American imagery into programs ripe for the audience's listening pleasure.[11] As John Lair said to an audience one night, the West was "an [i]mportant part of the history an [*sic*] musical culture of a mighty great nation—the nation the makers of these songs helped to build."[12] Annie Oakley and Hollywood movie Westerns (which became popular in the 1910s and 1920s, but experienced a decline in popularity in the 1930s) had taught audiences that the West was a premodern place with little or no industrial development.[13] The supposed lack of industrialism reminded listeners that there were places where closed factories did not exist: on the prairie, a person could be free from the restraints caused by industrialism and perhaps make a new start. It was an area that needed to be tamed, and one of the crucial actors in civilizing that savage place was the "good woman" who promised the redemption of those who wandered on the prairies, searching for a new life.[14] Annie Oakley and Mommie Gray certainly symbolized that good woman on vaudeville stages as did lesser-known women on Hollywood movie lots. Movies and vaudeville shaped radio listeners' expectations of Western music and stage plays in ways they never shaped expectations of the sentimental mother, since movies especially reached a mass audience using more consistent material (a movie was a stable phenomena wherever it was shown, whereas a vaudeville show could differ from one stage to the next and even from one performance to the next).[15] Radio used the common clothing, naming practices, and song repertoires, albeit translated into the aural needs and business practices associated with radio. Performers had to wear hats and six shooters, and audiences expected certain songs and lyrical themes from those who appeared on stage.[16] The Girls catered to those audience expectations when creating their characters. First, they chose a stage name. They kept their first names but added "the Girls of the Golden West" to their act and changed the spelling of their last names from Goad to Good. In Western mythology, there were the good guys and gals (cowboys and girls) and bad guys (outlaws, Native Americans, and others). The spelling change was one way to lay claim to the good woman whose virtuous, civilizing hand holding a rifle was so important. It also minimized the audience's tendency to misspell their last name. A virtuous Western background also met audience expectations. Muleshoe, Texas, a town chosen from a map, became their main claim to a Western past, and their supposed childhood on the Texas frontier implied that it continued to influence their moral and ethical choices, even in industrial Chicago.[17] Milly's strict Protestant work ethic, *Stand By!* reported, had been forged in her Texas hometown: "Milly went to a high school for a short time but decided she would rather stop school and start earning her own money. This she did by taking care of the neighbors' children. She also helped with the farm work, milking cows, churning, hoeing corn, and driving a horse in front of the binder while the menfolks were cutting wheat."[18] That hard work was as valued as any work a sentimental mother did around the home and whenever announcers introduced them, they reminded listeners of their virtuous beginning. John Lair announced one night that he wanted the Girls "to sing about them big hills you crossed when you came here from Muleshoe, Texas," before they sang their version of "On the Sunny Side of the Rockies."[19] Lest they worry about the authenticity of the Girls' Western birthplace (or its moral hold on them), Lair told his listeners to "Look it up on the map if you don't believe there's a town by the name Mule Shoe [*sic*]!"[20]

Their costumes, complete with fringe and guns, also invoked familiar Western mythology where weaponry served as a civilizing tool alongside the Bible and plow. Fans wrote letters to *Stand By!* querying what the Girls wore on stage, and magazine writers assured them that "The Golden West Girls wear handsome cowgirl outfits consisting of 10-gallon hats, high boots, leather skirts, white or black silk blouses, and leather bolero jackets."[21] Milly remembered the impact of their costuming:

> We started out with the publicity following us that our outfits were all handmade, and a big deal about that. We did make them ourselves and it was made out of velvet and then we had more like a drapery fringe just on the bottom of the skirt. But where we got the idea of how to dress like cowgirls with fringe, I guess it would be like the cowboy outfits because there were no cowgirls at that time that I know of. The fringe and the boots and the gun and the holsters . . . They were real guns, but they didn't have any bullets in them. Then we had vests with fringe on, and skirts under that, and bought cowboy hats.[22]

Audiences required photographic evidence to verify the Girls' authentic clothing and character. *Stand By!* and WLS's yearly Family Albums featured the Girls as well as their good friend, Patsy Montana, standing next to a campfire in their costumes. They complemented their costumes in those pictures with other symbols from the West: a log to stand against, a guitar to serenade cows (or listeners), and fake trees.[23] WLS broadcasters and performers showed a real cost consciousness (it was the Depression, after all) when it came to these pictures: both the Girls and Patsy Montana made their publicity photos using the exact same props and scenery.

Yet like those who played mountain women on radio stages, Western women incorporated vaudeville assumptions about women and their sexuality into their act. In St. Louis, broadcasters kept the Girls from wearing cowboy boots so their legs would show. Physical descriptions appeared in fan documents, reinforcing the sale of their sexuality. According to *Stand By!* Dolly was "a tall, well-built girl, with a height of five feet, seven inches, and a weight of 140 pounds. Her dancing eyes are hazel and she wears her light brown hair in a curly long bob."[24] In case fans missed how pretty she was, Dolly's face graced the cover of the magazine, spotlighted in a close-up picture that did not show her body. John Lair reminded his listeners that the Girls looked as pretty as they sang when he said on the air one night, "an folks these girls look jest as sweet as they sound. If you don't believe it drop around an see 'em on some of ther personal appearances."[25]

The Girls invoked the mythic West most successfully with their musical repertoire. Many songs such as "Old Chisholm Trail" and "Whoopee-Ti-Yi-Yo, Git Along Little Doggies" were standards that were as old as the mythology itself, or favorites from vaudeville stages that Mommie Gray or Annie Oakley may have sung.[26] When the Girls sang "Oh it's bacon and beans most every day soon to be eating prairie hay, come ti yi yippee yippee yea yippee yea," part of "Old Chisholm Trail's" familiar refrain, listeners recognized it as one they may have heard in movies or at a traveling vaudeville show.[27] More than a song's age invoked the Old West, however. Inherited themes dominated the Girls' repertoire, whether the song was a favorite from the past or one they wrote themselves. One common theme was rugged individualism forged on a seemingly endless prairie. The Western frontier promised hardy individuals redemption or riches if they could withstand its rigors. In "Oregon Trail," the Girls sang about the wealth waiting for pioneers once they finished their long, arduous trek on the Oregon Trail:

> There'll be apples on each branch in Oregon
> There'll be valleys filled with golden grain
> There'll be cattle on each ranch in Oregon
> For there'll be plenty of sun and rain.
>
> Hurry up oh pioneer keep movin'
> Your faithful little band must never fail
> Cross the Great Divide side by side we'll ride
> Down the Oregon Trail.[28]

Images of rain and a surplus of apples, of course, would have been especially enticing to listeners in the Midwest who suffered from the droughts and dust storms that plagued the region in the 1930s.

Paeans to nature were also a common lyrical theme. For those who believed the modern urban world had caused the Great Depression, the West's pastoral quality stood ready to rejuvenate them. As one scholar noted, the Western past was "an exotic land where one could find happiness and freedom," not pain or despair as listeners found in the industrial present.[29] John Lair told listeners on his *Bunk House and Cabin Songs* program, "There's a sort of a romance about old songs of that strange wild land that lay beyond the Mississippi. That makes songs of the early cowboy mean a lot to the romantic girl singer of radio today."[30] The Girls conjured this pastoral image in "Take Me Back to My Boots and Saddle" when they sang:

> Take me back to my boots and saddle
> Let me see the general store

Let me ride the range once more.
Give me my boots and saddle.[31]

Yet all consumption was not bad; if one bought from a general store set in a simple place, consumerism was just fine by the Girls.

The Girls' song selection also declared the West to be a class leveler; a place where anyone who worked hard enough could build a good life was an easy sell to Depression-era listeners who believed unethical elites had caused the economic crisis. John Lair described the West as "a new frontier," a "new land—a wild, free land, where everbody had a chance to git a new start."[32] The Girls summoned that image with their self-penned "Two Cowgirls on the Lone Prairie":

I have no longing to live in a town
And cook all my grub on a stove
Oh give me a barrel on the lone prairie
As a cowgirl, I will always roam.[33]

But the West also leveled differences between the sexes. The Girls laid claim to an independent woman's West in three distinct lyrical ways. The music they wrote, first, claimed male activities as their own. Their song "I Wanna Be a Real Cowboy Girl" declared a life lived on a prairie, wearing cowboy garb, preferable to living in a city in silk and satin:

I wanna be a real cowboy girl
And wear all the buckles and straps
And know how it feels to wear spurs on my heels
And strut about in my chaps
I want to tote a six shooter, too
Wear a belt that is four inches wide
Then ride like the dude on a buckskin cayuse
With the cowboy I love by my side [yodel].[34]

While she might consider fashionable cowgirl clothing fun, riding a horse with a good gun and with her cowboy by her side were just as important.

The Girls also declared cowgirl independence by using the male authorial voice. Rather than changing pronouns to reflect their femininity, the Girls instead sang songs as if they were the male narrator. Their song "I'm Lonesome for You, Caroline" is just one example:

You broke my heart when you said goodbye
I'm to blame our romance is through

> You never know how you made me cry
> I have nothing to live for but you.
>
> Gee but I'm lonesome for you, Caroline
> So lonesome, pal of mine, without you
> I'm always yearning for you, Caroline
> Please soothe this aching heart of mine.[35]

The Girls were certainly not the first to use the male authorial voice nor would they be the last. Eventually, it became standard for country and western music women to use men's songs to demand independence or to construct a new character.[36]

Finally, the Girls used lyrics to eschew the conventional roles that Linda Parker claimed for women on stage, namely marriage and motherhood, but did so in ways that mimicked Lulu Belle and her implicit rendering of the independent mountain woman on stage. As Lulu Belle did with "Single Girl, Married Girl," the Girls' music sometimes suggested marriage and motherhood were poor choices. Their song, "Two Cowgirls on the Lone Prairie," decreed (in what might be described as a Freudian field day) their horse to be the best husband of all:

> Oh I have no hankering ever to wed
> A husband I never could see
> My horse is my sweetheart and he loves me, too
> A married life won't do for me (no sir).[37]

Their sound invoked the West as much as any lyric did. The vast majority of their songs used uncomplicated harmonies with Dolly's guitar strumming modestly in the background. Since instrumental flourishes detracted from the image, plain and simple music summoned a plain and simple West. Moreover, the tempo they used was, in most cases, slow-paced (with the exception of older, fast-paced songs such as "Old Chisholm Trail"). The Girls rarely punctuated any of their notes, typically sliding into them to conjure the "lonesome," or mournful, sound that evoked lonely, widespread prairies and cattle lowing on a drive across the plains, but that also referred to former boss Rudy Vallee's style of singing.

Just about every song included a yodel done in close harmony. There is little historical evidence that real cowboys and girls ever yodeled, but by the late 1920s, Blue Yodeler Jimmie Rodgers (country and western music's first superstar) used yodels in his act. Rodgers called them "blue yodels" because blues men taught him the vocal form. Scholar Douglas Green described blue yodels as Rodgers sang them: "Blue yodels were powerfully evocative, expressing loneliness, alienation, dejection, and pain, as well as freedom and joy. They were relatively easy to master by any singer with the ability to break his voice, and the next generation of cowboy singers made yodeling a musical challenge."[38] Depression-era radio programs transformed the blue yodel from its lonely, pain-filled, harsh sound to a lighter, sweeter, and softer sound in keeping with shows' premise that they soothed listeners rather than depressed them. Performers like Patsy Montana used the tricky vocal technique to awe and amaze listeners in what historian Bill C. Malone called a more "sophisticated Swiss style."[39] The Girls used a different, slower-paced, less technically proficient yodel, one modeled on a softer sound like Rudy Vallee's that did not refer to Rodgers' explicit blues sound or Montana's Swiss style. Milly recalled they preferred things a little slower because "we thought it went with our style and type, we just liked them better."[40]

While audiences might have expected certain Western conventions on barn dance stages, the Girls usually combined references to multiple characters and places into their act. On barn dance radio, melding together elements from both the West and South was especially easy, given the subtle similarities between the two. Both images relied on mythological representations rather than historical reality. Each place had not evolved from its frontier history into an industrialized place, at least on stage, and that mythic quality made each region devoid of the politics, crises, and controversy that infused the everyday life of Depression-era listeners. The difference, of course, was the West seemed to be a contemporary frontier, one still able to be accessed, while the South seemed to be one from the past. Because both were symbolic frontiers, both regions were protected from the potential contamination of pioneering values. Westerners, like mountain folks, were wholesome and believed in old-time fun, but in the West, they had their play parties with cows.

This intermingling of West and South was not simply the placement of cowgirls and sentimental mothers side by side on the same stage. Performers also mingled elements from both regions into their characters. For a cowgirl, the Southern sentimental mother was a subtle, but common, component of her character. While she might be independent, a cowgirl could not be too independent or she risked the audience perceiving her as immoral. *Stand By!* magazine noted that both Milly and Dolly were married and Milly's husband, Bill McCluskey, reportedly told *Stand By!*, "She's a mighty good cook . . . and she's not letting her radio career interfere with being a wife and mother."[41] Dolly's marital problems with husband Tex Atchison, a member of Patsy Montana's Prairie Ramblers, were never discussed nor was her eventual divorce. The Girls knew their children countered their independence since the audience knew they had responsibilities waiting for them at home, and they included them on stage whenever possible. When asked if she talked about her five children on the air, Milly responded, "We would mention it if it would come in handy. One time I had the four boys down on our show."[42] *Stand By!* regularly included pictures of the kids; in a 1935 Thanksgiving article, Milly told the magazine she was most thankful for "my two boys and Bill."[43] The downside, of course, was that investing their characters with elements from the sentimental mother (which tied them to the home) contradicted the cowgirls' desire to ride the open range, free from worry and duty.

When radio performers and broadcasters mingled Southern and Western imagery, they did so knowing they operated on a frontier of their own. Advertising techniques developed in the late nineteenth century were based on visual media such as magazines or newspapers. Selling products using sound required new techniques.[44] Those techniques, called "scientific advertising," used multiple practices to rationalize consumer behavior when it seemed anything but. Those approaches, which began to appear when Bradley Kincaid starred on WLS's stage, included an intimate, emotional tone of speaking to the audience and addressing the audience as "you" rather than in the third person. Announcers and performers also used the "soft sell," personal pitches to the audience, that erased the line between ad and entertainment and that promised therapy for weary, anxious listeners.[45] Products reinforced the image of shows as healers. Medicinal products like Alka Seltzer and Pinex Cough Syrup in the early and mid-1930s bolstered the claims of health and healing. Tobacco and cigarette products made similar claims. In 1940, John Lair sold Big Ben Tobacco as a tobacco "mild and mellow, fragrant and rich in flavor," adjectives that suggested it was a product with healthful properties. Broadcasters sold Allis Chalmers tractors, too, as therapeutic for farmers. Tractors in this instance eased a farmer's life, which fit both the show's rustic appeal and its images of health and comfort.[46]

The human voice repeatedly sold the product over a fifteen- or thirty-minute show. An ad was not merely copy inserted at the beginning and end of a show, but was apparent every minute it was on the air. When an actual ad did appear, the announcer was typically a man since the conventional wisdom in the industry by the early 1930s was that women made poor announcers (and therefore, advertisers) because listeners (and the scholars studying them) judged their voices to be artificial and strident. As one scholar who studied radio ads noted in 1933, "a gruff, friendly, masculine voice engenders confidence, while the unctuous tone, which women find so hard to overcome when speaking on the radio, makes the listener feel unconsciously that he is being patronized, and as such, probably has a great deal to do with the marked unpopularity of women lecturers or announcers."[47] Women selling on the air gave the impression of "affectation and unnaturalness" because commerce was not conventionally considered part of their "natural" sphere.[48] Industry insiders further justified men's role as advertisers because they were "more persuasive and more interested in the material they read."[49]

While prejudice kept women from announcing ads, symbolic women were still used in "direct ads," the portions of a radio show set aside to publicly proclaim a product's attractive attributes. Ads constantly referred to that most uncommercial of images, Mother and her old-fashioned ways, using her to mask the direct sales pitch. One announcer told the audience, "Folks—do you remember Mother's home-made cherry pie and that devil's food cake that just melted in your mouth? *Sure* you do! And there's another home-mixed favorite you'll all remember. That's PINEX—that good dependable cough syrup that Mother mixed right in her own kitchen—that brought such quick, comforting relief for those coughs due to colds. Well, folks—PINEX is *still* the family favorite after thirty long years!"[50] Buying Pinex, the announcer assured his audience, simulated "Mother's wise, old-fashioned ideas that bear the test of time."[51] In other cases, one could recreate the past by buying a product Mother used to use. Lair auditioned for the Pinex account, using an ad that touted this link with the past: "Perhaps your mother used to prepare this mixture in your own home."[52]

At times, announcers recognized that women were the primary consumers in the household and spoke directly to Mother, selling their product as a way to economize.[53] But surviving scripts suggest that speaking directly to women was rare. More common were ads for products like Allis Chalmers tractors that touted the tractor's ability to ease the "women folks'" labor. John Lair asked men if they were willing to ease their wives' lives by buying a tractor (tractors would eliminate hired threshers for whom women would cook). He read aloud a letter from Mrs. Jess Francis, who wrote after her husband bought an Allis Chalmers All-Crop Harvester, telling him how delighted she was with the new harvester. Mrs. Francis wrote that no longer would she stay up late cooking for threshers. "Which will it be for your wife?" Lair asked after reading her letter on the air, "drudgery or an All-Crop Harvester?"[54]

Using women's singing voices to sell Pinex and other products proved far more effective than using them as passive symbols. Their musical sales pitch reproduced a kind of salesmanship called the croon or personal pitch and mimicked the motherly crooning that Linda Parker used to sing to her listeners. Microphones, which had already changed who sang on the air, contributed by causing listeners to think that the singer sang personally to each one through the radio speaker sitting within a living room.[55] Cowgirls called the singing personal pitch by a familiar name associated with the West, yodeling.[56] The Girls' rendering of yodels, with their slow-paced articulation, made them use the yodel in order to lull their listeners into a feeling of comfortable languor that would make customers out of listeners.

The Lair-produced Pinex Cough Syrup shows were the primary place the Girls used yodeling sales pitches, first in Chicago and later at Cincinnati's WLW. They began as half-hour Sunday programs in January 1936 and quickly added a daily noontime program. By October 1936, the show's cast, now called the Pine Mountain Merrymakers, included the Girls, Red Foley, and (for a time) Lily May Ledford.[57] The troupe's name sold Pinex even when the radio was turned off, in what was called indirect advertising, since the troupe then "played out," or appeared at local concerts bearing that name.[58] By the time the show moved to Cincinnati in 1937, the Merrymakers followed a familiar format that incorporated the hallmarks of scientific advertising on their transcribed shows with performers integrating ads, music, and yodels so smoothly that listeners knew an ad only when Whitey Ford mentioned that Pinex was bringing them "a lively program of music and song," or "wholesome transcribed entertainment."[59] Featured performers on the show, the Girls typically appeared near the beginning and the end of the show yodeling songs about the West like "Texas Moon" or their standard "Two Cowgirls on the Lone Prairie," invoking in their song selections that sales pitch that lulled listeners into a buying mood.

Yodeling sales pitches had other benefits. Erasing the line between ad and entertainment also helped decrease the distance between performer and listener. Where miles could separate listeners from performers offstage, on the air the distance seemed inconsequential, as if the radio friends were next-door neighbors. On one show after the Girls sang "By the River Rio Grande," master of ceremonies Whitey Ford remarked, "That was a mighty pretty song, girls. Bet the neighbors out there liked it, too."[60] Announcers and performers also invited listeners to stand on stage with them. In one case, Whitey Ford told listeners that fiddler Slim Miller played a song that was a "special request from friends on the east coast of Maine."[61] In other cases, he invited listeners to request a song from the Girls, saying, "If you'd like to have the girls sing a special song for you, drop a card or letter."[62]

Pinex brought the "cheerful entertainers" to its listeners, and the audience clearly loved the Merrymakers, whether they were in Chicago or in Cincinnati.[63] One listener wrote, "Just want to tell you how much I enjoy the new members in your family. Lily May, Red, Milly and Dolly make a wonderful program and let's have more of Red and the Girls of the Golden West as a trio. It is great."[64] Announcers told those listeners who enjoyed the show so much that they owed Pinex a debt of gratitude for bringing good, wholesome entertainment to the radio. It was "through the kindness of the people who make that good Pinex cough syrup, we kin reach right out over the air an invite everybody, everywhere, to attend our little getherin's [*sic*] by radio."[65] In other words, listeners should buy some Pinex cough syrup so the program could continue.

Yodeling to cows (and listeners) may not have seemed like it on the surface, but the seemingly old vocal form masked a modern sales technique called the soft sell, or personal approach, a core element in the new scientific advertising. The Girls of the Golden West's yodels masked that new approach, making shows seem like endless entertainment, not sponsored programs designed to sell a product. The ads that did appear were simply musical tributes to a virtuous frontier past, one that promised Depression-weary listeners a respite from their modern lives.

Banjo Pickin' Girl

Lily May Ledford, the Roosevelts, and Constructing National Identity

I'm going round the world, baby mine
I'm going round the world, baby mine
I'm going round the world,
I'm a banjo pickin' girl
I'm going round the world, baby mine.

—Coon Creek Girls, *Early Radio Favorites*

It was an auspicious night for the young woman from Red River Gorge, Kentucky. On June 8, 1939, "banjo pickin' girl" Lily May Ledford stood in the White House's East Room ready to play for President and Mrs. Roosevelt, the king and queen of England, and some 300 other American and British dignitaries. A highlight of her career as a barn dance radio star and folk musician, Lily May remembered that performance in her unpublished autobiography:

> We were scared. This was no school house or movie theatre. All that splendor! Dresses, white tie and tails, jewels, jewels, jewels! ... When I began to gather my wits about me Lord! Right there in the front row about 5 feet from stage sat the King and Queen and the Roosevelts! I like to dropped a stitch or two on my banjo, but recovered and went on and tried not to stare, tho I was able to size them up from the corner of my eye.

Our spirits rose as we realized that the Queen and Mrs. Roosevelt were smiling as well as Pres. Roosevelt, but the King!, with a rather long faced dour, dead pan look worried me a little, then as I glanced down, I caught him patting his foot ever so little then I knew we had him![1]

By 1939, when Lily May Ledford (1917–85) played for British royalty, barn dance women's popularity and the assumptions made about their music made their performances fit for a king. Ledford's performance, done a mere three months before World War II began, had ramifications for the making of American national identity. As the new crisis neared, the Roosevelts sought to define who we were and what we stood for as a nation, using the cultural work they had started with the New Deal. They used that cultural work not only to rejuvenate American culture, but to tout our ideological mightiness to the international community. As the most genuine (legitimate, virtuous) nation on earth, the Roosevelts and those working with them tapped Lily May to perform (witness an example of that virtue, our authentic musician on stage) in ways that reflected the New Deal's cultural agenda and incipient foreign policy. While others may have planned the event (Works Progress Administration officials, folklorists with close ties to the White House), documents from the Roosevelt Papers suggest that President and Mrs. Roosevelt were fully aware of the musical events for that night, approved of the performers and their musical selections, and were ready to use those performances to make the transition from an isolationist American culture to one that was ready to fight the Nazis.

By 1939, even President Roosevelt, well versed in the potential of radio because of the success of his Fireside Chats, used barn dance music to help ready Americans for a new war. There were two contradictory elements, however, in his and Mrs. Roosevelt's use of Ledford's music. First, the image the government used was forged on a commercial stage rather than straight out of the mountains: threads of that tradition had first been brought to urban venues by British folklorist Cecil Sharp and vetted before a mass audience on the radio. Second, banjo pickin' girls disrupted a smooth, seamless national identity based on flags waving and Ledford's hearty rendition of "The Soldier and the Lady." Tension and chaos dictated American national identity in the 1930s and 1940s, not slogans and songs declaring "United We Stand." This is particularly apparent considering the entire slate of performers who appeared with Lily May, especially African-American opera singer Marian Anderson, who performed Western art music. The juxtaposition of a white mountain woman and a black opera singer suggests that, as the Roosevelts tried to embrace our diversity by using Anderson (rather than John Lair's powerless metaphor of slavery), white Americans challenged and even rejected that national identity because it did not validate their sense of racial superiority.[2]

If portraying a musician who could revitalize American democracy was hard, so, too, was embodying the tensions implicit in being a banjo pickin' girl, particularly when it contradicted her own ambitions and experiences. This is especially important since Ledford's career on barn dance radio represents a shift in the genre as a whole, where broadcasters like John Lair learned that Southern and Western performers like Lulu Belle Wiseman and the Girls of the Golden West and their brand of barn dance music were the most popular. They searched more and more for performers who could become Southern or Western images and, in Lair's case, left established programs like the *National Barn Dance* (which still maintained the eclectic immigrant mix that had made it popular in the early 1930s) in order to make those metaphors more consistent, apparent, and dominant in the mid- to late 1930s. Lily May's handwritten autobiography, written in the 1970s and rarely cited by scholars (it has never been published in its entirety and few scholars have used even those truncated versions that are available), displays her first encounters with this new stage and throws into broad relief her insecurities.[3] In short, she failed to recognize the limits of being an authentic performer able to ready a nation ideologically for war, and she suffered for it personally and professionally.

❧ ❧ ❧

I was born March 17, 1917, to White and Stella May Ledford in a remote section of Powell County, Ky called the Red River Gorge, one of the most unusual places of natural beauty I've ever seen.
—Lily May Ledford, autobiography

Strengthening American national identity required a performer whose roots were intricately linked with an isolated, mountain South where pure British ballads had thrived unadulterated by commercial forces. Lily May Ledford had lived the rural life that barn dance radio sold (and which the federal government used), and her rural Kentucky upbringing contributed significantly to her development as a musician and to her first painful experiences on the air. But her autobiography exposes the false aspects of the image sold by broadcasters and government officials who suggested that she lived in an isolated mountain holler. Ledford's true upbringing, as well as her desire to leave much of it behind, warred constantly with the image of the South she was to perform.

Rather than living in isolated self-reliance as touted by Bradley Kincaid and John Lair, the Ledfords and other rural Kentuckians had become subject to the whims of outside markets in the late nineteenth and early twentieth centuries. Rural folk labored in extractive industries such as coal mining and timber, entertained tourists who traveled to their remote section of the South, listened to Jimmie Rodgers and classical records on old Edison phonographs, and bought consumer goods such as cloth when finances permitted.[4] They were also subject to the economic downturns that accompanied the market. In response, Kentucky families developed a collective, or family economy, approach to their survival in which they depended on each member's giving her or his labor to stave off poverty and, perhaps, provide a few luxuries. Ledford family members supported themselves by mingling together money earned from various kinds of work including sharecropping, mining coal, working on the railroad, and selling domestically produced goods. They also farmed, growing corn and sorghum cane, and, as Lily May remembered, her family "raised many vegetables in smaller patches of ground closer to the house. We supplemented this with wild game and fresh berries, grapes, and nuts and many kinds of wild greens. We raised hogs for our meat and kept a milk cow or two. When it was too wet to work in the crops the whole family would take to the hills to hunt for gensing and yellow root to be taken to the nearest general store and sold to buy school books, pencils and tablets and several bolts of dry goods for making dresses and shirts."[5]

Market whims forced the frequently impoverished Ledfords to develop substantial ties with local residents for support in bad times. Music mingled with and reinforced those ties, especially at square dances that accompanied work parties. Called "workings," music accompanied bean stringings, barn raisings, and corn shuckings, and much of the warmth that Ledford had for her home centered on her musical and working relationships with others.[6] When she prepared to move to Chicago in 1936, "Every body had tried to help me get ready to go," she recalled. Neighbors contributed odds and ends to her suitcase, threw her a going-away square dance, and then drove her to the train station.[7]

While the family economy approach was an innovative response to exploitive market conditions, there were drawbacks for individual members. In Lily May's case, the family economy induced in her a dependency upon others that caused her to avoid questioning decisions made for her, according to her granddaughter, Cari Norris. She relied on her parents, who told her when to work and when to have fun. Moreover, she assumed that women did not question men's authority in the family even though, in the Ledford house, her mother was in charge because her father was a "weakly man."[8] This dependence had ramifications for her later on because it formed the basis of her relationship with her manager, John Lair.

In an area where family, community, and music were intimately tied, it seems fitting that her father, White Ledford, was Lily May's first music teacher, and siblings and local friends the members of her first band. It was during a jam session with her father and some neighbors that she discovered her talent. She said in an interview, "They [the neighbors] brought their fiddle and banjo, and I heard three instruments playing together for the first time. And I can't tell you! Before that, Daddy just played the fiddle, and I felt a rhythm in me of some kind, but it was never carried out in my hearing. But when the banjo played along with the fiddles, I began to feel something I'd never really felt before—a rhythm in music. And oh my goodness!"[9] Her mother, Stella, also influenced Lily May's musical development, passing on her knowledge of ballads that folklorists had identified as survivals from the British Isles. But Stella frowned on her daughter's music making, fearing she spent too much time playing: work represented the difference between starving and surviving. Lily May recalled, "She would sing only while rocking the little ones or as she went about her chores, Mama was a great one for slipping a little work into all pleasures and believed that work and plenty of it was a cure-all for everything and should be enforced with a good keen switch when necessary. She loved my papa's music, but hadn't counted on us taking it up. What frustrations it must have caused her as one by one, we began to play on such old pieced up instruments as could be rigged up."[10] Even the music Stella taught focused on work. Lily May said, "She was so work minded, one of them [songs] was typical of her: 'We'll work till Jesus comes, we'll work till Jesus comes.'"[11]

Exhibiting what would be a long-term trend, Lily May subtly challenged her mother's authority over her music making. She remembered, "And now when I started to play, poor old Momma fussed all the time, but she couldn't hardly get a lick of work out of me until that old fiddle fell apart—which was in a couple of years."[12] By the age of seven, Lily May regularly shirked her chores in order to play the family's homemade banjo, made from a hedgehog hide, hickory sticks, and ten cents' worth of strings from Montgomery Ward. She also traded neighborhood children "pretties" (an old flashlight, her "precious box of crayons") for used, battered fiddles.[13]

It took more than skill and family ties to develop Lily May's musicianship. She also learned to please a diverse audience by playing for outsiders who traveled to Red River Gorge to see its lush, natural beauty (commented on by Ledford in the opening epigraph to this section). She found she "possessed something that outsiders were willing to pay for," scholar Lisa Yarger argued.[14] To capitalize on that money-making potential, Lily May formed a band, which included her brother Coyen, sister Rosie, and neighborhood friend Morgan Skidmore, called the Red River Ramblers. They then moved to Rochester, Indiana, in 1934 or 1935 where they played small theaters that catered to migrant Southerners. They were so successful one theater manager wrote WLS in Chicago for an audition, saying, "I have four Kentuckians who have real talent . . . They use guitars and violins and sing all hill-billy music and songs some eighty in their repertoire. Aryton Howard, for instance, says they are the best he ever heard on air or stage . . . Am enclosing a picture of them. You see they are not bad looking kids."[15]

Lily May Ledford auditioned for John Lair in 1935 as he was preparing to start a new barn dance program called the *Renfro Valley Barn Dance*. He most likely chose her because of her talent (she was extraordinarily skilled as a musician and had a certain sophistication learned in Red River Gorge and on the road in Indiana). But he had learned with Lulu Belle that a performer with a background similar to the mountain mother was useful in selling her to his audiences. Lily May also helped frame his new program in specific and distinct ways. For Ledford, signing with Lair meant she had someone who would care for business details, but it also meant she had to deal with Lair's imperious nature. In his mind, he was not simply her boss; he was also a steward who should guide her through Chicago's modern environment where urbanites valued pleasure over virtue. His stewardship reminded Lily May of her family's authority structure and caused her to rely heavily on his advice and guidance. That combination—her dependence, the portrayal of a constructed image of authenticity, the large sums of money involved—invoked in Ledford a constant stream of insecurity and grief. But Lair's expertise and the WLS star-making machinery also put her in position to become a famous musician, one who caught the eye of the White House.

Lair's Southern background prompted Lily May to choose him over another WLS manager who, she remembered, had a "clipped Yankee brogue which I hadn't heard much of, and he had a twitch in his face, and was a very nervous man. I was half afraid to sign with him."[16] She signed with Lair, saying, "All right. I'll sign a contract with you, Mr. Lair, because I trust you. You're a Kentuckian, you talk a little more like we do, and yes, I'll be glad to do that."[17] She recognized that they came from different backgrounds: Lair was middle class, had a high school diploma (an elite degree in the mid 1930s), and was more urbane, but she signed with him because he knew the business, something she knew limited her. Lily May wrote in her autobiography, "My lack of levelheadedness and with no business sense what so ever, I began to worry about how and which way to run my life. Which way to ruin it might be a better word."[18] She remembered that she never "had much ambition with my music," which caused her to feel "fearful, inadequate, apprehensive" about performing on stage.[19] Lair seemed the correct choice since he provided the ambition and the business expertise while she provided the talent.

Lair believed Lily May needed more than his business expertise. She also needed his superior morals and knowledge that would guard her against Chicago's big-city temptations. Those temptations, of course, could undermine his attempt to promote performers whose geographic isolation kept them less materialistic. To keep her the pure mountaineer, he admonished her, "Stay a mountain girl, just like you were when you came here. Be genuine and plain at all times."[20] Barn dance performer Cousin Emmy served as Lair's example of a mountain musician whose morals had succumbed to the modern world's commercialism. He told Ledford, "We done know all about Cousin Emmy. She's been all around the country in radio, she's much older than you and she's wearing diamond rings big as hickory nuts and she's got a pair of Cadillacs."[21] Lily May realized, "I must serve as an apprentice to these experienced people and yet retain a natural, casual attitude with my old fashioned music."[22]

Lair and Ledford turned once again to vaudeville to find the roots of her new character, an early incarnation of the banjo pickin' girl called the mountain girl, based on solo women who performed on vaudeville stages with banjos. The character was a solo act and Lair hired only Lily May, sending the remaining Red River Ramblers home. Lily May's musical upbringing emphasized music as a collective enterprise, and it ill-prepared her to act on her own even though it was her talent that made the troupe stand out. As the Ramblers returned to Kentucky, Ledford recalled feeling that "with them went much of my own confidence for we had been very happy with our music together and now began the battle with myself as I realized without them, I had less to offer for they had done most of the singing, so without them I found I had to handle each tune from beginning to end myself."[23]

Not only was a mountain girl a solo performer, she also lived in an isolated Kentucky "holler" where old-time musical skills and instruments were preserved. Her instrument of choice had to change—from fiddle to banjo—to meet the professional image of Appalachia on barn dance radio. She recalled in her autobiography the day Lair asked if she had "ever fooled around with a 5 string banjo." When she showed him her "old fashioned" banjo skills, "Mr. Lair and every body gathered around and cheered me on."[24] At the end of her performance, Lily May recalled, "Mr. Lair said, 'You stay on that banjo from now on and let the fiddle be incidental for we've plenty of good fiddlers but that banjo is what you'll make it on.' I said, 'Mr. Lair I'd rather fiddle, I don't know many banjo songs.' He assured me that would be no problem as he had a library full of banjo songs and he would write me some more."[25] The banjo fit the isolated mountaineer image as did Ledford's picking style, called clawhammer style, which required her to shape her hand like a claw to pick the strings, a picking style that differed substantially from the three-finger picking style associated with Earl Scruggs and current bluegrass music. Press releases assumed a Northern or Western audience that had no knowledge of banjos (Southerners were more likely familiar with the technique) and touted her particular way of picking as one "rarely met with outside the Southern Mountain Area."[26]

The disconcerting change reinforced her feeling that she was an archaic oddity in a modern world. Also alienating was the new banjo Lair chose for her, a Vega "White Lady." Her family's hedgehog banjos needed to be picked loudly in order to produce sound, especially when she played live and without microphones for large groups of Red River Gorge tourists. Her loud playing overwhelmed WLS microphones when she played the strong-toned Vega, and she had to learn to pick in a softer, quieter manner, one more suitable for the mikes. She wrote, "It [the Vega] was so loud and strong the producer was on my neck constantly to pipe down and I was scolded by producers and directors a great deal and some times I cried."[27] A mountain girl also had a different tone to her voice than Linda Parker's crooning style, and it had a similar effect as the Vega on WLS's microphones. Ledford had a higher, nasal tonality endemic to Kentucky and Tennessee before age, musical training, and cigarettes lowered her voice. That tonality, too, had to be toned down before the mikes worked adequately with her voice.

"Lair was basically asking her to continue to represent the very way of life that her musical talents allowed her to leave behind," scholar Lisa Yarger argued.[28] Yet Ledford desired to escape the hardships of her past and experience the pleasures of her present. Costuming was one place where she contested his demands. Lair had his secretary sew calico dresses with "ric rack" for Ledford's stage costume, the calico once again serving as a modern version of Appalachian homespun.[29] Her dresses were a "colorful spot" on shows and were "carefully made so as to be just the type of thing they used to wear at home," Lair later wrote National Folk Festival organizer Sarah Gertrude Knott.[30] He found high-topped shoes for her to wear and required that she wear her hair in a bun on stage. Lily May "felt like an old lady and not at all pretty . . . Mr. Lair discouraged my buying clothes, curling my hair and going in for make up or improving my english," she wrote. She wanted to look like her WLS friends, to buy the makeup and clothing she could now afford, to accede to friends like Dolly Good who scolded Ledford for not "glamorizing" herself. "How I did want to look like the others, and did a little fixing up in spite of him and would not wear my hair pulled back in the bun except on stage," Ledford remembered.[31]

When Lily May initially appeared on the air, Lair emphasized her physical attractiveness, the dark holler she supposedly grew up in, and her musical ability and its links with the past. As Lair blended the fact and fiction of her Kentucky upbringing on the air, he simultaneously linked her to the images of the authentic mountain woman who preserved folk songs and pioneer values. Lair introduced the *National Barn Dance*'s audience to Lily May in September 1936, saying,

An now, folks, we're ready to interduce to ye the newest member of the big WLS family. You've read about her, an heard about her this week, an of course you're anxious to meet her an see what she's like. Her name is Lily May Ledford. She comes frum the Kintucky mountains, from back in one of them dark hollers five miles off the road. She's five feet an about 9 inches tall, with brown eyes an one of the nicest smiles we've seen in a long time . . . Lily May hasn't always had such an easy time of it. When there's ten mouths to feed in one family everbody hasta do ther part—speshilly when the livin hasta be dug out of a little hillside farm—an many a time she's had to go out an do a mans work in the corn field er the tobacker patch.

Somehow, tho, she found time to do a lot of practicin on her granpappy's old fiddle an the one ambition of her life has bin to git to Chicago an play on the old barn dance.

An now, Lily May, yore big moment has come . . . all yore frens an kinfolks are gethered round radios waitin to hera ye, an out there on the air, all over the country, thousands of frens you aint met are waitin to hear ye, too, so step right up here with that old sushaw fiddle an show em what you got.[32]

Stand By! magazine used its popular columns to tell fans even more about her mountain home and lifestyle. The Hired Man reported (incorrectly) in his rural-style gossip column, "The Old Hayloft," that Ledford "hitch-hiked 20 miles, both ways, over the Kentucky mountains to buy a 5-string banjo after she was invited to come to Chicago and the old hayloft . . . She walked about three-fourths of the way, however."[33] A contrived dialect emphasized that isolation, and John Lair told audiences that she "talks in her natural voice on the air."[34] *Stand By!* used her dialect, quoting her on Groundhog Day in 1937, "Sure, us folks believe if he sees his shadder there will be bad weather to foller."[35] Again, as in the case of Linda Parker, dialect marked her as different and outside of mainstream culture.

In an odd bit of promotion, Lair used a comic strip to both idealize and parody Lily May's upbringing. Entitled "Lily May, The Mountain Gal" and published in *Stand By!*, it featured Ledford, beautifully coiffed and well-endowed but barefoot, in various scenarios in her fictitious homeplace, "Pinchemtite Holler." Characters "Mammy" and "Pappy" joined her, and readers laughed at their quaint and archaic ways or at their misperceptions of modern life.[36] One comic strip depicted Lily May telling Mammy and Pappy that she had won a five dollar "gol' piece" at a fiddle contest.[37] The comic continued with Mammy and Pappy's gleeful statements:

Mammy: Goody! Now Ah kin have me a new hat an'a new pockit book an'a. . . . .
Pappy: An' I kin have a new pipe an'a jar o'tobaccy. But Lily May What'll YOU have?
Lily May (sheepishly): Mebby I'll have me a bag o' popcorn.[38]

Especially intriguing is the parents' desire for trinkets (a new hat, a pipe) since commerce was perceived to be antithetical to the mountain South. Their desire for goods made them seem more like city dwellers dressed up in overalls. Thus, while comic strips could be read as Lair's willingness to allow popular caricatures of hillbillies on stage, comics intermingled the subtle blend of past and present that had always been a part of barn dance radio. Lily May may have been barefoot in the comic, but she was still attractive to modern eyes.[39]

In comic strips and on stage, Lair made Ledford's poverty benign and Red River Gorge a place of quaint people and banjo playing, not of hard work and hardship. Mountaineers' real poverty and desperation could never be a part of Lily May's stage character or the comic strips because fans used the radio to escape their own Depression-inspired desperation. The audience knew about Ledford's family and community of musicians, but they never knew that, for example, she and her siblings wore underwear made from flour sacks. Moreover, no matter how isolated Lair wanted the mountain girl to be, the modern world had already transformed Lily May and her music. Radio and records had already affected her repertoire and sound. Red River Gorge friends owned Carter Family and Jimmie Rodgers records, and at least one neighbor owned a radio. She had been performing for pay for several years and already knew how to please an audience when she came to the *National Barn Dance*. In fact, Lair probably hired her because she would not seem too alien to listeners.[40]

If the fiction of her stage character camouflaged her less-than-isolated and difficult upbringing, it also hid her very modern desire to earn money. Sent out like her siblings to earn money, Lily May reveled in her ability to support her family, remembering forty years later that she earned sixty dollars per week (plus ten dollars per personal appearance), her pride in buying a forty-dollar diamond ring for a relative, and the presents she bought that first Christmas for her family. She wrote, "I shopped and shopped for Christmas, for the family, for the 'Skiddies' [Skidmores] as I loved them and owed them so much for the great help in the past. That's when I gave Aunt Carrie the diamond ring and some fussy lingerie, etc. for their daughter. For home I sent two sets of warm long underwear for all my brothers, towels, bed spreads, clothes, pictures to hang and dozens of other things."[41]

Even though it promised remarkable riches, being a radio mountaineer demanded a remarkable amount of energy, and no more than a year into her career, Lily May began to feel "a certain tiredness of my work."[42] She worked constantly: on the daily Pinex show, the Saturday night barn dance, and as many as seven personal appearances each week. Chicago's strange environment added to her exhaustion. She recalled "having to battle the strangeness of making my way thru the almost (to me) unsurmountable problems of just every day traveling, working, dealing with the broken English of half of the shop and restaurant people, each one inquiring where I came from soon as I opened my mouth to speak. I longed to hear familiar voices and be back where no one hurried, nor ever scolded nor teased me nor criticized my music and clothes."[43]

To combat the homesickness, she sent gifts and money home to family weekly, and "wrote home to nearly every body. I couldn't bear to be forgotten."[44] When Lair offered her the opportunity to join his new barn dance show, the *Renfro Valley (Kentucky) Barn Dance,* which would initially be broadcast from Cincinnati and later from Renfro Valley, she jumped at the chance to move.

Lair married barn dance radio's popularity to the tourist business to create his new radio program and his popular vacation complex, Renfro Valley in eastern Kentucky. Cars had emerged as a common part of American life in the 1920s (in fact, many Southern migrants who moved to the North worked in the automobile plants that produced these cars), and innovative businesspeople like Lair saw their potential for developing a tourist trade based on driving, rather than the railroad, as earlier Americans had done. Cars provided Americans more flexibility in terms of where they stopped (railroads stopped only in specified places), and roadside businesses such as motor hotels ("motels") and campgrounds sprang up everywhere to meet this trade. The New Deal helped by putting unemployed men to work, building or upgrading roads in rural and urban areas. But Lair took the new tourist trade a step further: he sold Renfro Valley as the valley where time stood still, an easy drive to a place where one could get good old-time food, stay in a cabin (although they had the modern conveniences like indoor plumbing demanded by customers), and listen to old-time performers like Lily May Ledford, the mountain girl.

Lair broadcast what he considered a purer image of the mountain South at Renfro Valley while simultaneously exploiting Americans' greater access to cars. It was his entrepreneurial spirit that led him to this new business venture, but the *Renfro Valley Barn Dance* was also a distinct departure from the *National Barn Dance,* which he seems to have thought had become too commercial and too focused on multiple acts from multiple regions in addition to the South and West. He did continue many of the professional practices he learned on WLS, however. The resort both replicated and idealized Renfro Valley's colonial days, an era that seemed pure and patriotic, in ways similar to Lair's early WLS shows. He wanted to bring the valley back to its original form, to "preserve the old fashioned friendliness and the neighborliness, the idea of helping people out when they were in trouble. We wanted to show how people had lived before us, how hard they'd had to work to establish the country and under what difficulties they'd done it, as we hoped it'd be an incentive to the present generation. In other words, just trying to keep alive a memory."[45]

Selling Renfro Valley as Saturday night fun "that you won't be ashamed of Sunday morning," he thought the resort could stave off what he perceived to be a creeping "cultural regression" precipitated by commercial leisure.[46] Entertainment, including tourist activities, should not simply make money but also guide tourists toward a better, more moral life.[47] "I see too danged many farm folks hanging around on the streets and out at the cheap dance halls on Saturday nights," Lair told his partner, advertising agent Freeman Keyes.[48] Renfro Valley represented a time that was "more neighborly, more solidly grounded, in the principals [sic] and not so carried away by every new idea that came along."[49] His new barn dance show would feature "a little more realism—a little less showmanship and a little more heart-felt sincerity," and hopefully, teach his audiences to behave.[50]

Yet Lair never drew too fine a line between making money and didactic entertainment designed to educate an audience in specific morals and values whether in Chicago or Kentucky, and in Renfro Valley he found he could easily meld the two. Press releases touted the resort and its radio shows as authentic interpretations of the past appropriate for contemporary sales:

> All broadcasts by the organization, headed by John Lair, will originate in "The Old Barn" in the valley . . . It is believed that the program will be the only one of its type originated in such fashion, with a rural background. John Lair, Red Foley, Whitey Ford (the "Duke of Paducah") already have reestablished their homes in the valley. There the men folk will hunt and fish and follow other rural pursuits, in addition to operating a rustic camp for visitors. Authentic reproduction of pioneer homes of the vicinity, together with barns, fences and other characteristic landmarks, has been undertaken.[51]

Ads published in *Variety's* radio directory told potential sponsors that Renfro Valley was "bringing clean, wholesome entertainment into thousands of homes, breaking box office records in theaters and auditoriums and doing a swell job for the sponsors."[52]

Lair's clean, wholesome entertainment featured Lily May, now called the "Banjo Pickin' Girl." Instead of a solo act as she had been on WLS's stage, at Renfro Valley Barn Dance, her music was a collective responsibility, performed with other skilled musicians who were friends and neighbors from the fictitious Pinchemtite Holler. The new neighbors included her "all-girl" band, the Coon Creek Girls, and press releases showcased their expert ability to perform real mountain music, implying that their expertise had been formed by their long-term neighborly relationship. The original group included Ledford's sister Rosie on guitar, Evelyn Lange on fiddle and bass, and ballad singer Ester Koehler on guitar and mandolin. Both Lange and Koehler were Midwesterners.[53]

The Coon Creek Girls attempted to fashion their own characters, but Lair stepped in and nixed their ideas when they conflicted with his own rendering of a "genuine" past. They chose their theme song, "Wild Wood Flowers" (a sentimental vaudeville tune made popular by the Carter Family), and Koehler and Lange changed their names (Ester to "Violet" and Evelyn to "Daisy") to mimic the Ledfords' flowery first names.[54] "The Wild Wood Flowers" seemed the perfect group name, but Lair told them, "Girls, I had thought a more country name would be best. How about 'Coon Creek Girls?' Any one hearing that name would know at once the type of music would be expected."[55] Lily May remembered that the girls replied, "'Mr. Lair, there ain't no Coon Creek where any of us is from.' And he said, 'Oh well, that doesn't matter in the least. Your audience out in radio land don't know that.' So he named us, and the Coon Creek Girls we became."[56]

Lair also insisted that Lily May and Rosie trade off singing lead vocals while Lange and Koehler sang backup or simply played their instruments. This angered Koehler, but her voice did not have the high nasal twang the Ledfords had. That twang was what Lair saw as traditional, and therefore commercially viable, since it served to remind the listeners of the Coon Creek Girls' difference from the mainstream American culture found on other radio channels. Ledford recalled, "Mr. Lair had always featured Sis [Rosie Ledford] and me more than them [Koehler and Lange]. Red River or Appalachian music wasn't all we played, but Mr. Lair had wanted to keep us typical of native Kentucky and didn't want anything that would show those two girls were from up North and Yankees. So they were kept in the background or at least not pushed for solos."[57]

Lair wanted the Coon Creek Girls to perform a repertoire that was at odds with the song mix the Ledfords desired. Lily May wanted tragedy, poverty, and hardship to dominate, since those themes mimicked a mountain girl's life. Folk songs such as "Omie Wise," a murdered girl ballad that recounted a North Carolina woman's death in 1808, imitated in tragic tones the prevalence of death and hardship in rural Kentucky and in Lily May's own life.[58] Of fourteen children born to her parents, four had died in infancy and two surviving siblings died in 1937 (one a suicide, the other from illness). The Ledfords therefore thought "lonesome songs," music that had a keening wail or a cry of grief and despair to it, appropriate because they depicted the grief that was a common part of their mountain upbringing.[59] Sentimental mother ballads and religious, "holy roller" tunes would round out their repertoire, if they had a choice.[60]

Lair wanted to entertain, not depress, his audiences who searched radio for relief from the Great Depression in 1936 and 1937. And in 1938 and 1939, when the Nazis began their drive across Europe, radio could provide relief from the terrifying new war hovering just over the horizon (and broadcast over another radio channel). "Funny" songs were Lair's main choice for entertainment like his composition "Old Uncle Dudy," which was a fast-paced, upbeat fiddle breakdown. The audience laughed when they heard the girls impersonate an old mountain man during the song:

> Well hi Uncle Dudy, how you feelin' today?
> Well, I hain't very well I bound fer to say.
> I can't fix my labor with a shovel and a hoe,
> But I sure can handle that fiddle and a bow.
>
> Keep fiddlin' on, Uncle Dudy Uncle Dudy.
> Keep fiddlin', just fiddle right on.
> Keep fiddlin' on, Uncle Dudy Uncle Dudy,
> Til the old man's home.[61]

In other words, when the Coon Creek Girls' definition of authentic music conflicted with Lair's ideas of authentic music—which were predicated on what was marketable—his ideas won out. His marketing sense was, after all, the main reason Ledford enlisted his management. For Koehler and Lange, however, disagreements over repertoire as well as salary angered them, and they left the troupe soon after their performance for British royalty.

Even as the Coon Creek Girls bristled at Lair's dictates, they still acceded to his authority, hiding anything that contradicted their made-for-radio mountaineer personality. Lily May had already learned that she "had to lie and fabricate a little in the business, and that you had to learn to politic around."[62] Evelyn ("Daisy") Lange said, "We didn't put on anything and whatever we said it was a natural thing . . . We always tried to dress and look very presentable . . . we didn't want to do anything to ruin our image."[63] Among those things that might ruin their image were Daisy's and Violet's "Yankee" backgrounds and Lily May's, Daisy's, and Rosie's smoking. Lange explained, "We never smoked anywhere where anybody would see us. We tried to be like people thought we were."[64]

It was this commercial view of the Southern mountains that Eleanor and Franklin Roosevelt wanted on their stage, but each had different aims when hiring the Coon Creek Girls. Eleanor Roosevelt was like many elites who believed mass consumption had disintegrated the morals of consumers who were willing to buy anything with little regard to quality. Hillbilly music presented an especially "grave cultural problem," according to scholar David Whisnant, because its performers sold sacred, pure mountain music for profit rather than preserving it for the ages.[65] Some, like Sarah Gertrude Knott, responded by organizing folk festivals (like the National Folk Festival) that provided an appropriate outlet for musicians so they would not sell their music over the radio or on records. Intriguingly, the National Committee for the Folk Festival included John Lair (listed as a "Student, Origins of American Folk Music," not as a radio broadcaster) in 1939.[66]

Knott invited Mrs. Roosevelt to the National Folk Festival in February 1939, knowing that the Roosevelts' support for folk festivals and folk music were part of their larger goals for the New Deal, which were on display the night Lily May played for the royals. Knott's letter mentioned, "Through your interest last year, we have developed a fine organization in West Virginia at Arthurdale . . . They will not only have presentations of the folk songs, music and dances on the stage, but brought along last year and will bring along again this year, Handicraft exhibits."[67] This odd juxtaposition of a government-sponsored, cooperative community in Arthurdale and folk music was in fact an intrinsic part of the New Deal effort. The Roosevelts and other government officials referred specifically to their New Deal programs as the "Three Rs": relief, recovery, and reform. By relief, they meant immediate palliative care from the crisis; by recovery, they meant an end to the current crisis; by reform, they meant to impose new structures that would diminish the likelihood of another devastating depression.[68] To eliminate that likelihood, reform-minded New Dealers focused on poverty, defining it as a problem of environment (in this case, the natural landscape in the traditional sense and as home and cultural life in a broader, more humanistic sense) that could be changed so that no depressions could harm Americans as deeply as the 1930s downturn had. This made the New Deal's cultural work as important as their economic work and, indeed, many times it was difficult to discern a difference between the two. The cooperative living arrangement begun in 1934 in Arthurdale primarily housed displaced miners and was a pet project of Eleanor Roosevelt's. It intermingled the skills and talents of multiple people and sought to alleviate long-term poverty by moving residents back to a simpler time where communities supposedly shared with each other, not unlike the image of community that the *Renfro Valley Barn Dance* and early WLS shows broadcast on the radio. In that community, folk music would serve as both a conduit to the past and as a reminder of the patriotic ideals and values of that earlier time when economic depression was not a part of everyday life.[69]

Folk music and folk crafts became part of the Arthurdale attack against poverty, but the New Deal avoided hillbilly music (too commercial and too immoral in the eyes of folklorists) and jazz (the boundaries between black and white musicians were too fluid for New Dealers). Folk artists played important parts in the government-sponsored culture that flaunted the folk as "embodiments of America's strength through diversity."[70] And as Emma Bell Miles, Cecil Sharp, and Maud Karpeles had asserted in their work, as well as much of the programming of barn dance radio, folk music supposedly came from an earlier time that was somehow better, a time where American ideals seemed to be purer and better. Folk music was used in a classically functionalist way, meaning that it was a method to move people back to the past, a past that would be a core part of an "official culture—the culture sustained, sanctioned, and deployed by the federal government," according to scholar Benjamin Filene.[71] That official culture was promoted in other venues, too, not just the experimental Arthurdale project (which eventually failed). Alan Lomax's work with the Library of Congress's Archive of American Folk-Song and the WPA's Artist Bureau were both important places where folk music was seen as an access point to the past. Both Lomax and a WPA choir performed at the concert for royalty, while much of the talent was secured by WPA officials.

Experimental projects like Arthurdale were ones that Eleanor Roosevelt explicitly supported. What Franklin Roosevelt wanted is unclear. Ever the chameleon who could say one thing to his staff and then act in another way, Roosevelt was an expert at hiding his true feelings about various projects. Moreover, as the 1930s waned, he had significant concerns in mind when he approved putting Ledford on stage, particularly in terms of foreign relations. In June 1939, he had several problems. The first was political and military isolationism, fostered by Americans' desire to avoid any entangling alliances. The United States was willing to sell guns to other countries but would not shoot the guns themselves. He knew that the British air strength against Hitler's bombing raids was weak. If it lost the battle for Britain (which it almost did), then Hitler would control all of Europe. The United States would then be the last country standing against Hitler's domination of the Western world.

Roosevelt knew he had to name the British his allies so he could support their military buildup, but he could not be assured that all Americans would be pro-British. The American Nazi Party had a substantial presence in the United States during the 1930s, attracting American luminaries such as Charles Lindbergh. American companies—General Motors, Ford, IBM, and Du Pont—sold materials to Hitler as he illegally rearmed Germany.[72] Finally, there was a substantial German-American population and an Irish-American population in the United States that was vehemently anti-British.

Roosevelt turned to his greatest strength—his ability to manipulate words and symbols—to tout the Germans as our enemy and the British as our friends. (Roosevelt proved so adept at using words and symbolism that Prime Minister Neville Chamberlain wrote his sister, "It is always best and safest to count on *nothing* from the Americans except words.")[73] He hoped to encourage ideologic shifts before most Americans considered them necessary. Before the 1938 boxing match between American Joe Louis and German Max Schmelling, for example, Roosevelt felt Louis's biceps and said, "Joe, we're depending on those muscles for America."[74] Lily May's folk music was another instance where he used cultural material to proclaim the British as our allies, since her music seemed to be an example of a timeless shared culture.

Thus Roosevelt intended Ledford's performance for British royalty in June 1939 to serve multiple purposes for multiple audiences, an act that would rejuvenate a depressed America by touting our authentic culture while simultaneously building ties with the British. Singers like the Coon Creek Girls represented our common history with the British; the Roosevelts eschewed singers like Paul Whiteman, the self-proclaimed King of Jazz, who offered to perform that night. They also avoided barn dance singers who suggested a more commercial folk music: the alternate appellation, "hillbilly" indicated not just commercialization but an earthier kind of singing, represented by Uncle Dave Macon's performances on the *Grand Ole Opry*. One Roosevelt advisor from the WPA said of the cowboy group that performed that night, "Their singing is natural although influenced to a certain degree by radio technique. However, it is not a hillbilly type."[75]

The special performance for royalty on June 8, 1939, began with Franklin Roosevelt's toast to the king, giving "thanks for the bonds of friendship that link our two peoples." Then the performance of "All-American" music, as newspapers heralded it, commenced in front of the American and British dignitaries.[76] The first portion was a mini folk festival featuring authentic musicians "whose talents have gone generally unheralded outside their own communities," one journalist reported.[77] A troupe of "Negro" singers from the WPA sang first; then the Coon Creek Girls performed, singing old British ballads like "The Soldier and the Lady." The Roosevelts touted the Girls' ability to perform those ballads in the evening's program, telling the audience that they were from "Pinchem-Tight Hollow in the Renfro Valley of Kentucky. They led the normal hard life of the mountaineers of that State until 1937 when they were 'discovered' by Mr. Lair and started their radio career."[78] "The Soldier and the Lady" was described in the evening's program as "an old English ballad with many variations, found throughout our Appalachian country."[79] The music they performed symbolized all that we shared with the English, and Lily May's appearance on stage suggested to all that the British, our trusted friends, were our true allies because of these common ties.

The Roosevelts did not claim the Coon Creek Girls' music was exclusively white folks' music, although that interpretation was possible. The program may have noted that "The Soldier and the Lady" was an old English ballad, but it also highlighted the mixed racial background of another song, "Cindy," which was described as "a 'cracker-jack' party tune with countless verses, probably of part Southern Mountain white and part Negro origin."[80] The Roosevelts thus recognized the interracial roots of folk music even when others sold it as pure white.

Noting the interracial context for music like "Cindy" was one place where the Roosevelts proposed a multiracial national identity before America's entrance into World War II. The second part of the evening's program was another. Here the repertoire moved to high culture and spotlighted black opera singer Marian Anderson, white popular singer Kate Smith, and white Metropolitan Opera baritone Lawrence Tibbett. Eleanor Roosevelt, well known for her progressive racial views, had used her position as first lady to welcome black Americans of talent and grace into the White House and, by extension, out of the segregated margins of American society and into the mainstream. Four months before the royals' visit, she had publicly resigned her membership from the Daughters of American Revolution because the elite white women's group excluded Anderson from its Constitution Hall. Eleanor's well-known views contrasted with her husband's more circumspect approach to race (perhaps to maintain support from white Southern Democrats in Congress), and they clearly made some Americans uncomfortable. When Anderson performed for the king and queen, she did not sing "Negro" slave spirituals, a repertoire that may have been more acceptable to whites since those songs reminded them of a time when blacks were powerless and reminded blacks of a time when they were enslaved (something many blacks most likely would not have forgotten as they attempted to carve out a meaningful life under segregation). Instead, Anderson sang opera, high-class music that claimed a powerful spot for African Americans that countered the passive or invisible place John Lair and other radio broadcasters had reserved for them on the air. As noted earlier, white listeners had become used to hearing minstrel shows (such as barn dance minstrel acts like Jamup and Honey) that entertained whites (and blacks, too) in a way that "encoded the air-waves as a domain of white pleasure and power produced at the literal and figurative expense of racialized African Americans," according to scholar Derek Vaillant.[81] Anderson's performances of opera were thus a direct counter to that common radio image.

Even though she was controversial, Anderson's presence on the program addressed several problems. First, some saw her as a way to mitigate the history of the British colonial past and the American war for independence. Newspapers made much ado over attempts to put that past to rest; highlighting shared British relatives was beneficial to the coming war effort, and the history of rebellion against those same relatives was not. The king laid this past to rest, literally, when he visited Mount Vernon and placed a memorial wreath on George Washington's grave. Anderson was also presented to the queen while the Daughters of the American Revolution, who excluded her from its concert hall, looked on. Newspaper editorialists noted (with a distinct tone of glee) the DAR's decidedly small role in festivities in honor of the royals; although they were members of the Washington elite, they were not introduced to the queen.[82]

Anderson may have also been seen as a counter to the Nazi's racial policies since her presence exhibited a racially liberal vision of American national identity: all Americans were included on our stages, not just those who fit a racially pure image. Contradicting that racially liberal view, however, were the original plans for the evening. While Eleanor Roosevelt was willing to promote a superficial racial equality in public, in private she still followed racial etiquette. The royals initially planned to dine twice at the White House, one evening featuring white artists, the other featuring black ones. An invitation to the British embassy scuttled the second dinner, and Eleanor Roosevelt remarked to an official that "in the white program, they [the white singers] will have to be told that they are appearing on the same program with colored people. We will have no supper so we will not have that complication," (meaning they would not have to worry about segregating white and black entertainers from each other at dinner).[83]

While it is unclear how the Roosevelts intended to showcase Marian Anderson specifically, what is clear is that Americans wrote Eleanor, especially, commenting on Anderson's performance (and the menu: Eleanor served hot dogs to the royals, an attempt to show them "real" American food). Many wrote denouncing attempts to construct American national identity in any way other than white. Many of the letters were sent anonymously (including one from a Ku Klux Klansman) while other missives warned of racial unrest in the South if the Roosevelts included blacks on any stage.[84] Yet some editorials and writers understood the international intentions behind the choice of performers. Oliver Huckel, president of the Hymn Society of America, wrote to suggest one of his works for the king and queen: "We feel that we [the British and the Americans] must stand together for true democracy, the plighted world, and peace among the nations of this warring world. We do feel that you are in the fullest sympathy in the work of cementing friendship with England in unifying the mutual purposes of our two great nations."[85] An editorial in the *Youngstown Vindicator* applauded President and Mrs. Roosevelt's hot dog and folk music diplomacy. Editors wrote, "Americans can count it a piece of good fortune to have had as their representatives in this critical period in the world's history two of their countrymen who could receive a King and Queen and be equal to the occasion."[86]

I do not know if Lily May understood the intentions behind her performance. By 1939, however, she had become used to portraying an archetype that fictionalized her Kentucky mountain upbringing for people like the Roosevelts, who used her for multiple purposes. They intended American citizens to see the United States as a nation with an international mission, righteous in its anger and horror at Nazi policies, ready to do battle with our trusted friends, the British, by our side. What the Roosevelts achieved, however, was a chaotic identity that said as much about our contradictions—indeed, what we feared we might be—as it did about what we wanted to be. At the center of that representation was a young, talented woman, a mountain singer who sang sweet ballads that had traveled with the original settlers to America, who simply wanted to make some money and some music to support her family.

*How many letters did you get
in the wrong box this morning*
Hartford

A publicity shot of Linda Parker and the Cumberland Ridge Runners. Note her pearls and high heels. *Lying in front:* Slim Miller. *Standing from left:* Karl Davis, John Lair, Linda Parker, Hartford Connecticut ("Harty") Taylor, "Red" Foley, Hugh Cross. Courtesy of the Southern Appalachian Archives, Berea College.

John Lair standing with his listener mail at WLS in Chicago. Courtesy of the Southern Appalachian Archives, Berea College.

An early promotional photo of Lulu Belle. Courtesy of the Southern Appalachian Archives, Berea College.

Lulu Belle and Scotty Wiseman, "The Hayloft Sweethearts." Courtesy of the Southern Appalachian Archives, Berea College.

Undated promotional photo of Dolly and Milly Good. Courtesy of the Southern
Appalachian Archives, Berea College.

From left: Milly Good, "Red" Foley, Dolly Good. Courtesy of the Southern Appalachian Archives, Berea College.

Above: The Coon Creek Girls just before their performance for British royalty. *From left:* Rosie Ledford, Ester "Violet" Koehler, Lily May Ledford, and Evelyn "Daisy" Lange. Courtesy of the Southern Appalachian Archives, Berea College.

Below: Lily May Ledford and Sarah Colley (aka Minnie Pearl) met at least once. This picture was taken most likely in Cincinnati during World War II. *Seated from left:* Judy Perkins, Lily May Ledford. *Standing from left:* Rod Brasfield, Sarah Colley, four unidentified men, Hugh Cross. Courtesy of the Grand Ole Opry.

Sarah Colley in street clothes. Courtesy of the Grand Ole Opry.

Left: An early incarnation of Minnie Pearl. Courtesy of the Grand Ole Opry.

Below: Sarah Colley Cannon in full Minnie Pearl regalia in a postwar, postmarriage photo. Hank Williams Sr. stands at her far right. Courtesy of the Grand Ole Opry.

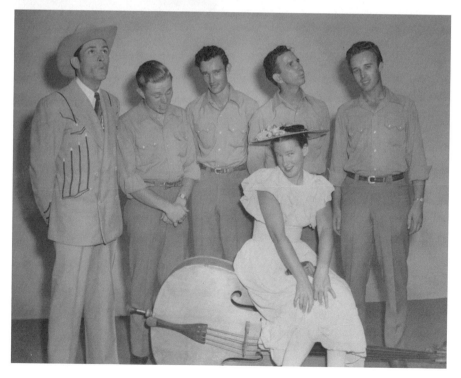

Rose Lee and Joe Maphis in an undated, signed promotional photo. Courtesy of the Grand Ole Opry.

6

"HOWDEE! I'M JES SO PROUD T'BE HERE"

Sarah Colley Cannon (Better Known as Minnie Pearl), World War II, and the Grand Ole Opry

"I wear a hat so folks can tell us apart."
—Minnie Pearl on Dolly Parton

Sarah Colley[1] remembered exactly where she was when the Japanese attacked Pearl Harbor, but it was not just the attack that caused her to remember that historic day. The day after, she was heckled for the first time by a drunk, scared soldier at Randolph Field in San Antonio, Texas. It was that event—and its effect on her career as Minnie Pearl—that solidified the day in her memory.

In December 1941, Sarah was traveling with the Camel Caravan, a troupe of *Grand Ole Opry* members who entertained military men at camps like Randolph Field. There, she performed for soldiers who roared with delight when the Caravan's sexy women entertained them, and they pinched the cigarette girls who traveled through the audience selling tobacco products. When it was Sarah's turn on stage, however, the soldiers did not want to hear a sexless country girl crack jokes about beaus and marriage.[2] Sarah remembered she "had to work awful hard" for men who only wanted to "get back to the girls."[3] A soldier began to mimic her in a "silly" voice, providing her punch lines before she could. She started to "stumble and stagger" in her timing and eventually ran from the stage in tears. Stage manager Ford Rush calmed her by pointing out a new historical reality: the war had already begun to intermingle heterogeneous groups of men who had different expectations of women on stage. To be successful, she had to learn to control those expectations by (in his words) acting silly. She recalled him saying,

> "Now the first time . . . you walked on the stage as a . . . woman and said, 'hey hey look at me, laugh at me,' you're letting yourself in for just what you got tonight." He said, "If you're going to say you're funny and are going to ask for laughs, you've got to be a buffoon. You're a target. And the sooner you learn that the better. And the woman who does it is even worse because it is putting her out of her natural habitat." And he said, "You've got a silly costume on and you go out there and you act silly and you got to take whatever comes. But you've got to learn to whip it."[4]

She used the remaining year on the Caravan doing just that; she learned to make fun of military men's (and others') expectations of women, a lesson she then used to help the *Grand Ole Opry* replace the *National Barn Dance* as the nation's favorite barn dance program. One famous joke, written after the heckling, acknowledged a lesson well-learned: "I felt so at home [coming onto the military base]. In fact, one fella told me I was the homeliest woman he'd ever seen. They had fellers to meet us at the gate and they was so cordial and so pleasant. They had my name on their sleeve. MP—Minnie Pearl. They got on the bus and searched every car until they found me." The joke became so popular that it followed her from camp to camp. Soldiers yelled out, "Tell us about the MPs," and in some places, the military police rushed the stage to grab her while others gave her their badges.[5]

World War II sparked a new evolution in barn dance characters as Americans mobilized for war. That mobilization created new audiences for barn dance radio who posed new questions about conventional roles for women who were moving into potentially revolutionary roles in war industries, and programs like the *Grand Ole Opry* rushed to provide answers. That evolution also indicated another shift from the 1930s barn dance genre: where once the eclectic, migrant nature of the *National Barn Dance* had been appropriate, the success of women like Minnie Pearl now promoted the popularity of programs like the *Grand Ole Opry,* which seemed almost exclusively Southern or Western.

The most successful comedienne on the *Grand Ole Opry*—or just about any other stage, for that matter—was Sarah Colley Cannon (1912–96), whose character best embodied these new circumstances. Called Minnie Pearl, she incorporated what she perceived to be her audience's evolving and often conflicting ideas about women's roles. But incorporating those multiple understandings of women made her an iconic character, meaning her character became so popular that she was able to transcend her place and time to become a beloved image to many.

Sarah's character provides us an opportunity to look through one performer's eyes at her audience just as America entered World War II. Through her eyes and the changes she made to her act, we can see how the 15 million Americans who moved to industrial cities to staff war plants and the 16 million others who served in the military evolved in their definitions of appropriate roles for women in an era when Rosie the Riveter and Wendy the Welder dominated the popular imagination. But what began in the war continued to evolve after it as well, allowing Sarah to use wartime tactics to meet the many challenges that national exposure proffered her, whether they were soldiers, network broadcasters, or ludicrous Southern stereotypes. The phrase "Sarah Colley Cannon, better known as Minnie Pearl" acknowledged the layered, multifaceted character that emerged in response, one that attempted to cater to every taste. It stabilized her own identity as she wrestled with the changes the war wrought on her personality and lifestyle.

❧ ❧ ❧

"I was a mistake from the start."
—Minnie Pearl, *Minnie Pearl*

While her background only hints that Sarah Colley Cannon would become country music's most famous comedienne, her autobiography does suggest she felt like an anomaly in her parents' upper-middle-class lives, "a mistake from the start." Because she saw herself as an aberration, she was able to make a break from her parents' elite lives, although never entirely, and construct a character that simultaneously defied and incorporated their expectations of appropriate female roles. The elite Colleys expected a demure, dainty daughter who drank tea; what they got was a tall, angular tomboy they called Ophie (for her middle name, Ophelia) who was at times a showoff and at others more like her Shakespearean namesake. That sense of difference and her natural theatrical flair led Sarah to her life as a comedienne.

Fannie and Thomas Colley, "proud, conventional Southern parents," as Sarah called them, were thirty-seven and fifty-five years old when she was born in Centerville, Tennessee, in 1912. They had four daughters by then, the oldest fourteen, the youngest seven. Her father was a New South businessman who owned a large lumber enterprise that employed both black and white laborers. His business prospered, providing a comfortable, upper-middle-class lifestyle for his family that included commercial goods such as a large and expensive house, a piano, Haviland china, Japanese tea cups, and Russian tea for the cultural circles his wife led in their home. Sarah recalled, "I think it made him proud to spoil [her mother]."[6]

Fannie Colley had a "drawing room upbringing" in the polite society of Franklin, Tennessee, and was "a slender, delicate-featured woman, very graceful and the epitome of a Southern lady. (I obviously did not take after her)," Sarah recalled.[7] Thomas's laborers' wives provided domestic labor for the family, so Fannie could pursue civic duties and volunteer work. She played organ in Centerville's Methodist Church and organized chapters of the Women's Missionary Society, a Chautauqua circle, and an Eastern Star chapter, making her one of the "social leaders of Centerville."[8] In short, she embraced the Victorian cultural and reform activities appropriate to a middle-class woman as well as the consumer goods that marked her as Southern, white, and elite.

Sarah tried to fit into her parents' world, but her active imagination and her desire to be on stage when, as she recalled, "*actor* still had naughty connotations" caused problems between them.[9] Piano lessons were one such conflict. Victorians considered a woman's piano playing important to keeping a moral home since it provided uplifting and educational entertainment for the family. As scholar Lynn Spigel wrote, piano playing "was associated with the spiritual talents of the True Woman who played hymns in the family parlor," along with other virtuous pursuits like Bible reading and domestic arts.[10] By the 1920s, piano playing had other, less uplifting uses that Sarah found more interesting. Silent movies required theater owners to hire local piano players to provide a musical backdrop for various scenes, whether scary, romantic, or action-oriented. Although Sarah had learned to play the piano because of her parents' desire for her to be a model Victorian woman, her skills, when she was ten, earned her daily admittance into the local movie theater. She remembered,

> I didn't receive enough allowance to go to the movies as often as I wanted (which would have been daily if it had been left up to me), so I made a deal with old Mr. Rulander who ran the theater. I told him if he'd let me in free I'd play background music during the films. He quickly agreed because he didn't have a regular pianist (undoubtedly owing to lack of funds). I'd play real sad songs during the sad scenes, romantic music during the love scenes and fast, exciting music during the action . . . I did this for several weeks before Mama found out about it, when she suggested, very firmly, that I was much too young to be hanging out at the movie house playing piano.[11]

Sarah's physical features reinforced her perception that she was unique and unconventional. She remembered, "I knew I wasn't pretty then—I had freckles, a knobby little body and straight, reddish blond hair." Her body added to her woes of being unable to fit into her parents' polite society. Sarah bemoaned her appearance, saying "if you're five foot eight and wear a size 9½ shoe you're going to have a very hard time looking demure!" Friends' comments bolstered that sense of weirdness. Her mother's friends said (when they thought she could not hear), "My, she's a plain little thing, isn't she?" In another instance, a friend set Sarah up with a blind date. She recalled, "I was still upstairs when the boys came, and I heard Ruthie say, 'You're gonna have a great time with Ophie. She's not real pretty, but she's the funniest girl at school.' Then she looked up the stairs, saw me coming down and called out, 'Say something funny, Ophie.' Her meaning was clear to me. I knew how I looked. I'd just left a mirror!"[12]

Sarah knew from an early age she wanted to be an actress and longed to follow in the footsteps of her idol, Katharine Hepburn. She took "expression" lessons, an early term for acting lessons, and then pursued theatrical training at Nashville's Ward-Belmont College, "the most fabulous finishing school in the state," she said, even though her father was about to lose his business to the Great Depression. Unmarried and with a degree in dramatics when she graduated in 1932, Sarah joined the Wayne P. Sewell Production Company from 1934 to 1940, a unique organization that produced musical shows for civic organizations throughout the South. Sewell's wife, a popular vaudevillian named Hettie Jane Dunaway, wrote most of the plays such as *Black-Eyed Susan, Rosetime,* and *Miss Blue*

Bonnet. "Winsome directors" such as Sarah learned the shows and then traveled to different communities, providing costumes and producing the plays featuring local actors.[13]

Traveling from town to town caused Sarah to construct a character that greeted residents in each new place. As a working "girl," Sarah operated outside her mother's accepted boundaries, and her reported shyness when meeting new people implicitly recognized this. But shyness did not stop Sarah Colley. Her new character, a mountain girl, had a friendliness that hid Sarah's doubts about her circumstances. It simultaneously diverted people's attention from Sarah the working girl, who posed a challenge to respectable society.

Named Minnie Pearl, Sarah's mountain girl was different from Lily May Ledford's. Sarah based her on a seventy-year-old farm woman from Alabama whose folksy sayings intrigued her, such as "I've had sixteen young'uns and never failed to make a crop."[14] Sarah began to gather stories, jokes, and sayings from northern Alabama, eastern Tennessee, and western North Carolina that brought the dainty, demure mountain girl to life. The jokes she told entertained locals, and she found that "it was a lot easier than standing up there as Ophelia Cannon, and the people really seemed to enjoy her."[15]

At first, Minnie reflected Sarah's own class status. Minnie was genteel, "much gentler and much quieter then and the character would get chuckles instead of loud laughs," Sarah remembered.[16] Minnie rendered her traditional greeting as a gentle salutation that seemed more like Fannie Colley than the exuberant Sarah. She would say, "I'd like to give you my impression of a mountain girl, Minnie Pearl [and in a soft drawl said], 'Howdy. I'm just so proud to be here.'"[17] The mountain girl's early jokes were equally demure and gentle. For example, she once poked fun at weddings:

> My feller and me went to a wedding the other night and oh it was so pretty and it was so sad. Everybody was crying. Cried and cried. I had the best time. And the bride she came down the issle [aisle] and she had on a white dress . . . it was all right in the front but sagged something awful down the back. Two of her younguns had to come along behind her and tote it for her. Why, if she'd a had to get away from there in a hurry that long thing swingin' out behind her she'd a fell and broke her leg they'd a had to shoot her . . . The groom was waiting for her at the halter . . . The bride looked stunning. He just looked stunned.[18]

Her early emphasis on demure behavior was one technique Sarah used to calm fears (whether hers or those in the audience) about her status as a working girl.

Like other female performers, Sarah found that clothing aided her transformation into Minnie. Beginning in 1939, she dressed in clothing she thought a mountain girl would wear to town on a Saturday afternoon outing—an old, cheap, yellow organdy dress, a hat with flowers on it (the price tag came later), white shoes, and cotton stockings. When she performed in costume, she remembered, "It was the first time that I had really had a sense of being somebody else."[19] At other performances, dressed in full regalia, Sarah felt herself "moving out of Sarah Ophelia Colley into Minnie Pearl. I felt more uninhibited than I ever had felt doing her before, but it was more than that. I *became* the character. It was the first time I had ever really changed places with her, and it gave me a wonderful sense of freedom I hadn't had before."[20] Because she recognized the effects of wearing a costume, she was adamant that, when she was not on stage, she wore modern, fashionable clothing she thought suited Sarah Colley. Changing clothes immediately after a performance thus marked an important step in delineating her offstage self from the Minnie Pearl character.

Although clothing helped, becoming Minnie Pearl was still an evolution that took several years of botched performances and travel to various military installations before Sarah perfected the persona. "It was still me talking like a character named Minnie Pearl. It was not me *becoming* that person," she said. Ever mindful of the polite society she had grown up in, Sarah refused to fully commit to Minnie until the heckler confronted her. In the late 1930s, she still considered Minnie Pearl a temporary thing that "would make me enough money to go to the American Academy . . . I didn't want to be a clown. I wanted to be Katharine Hepburn."[21]

Radio and the Great Depression together ended vaudeville shows like Sewell's, and she struggled with major financial problems beginning in 1940. These were desperate times for Sarah. She supported her mother, who had extravagant tastes (Thomas Colley died in 1937 after losing his business), and Sarah did what she could to cater to her. Twenty-seven years old and unmarried, she quit Sewell's employ in 1940, found work with the Works Progress Administration's Actors Project, and tried to support herself and her mother on the WPA's fifty dollars per month salary.[22] The Minnie Pearl character became a financial boon in this desperate time because she could perform her at local functions to earn extra money. In November 1940, she auditioned for the Grand Ole Opry and was hired for regional Saturday night broadcasts. Initially, broadcasters doubted the audience would like her because of her elite background. One manager said to her, "I don't know if these Opry people will take to you. I'm afraid they'll think you're sort of putting them down. That you're not a country girl."[23] Broadcasters put her on at 11:05 P.M. after the network had signed off so she would not offend anyone. She proved them wrong. When she picked up her paycheck the next week, some 250 letters and telegrams from new radio friends awaited her, congratulating her on her performance.

Her successful first night aside, Sarah still had to learn to act silly so she could make fun of her and her audience's perceptions of women. That education caused her significant heartache before the heckling incident because she was so stiff as a performer. In early 1941, Roy Acuff hired her to "spice up" his act (by 1941, it was an industry standard that a comedian be part of a troupe), but, she said, "I had really had not had enough experience of one night stands to really perfect the act and put this veneer on or begin layering the veneer."[24] She recalled joining Acuff: "We played Evansville [Indiana] and I met all those hillbillies and they say now that they liked me. They don't remember. I think they thought I sounded stupid. I didn't know their language. Not racy language . . . I did not speak their language spelled in capital letters. I did not know how to talk to them. I hadn't anything to talk to them about. I had this different background. My background was better, it was not better, it was different."[25]

That difference in background added to her difficulty loosening up and acting silly on stage. Another Acuff performer, "Bashful Brother Oswald," remembered, "She said her jokes so fast people couldn't understand them. She was nervous—like everybody starting out. Roy [Acuff] told her to slow down and people would enjoy her better that way. People couldn't laugh, 'cause she was goin' so fast, they'd miss the next joke."[26]

Sarah knew that she was not working out. "It killed me, but I couldn't cope with it. I was still undecided about whether I really wanted to be a comic, and there's nothing as sad as that because in order to be a comic, in particularly as a woman, you gotta turn it loose and let it fly. It's just got to go and you gotta be silly and I just couldn't be all that silly. I felt embarrassed, and you cannot be embarrassed and be a comic."[27] After Acuff fired her, Sarah joined the Camel Caravan, a traveling road show that sold R. J. Reynolds' products at military installations while entertaining the troops. It was that experience that taught her to open up and "let fly," as Sarah said.

Those military installations where she honed her craft were new in 1940. By that year, the United States had begun to prepare for what Franklin Delano Roosevelt believed to be our inevitable entrance into the European war. Turning once again to his strength (words), Roosevelt proclaimed in December 1940 that America "must be the great arsenal of democracy." In his State of the Union address just a month later, he declared his Lend-Lease Bill (initially discussed when the king of England visited in 1939) was important in securing democracy for the world, although it was really designed to subvert American isolationism by lending surplus military supplies to the British. But securing the national defense was as important as providing scarce military goods to Britain, and military expenditures increased from $2.2 billion in 1940 to more than $20 billion in 1941. Military draftees were one consequence of the massive expansion in spending, and almost 1 million new soldiers joined the military in 1941, well before Pearl Harbor. As a result, America's unemployment rate dropped below 10 percent for the first time since 1930.[28]

When soldiers were drafted, they found a decidedly different military than in previous wars. During the Civil War and the Spanish-American War, soldiers mustered into units from their hometowns. When one of those units fought in a battle, soldiers died alongside friends they had known all of their lives. Towns faced the devastating loss of many young men at the same time, certainly not a boost for civilian morale. During World War I, universal military training professionalized the American military, and a soldier's main attachment was no longer to his hometown but to his unit. Administrators randomly assigned men to those units, regardless of birthplace, and units continued to exist even when there was no war. The Big Red One in Kansas and the 101st Airborne in Kentucky were typical of these new units.[29]

As World War II loomed, military officials continued to combine dissimilar men into units. The effects were far more significant than in World War I, however. First, American involvement in World War II lasted much longer than the Great War did. The United States fought in World War I a mere eighteen months; the World War II peacetime draft began in 1940, and Japan did not sign the armistice until September 1945. World War II also required far more men. As historian David Kennedy argued, "The army tossed the remaining millions of men into the mother and father of all melting pots. The dozens of conscript divisions were all-American mixtures recruited from north, south, east, and west. They jumbled together farm boys and factory hands, old-stock Yankees and new immigrants, rich as well as poor, Protestants, Catholics and Jews. Many young men who had never left their rural county or urban neighborhood confronted in the army more social, ethnic, and religious diversity than they had ever encountered, perhaps ever imagined."[30] New York resident Art Buchwald, later to become well known as a newspaper columnist, joined the Marines and fought alongside men who had never seen a Jew before. South Dakotan Al Neuharth recalled, "When I first went in the infantry, I met people from Brooklyn who talked funny and people from Texas who you couldn't understand at all. I realized for the first time that the world is not made up of the white Germans and Scandinavians who settled my part of South Dakota."[31]

The military also provided different recreational outlets for its soldiers than it had in the past, catering to their diverse needs through modern technology like the radio. The Armed Forces Radio Service (AFRS), organized in 1942, recorded radio shows that were then broadcast to the men overseas. Shows proved so popular that the AFRS increased its number of outlets from 21 to 306.[32] Both the *National Barn Dance* and the *Grand Ole Opry* were broadcast to soldiers, who seemed to have liked the *Grand Ole Opry*'s mix of performers and comedians especially well.

At first on the Camel Caravan and later on AFRS, Sarah performed for that diverse group of men who had regional, ethnic, and class-specific definitions of appropriate roles for women. She was sensitive to how odd she seemed to her military audiences as she followed Dainty Dolly Dinkins, glamorous Kay Carlisle, San Antonio Rose, and the singing trio the Camelettes on stage since all were attractive women who sold sex as well as cigarettes. But it was not until Pearl Harbor when the frightened, drunk soldier heckled her that she felt the consequences of being different. While it is not clear what soldiers specifically expected (except sexy women with rear ends to pinch), Sarah did note the effect of "soldier shows" on Minnie's development: "There's nothing in the world as good for polishing an act as a soldier audience because they were rough . . . at that time it was good for me because I was doing so many shows and that's what it takes . . . there's no substituting for show hours . . . you pick up tricks and you enlarge your act because you are continually [working]."[33]

Sarah turned to a number of influences to create "Sarah Colley Cannon, better known as Minnie Pearl," the comedienne who wowed her heterogeneous soldier audiences with jokes about MPs. Her character developed over the course of the 1940s. One significant influence was the "network men" who attempted to dictate how Sarah and others should act on stage. Prince Albert Tobacco's *Grand Ole Opry* became a part of the National Broadcast Corporation's Saturday night lineup in 1939, and eventually NBC's 151 stations nationwide (including stations in New York City, Boston, and Seattle) featured the show on Saturday nights.[34] Not all of those listeners may have been used to the *Grand Ole Opry*'s particular charms, however. As a consequence, "network men," typically New York advertising executives, imposed new rules on Opry performers, just as they had done with other programs in the 1930s. The letters and telegrams ad men exchanged suggest they monitored Opry performers carefully. Perhaps it was the earlier reputation for earthy, natural "Dixie Dewdrops," jugs of liquor on stage, and other potentially scandalous behavior that scared network executives. Whatever the issue was, those executives wrote to each other throughout the 1940s to keep "the same careful supervision and production . . . of the Grand Ole Opry" and to "follow 'Grand Ole Opry' closely."[35]

Network men not only watched the Opry closely; they also tinkered with comedy routines to broaden a performer's appeal. They wanted the audience to participate in Sarah's act while she wanted the fans to remain passive participants as any professionally trained Broadway actress expected. It was all right with her if they applauded or laughed, but the audience had to remain otherwise passive. She remembered one network man said, "'Why don't you say a howdee real loud and let the audience holler it back.' That's not in character. I said she just doesn't say that loudly. She says it like a country girl. She says howdy like country people say, howdy. And that's the way I was saying it when I walked out on the stage."[36] But network men could fire her if she did not comply, and eventually it became standard for audiences to holler "Howdee!" back when Sarah greeted them from the stage.

Executives also inserted urban situations into rural scenes. "They wanted me to get boffo laughs," Cannon said, and they wrote jokes that did not fit the nostalgic country feeling with which she sought to imbue Minnie Pearl. Their jokes referred to explicitly Northern urban situations, not to country parties and candy pulls. She remembered they wanted her to say, "'The clothes my brother wore they were enough to take the heart out of Hartshackle and Marks [a city department store].' We didn't know about Hartshackle and Marks in the country. We knew Duckhead overalls and Buster Brown shoes . . . The material was not my material, it wasn't good."[37] Sarah said, "They never did understand what they were doing. They didn't understand the country feeling that Rod [Brasfield, another *Grand Ole Opry* comedian] and I were trying to put across."[38] Finally, executives recognized the performers' knowledge of their audiences and allowed both comedians to edit scripts once the show went on television in the 1950s.

Network men may have had a significant effect on Minnie's development, but female clowns from vaudeville also influenced her. Sarah had (of course) attended the traveling vaudeville shows that came to Centerville and worked for former vaudevillians while with the Sewell Company. But she had to translate vaudeville tricks so that they would fit the barn dance genre's nostalgic world where communities worked hard, praised God, and sang old-time music. Marriage provided stability to those communities; recall that the genre regularly featured married couples like Lulu Belle and Scotty. An old maid who would never marry was not just funny but, quite possibly, not a woman, just as vaudeville comedienne Kate Elinore had been perceived to be. Playing male characters on stage questioned a comedienne's gender even more so. On a televised *Grand Ole Opry* show from the 1950s, Sarah played Santa Claus, and her friend Rod Brasfield guessed that Ernest Tubb, Little Jimmie Dickens, and every other male *Grand Ole Opry* performer masqueraded as Santa before Sarah revealed herself. Indeed, she so successfully played an old maid that *Grand Ole Opry* broadcaster George D. Hay called her "one of the boys."[39]

The old maid was additionally a gossip. Although an old maid might wink at tradition by not marrying, ultimately, the gossip respected traditional relationships. In fact, she reinforced them by using shared information to build relationships between members of the community. As scholar Sally Yerkovich wrote, "To be able to gossip together, individuals must know one another. They need not be friends or intimates, but they must be familiar enough with one another to minimize intervening social distance."[40] The barn dance gossip reinforced traditional ties, then, by interacting sociably with radio friends connected by radio's long-range signal.[41] Radio's ritualistic qualities—where the audience listened to its favorite performers each week—augmented the gossip's relationships with her listeners when they tuned in.

Other comediennes had already had success with the old maid/gossip character on other barn dance stages. Old maid Tillie Boggs frolicked as the mayor of Sunset Corners on the *Iowa Barn Dance* on WHO in Des Moines. *Rural Radio* magazine told its readers that Boggs had "set her cap time and time again for some unsuspecting male resident of Sunset Corners but something always happens to save the fellow."[42] *Grand Ole Opry* audiences knew intimately the spinster/gossip character thanks to the comedy team Sarie and Sally, who appeared on the *Grand Ole*

Opry from 1934 to 1939. Edna Wilson (Sarie) and her sister Margaret Waters (Sally) staged a five-minute repartee each Saturday night in which they gossiped about *Grand Ole Opry* performers, home remedies, local women's clubs, and snuff-chewing contests. They spiced their dialogue with informal "home folks" phrases such as "a man of words and not of deeds is the same as a garden full of weeds," "flutterin' flutterflies," "Ah, the gnat's pappy," and "dear lesperdeezer."[43] What little remains of their act (few *Grand Ole Opry* scripts exist from this era) suggests that Sarie and Sally did not chase men on stage. Instead, they made fun of the Opry's prescriptions against women doing public work by being two freewheeling women who chewed snuff and gossiped about fellow Opry performers. In 1935, their repartee included this exchange:

> Sally: En do ye reckon [Opry performer] Arthur Smith shore nuff had air live mockin bird, whenever he wuz a playin "Listen to the Mocking Bird?"
> Sarie: Now whut about hit, what about hit? Why hit sounded so true ter the be ind air mockin bird thet I do berlieve I seed fethers fly whenever Arthur set his fiddle down.[44]

Sarah does not cite any specific influence by these women who were popular in the pre-NBC 1930s, but her *Grand Ole Opry* audience was prepared to accept her as old maid Minnie Pearl because they had already laughed at gossipy spinster comediennes.

While tapping into her audience's familiarity with the spinster, Sarah also used barn dance radio's assumptions about mountain women and their stability in a chaotic time. Minnie seemed to be unchangeable, enduring, and constant even though the world around her changed rapidly. Sarah said, "She has withstood the rigors of time because she's no threat to anybody. She's not pretty. She's not sexy. She's not smart and people just sort of think they're safe with her. Wives know that the husbands are not going to flirt with her."[45] Certainly that stability was critical to Americans who faced yet another set of challenges fostered by a two-front war.

Minnie Pearl, influenced by a variety of traditions, attempted to meet the varied expectations of broadcasters, network executives, sponsors, and audiences. The changes affected even Minnie's most identifiable trademark, her greeting. What was once a gentle "howdy" became by the postwar era a boisterous howl that greeted her audience each time she appeared on stage: "HOWDEE, I'm jes so proud t'be here."[46] After that greeting, Sarah reminded her audience about Minnie Pearl's unmarried status, her old age, and her ugly face before settling down for a good gossip. This example, from a February 1950 *Grand Ole Opry* show, is typical:

> MC Ernest Tubb: Right now let's do a little catchin' up on what's been goin' on down in Grinders Switch the past week—and here to tell us all about it is the gossip of Grinders Switch herself, Cousin Minnie Pearl!
>
> Minnie: How-dee! I'm jes' so proud t'be here!
>
> Y'know, I'm gettin' awful tired of havin' the fellers chase after me— and not bein' able to catch me!
>
> Seems like the gal who has the best chance to catch a feller is the one with short legs and long arms.
>
> It just don't avail a gal nothin' to be too persnickety. In her teens she wants a handsome man—in her twenties she wants a rich man—in her thirties she wants a good man—after that—just a man![47]

In another instance, she said of her boyfriend, Hezzy: "I guess I'm in love with him, no matter how old he is. He's on my mind all the time . . . him or some other fellow!"[48] On still another evening, she told her audience, "Over a million people was married last year and *half of 'em was women!* I ain't givin' up hope."[49] A popular song she sang captured the heart of Minnie Pearl, spinster comedienne, who, in desperation to marry, would settle for any man:

> He's not so good at idle conversation
> He never whispers love words to me
> He fills me full of joy
> He's a treasure, he's a boy
> And that's good enough for me.[50]

Jokes also stressed her ugly facial features and the effect of them on her marital status. Minnie said, "Hezzy—that's my feller—Hezzy thinks I'm purty. The other night we was a-settin' there on the sofa, when Hezzy says, 'Minnie Pearl, I got somethin' to speak to you about,' I said, 'Oh goody, Hezzy, I'm all ears!' And he said, 'Yeah, I know that . . . but maybe you wouldn't look so bad if you pull your hair down over them.'"[51] Coupled with jokes about her ugliness were ones about her age. On one 1947 show, she joked, "Somebody asked me my age and I said when I got to be 21 I stopped counting my age and they said, yes, but your face didn't."[52]

The jokes about catching a man and being old and ugly served several purposes. First, Minnie's ugliness provided her a chaperone whereas other women used men or older women. As long as the audience assumed that Minnie Pearl was old, ugly, and a spinster, her sexual attractiveness was no threat. Later on, Sarah's husband, Henry Cannon (who married her, ostensibly, because she was attractive), was her offstage chaperone. Second, as long as she chased (but never caught) men, audiences could assume she was heterosexual and still liked men. She was not an old maid because she had secret lesbian longings society would never let her fulfill.

Once she reminded her audience of her old maid, man-hungry ways, she settled down for a visit with her radio friends. If Minnie was odd, she was still a stalwart in an old-time rural community, the fictitious Grinder's Switch. A "hopelessly bucolic" place, as one reviewer derisively described it, Grinder's Switch was peopled with a variety (more than two hundred) of rural characters.[53] Listeners waited eagerly to hear the antics of Hezzy (the boyfriend who never proposed to her), Aunt Ambrosy, Uncle Nabob, Brother, Unicorn Buttelscut, Luly Belle Scully (possibly a jab at performers Lulu Belle and Scotty), and a host of other characters who had "no truck with modern things." Neighborliness still existed in Grinder's Switch, and residents played games that seemed to be from years past: "Pin the Tail on the Donkey," candy pulls, and dipping for apples.

Everyday rituals—especially local weddings (of course)—and the daily goings-on in Grinder's Switch dominated her gossip. Impish children were one important topic. She told audiences, "Missus Timkum had some trouble with one o' her younguns last Tuesday. Seems the little codger's picked up some cuss words some place. His mammy has been tryin' to break him of saying things like that so she says to him, 'Son, every time you say one o' them cuss words it makes a chill go down my back.' And the youngun says, 'Mammy, if you'd been around when pappy banged his thumb with the hammer you'd of *froze to death.*'"[54]

Catering in part to ad executives' (as well as some in her audience) stereotypes of the rural South, Sarah included buffoons and oddities in her act who resembled hillbillies. The fictitious Brother (who was arrested once, Minnie said slyly, for driving while ignorant) was that buffoon. She joked once that "Brother is a very important person in Grinders . . . Every place has its village *square* . . . in our town, it's Brother!" Other oddities included Mrs. Orson Tugwell who had "23 younguns."[55] Sarah used stereotypical assumptions about Southern life—women whose rampant sexuality caused them to have a large number of children, men such as Brother or Uncle Nabob who stole or drank—and put them at the center of her comedy. In Sarah's world, Minnie's friends and neighbors were not only examples of wholesome behavior but caricatures as well.[56]

Her emphasis remained on Southerners as clean and wholesome people who lived better, more honest lives than modern city dwellers, however. Grinder's Switch remained constant and did not change on a whim even as the world around Minnie's listeners changed rapidly. Grinder's Switch residents, for example, relied on time-tested methods with their parenting rather than on expert advice to raise their children. One evening, she said, "Link Shank's wife says she don't have no truck with modern ways o' raisin' kids. She sez she don't need no thermometers or gadgets to tell 'er how to give the younguns a bath. She sez if they turn red, the water's too hot. If they turn blue, the water's too cold . . . and if they turn white, they sure needed a bath!"[57] Modern technology also warranted a warning from Minnie Pearl. In a *Grinder's Switch Gazette* editorial, a fan newspaper she wrote and edited from 1944 to 1946, she wrote, "Yessir, science is wonderful. But there's one of them contraptions that science has turned out that has got me worried—Mammy too—and that's the Atomic Bum [bomb]. Law, it like Mammy sez, 'Science is all right till its gets to monkeying with the Laws of Nature, and that should be in the hands of the Lord.'"[58] Old-fashioned Southerners from Grinder's Switch also lauded what Sarah thought were old-fashioned ideals of hard work and industry, and cautioned against the perils of modern consumer items like lipstick, especially when it affected how hard people should work. Minnie Pearl's Mammy, she wrote in one *Grinder's Switch* editorial, kept giving Brother advice about marriage. "It's alright to flirt with the girls that wears the *lipstick*," she supposedly said, "but always marry one that can push a *broomstick*."[59]

Nature was an intrinsic part of this rural, old-fashioned landscape, and nature kept Grinder's Switch not only from modern conveniences and modern skylines, but crass modern values and a lack of faith in a Christian God as well. Sarah regularly wrote or told jokes that were paeans to nature and called on readers to not tinker with the God-given laws of nature, albeit in an ironic way that recognized nature was not perfect. She saluted fall one November in the *Grinder's Switch Gazette:* "There's beauty in the green leaves a'takin' on their reddish yellow hues, and the dogwood berries glimmerin' red on the bushes. Tall sheafs of golden-rod stalk there yellow heads along the road, givin' pleasure and hay fever to the passers-by."[60] Mammy's admonition against the atomic bomb was one place where readers needed to leave God's natural world alone.

That rural landscape ill-prepared its residents for the big city, and Sarah parodied that rural naïveté in a simple acknowledgment that many in her audience faced an uneasy transition from a rural lifestyle to an urban one for war work. If they could laugh at Minnie's antics, maybe they could laugh at their own as well or at least realize they had evolved past Minnie's naïveté.[61] Grinder's Switch residents encountered their first car and, typical of some people's reaction to new technology, thought it a monster rather than something new and intriguing:

> The first car came through Grinder's Switch on a hot summer morning when Aunt Ambrosy was sitting on the front porch shelling peas. She heard the noise, then looked up and saw this thing coming at her, so she jumped up flinging peas everywhere, and ran into the house hollering for Uncle Nabob.
>
> "Come quick," she screamed. "There's a varmint—biggest one I ever saw—just a-roarin' down the road."
>
> Uncle Nabob went running out on the porch with his shotgun and fired at the automobile. It terrified the man driving, who jumped out and ran for the woods. When Aunt Ambrosy heard the shot she called out from her hiding place in the parlor, "Did ya kill it?"
>
> "Naw," Uncle Nabob answered. "But I made it turn that fella a-loose."[62]

By 1943, Sarah seemed well in control of Minnie and the multiple influences that made Minnie possible. The plethora of one-night stands in front of soldier audiences helped, but so did her realization that Minnie would restore her elite status. Minnie's success was Sarah's financial "salvation," and it was soon clear that salvation would have significant financial rewards. In 1943, Sarah earned fifty dollars a week for performing on the Caravan, fifty dollars a week for acting as the cigarette girls' chaperone, and ten dollars a week for performing on the Saturday night *Grand Ole Opry*. She also appeared at shows outside of the South because the Prince Albert shows made her popular nationally. At those shows, she met dozens of men who had originally seen her while they served at military bases where she had performed for them during the war.

Experience and the financial rewards were not the only reasons Sarah became more in control of Minnie. She also found a way to manage giving up her "sex appeal" and becoming an old maid.[63] She constructed another character, Sarah Colley Cannon, who embraced exactly that which Minnie seemed to give up. The offstage personality further reassured Sarah (and her audiences) that she was not a masculine oddity when she portrayed Minnie because she had a "feminine" personality waiting in her dressing room. This helped Sarah preserve her own femininity even as she eliminated important components of it for the Minnie character.

New fan magazines and her comedy albums were the main places Sarah showed off her other character, called Sarah Colley (after her marriage in 1947, Sarah Colley Cannon), who evolved throughout the 1940s. In 1941, industry magazine *Radio Varieties* called her "the girl with the big future at WSM."[64] That 1941 article also set out the outlines of that offstage personality by noting Sarah was from a "family [with] above the average means" and mentioning her stint at Ward-Belmont College, described as a "superb finishing school."[65] A *Record Roundup* article, published in 1947, remarked that a "College Graduate Scores on 'Opry' as Girl Hillbilly."[66] Additions to the character were made when Sarah had life changes of her own. For example, when *The Tennessean* announced her engagement to Henry Cannon in 1947, it noted, "The bride-elect, [was] known professionally as 'Minnie Pearl.'"[67] In some cases, her duality was implied. As a "Furrin' Correspondent" for *Country Song Roundup* when the *Grand Ole Opry* cast went to Europe in 1950, Sarah appeared in photos that accompanied the article as both Minnie Pearl and as a well-dressed society matron.[68] Lest fans bristle at an elite woman poking fun at rural life, articles documented her country girl ways: a *Mountain Broadcast* article pictured Sarah making hush puppies.[69] By the 1950s, the two characters had become joined as one, and her comedy albums and other publicity displayed that duality. On the liner notes to her 1961 comedy record, the anonymous author wrote, "Minnie says that she and Sarah Cannon are growing more and more into one person. 'I just love to hear people laugh,' she says, 'whether I'm Sarah or Minnie.'" The liner notes also acknowledged her husband, Henry Cannon, reporting, "Although Minnie Pearl has always seemed desperate in her search for a man, things are not really that bad. In reality, she is married to Henry R. Cannon who operates a charter airline service out of Nashville. Henry has taken over the job as Minnie's business manager and flies her on all of her engagements in his Beechcraft Bonanza."[70]

Sarah's multiple character, labeled "Sarah Colley Cannon, better known as Minnie Pearl," allowed her to successfully pursue a business career, mold political debates, and (ironically) pursue the life of a Southern matron in ways similar to her mother. First and foremost, Sarah wanted to make money and have the lifestyle she had enjoyed as a child. While she was Sarah's alter ego, Minnie was her financial savior whose commodification made Sarah millions. Her fame as well as her lack of family responsibilities (she never had children) allowed her to explore barn dance radio's entrepreneurial sidelines. Sarah began early, in 1944, with her sale of the *Grinder's Switch Gazette,* which was the *Grand Ole Opry*'s official fan magazine during its run. She also sold items via the *Gazette;* when she offered a Minnie Pearl replica doll for sale in 1945, she announced in the magazine, "For Sale!-'Minnie Pearl.' Now, jest look at that there head line, a feller'd think that I was offerin' myself to the country at large, for sale-like a horse 'n' buggy or a good used plow. I ain't. I am offerin' a doll fer sale. You can't really see how cute the new Minnie Pearl is lessen you take her and hold her in your arms and hug her, jest like you'll want to the very minit you lay eyes on her."[71]

In 1953, she published a book entitled *Minnie Pearl's Diary,* a diary with fictitious entries that played on her *Grand Ole Opry* jokes. She opened a chain of chicken shops called Minnie Pearl's Chicken (it eventually went bankrupt) and ran the Minnie Pearl Museum.[72] Another moneymaker was her cookbook, titled *Minnie Pearl Cooks* (published in 1970), which used her dual personality to sell the book. In the preface, she wrote, "Ever since I became two people, Minnie Pearl and Sarah Ophelia Cannon, I've been faced with the problem of when to be Minnie and when to be Sarah Ophelia. In creating this book I've decided to be both."[73] And both she was. The front cover pictured Sarah in her Minnie Pearl costume—gingham dress, black Mary Jane shoes, and a flowered hat with the price tag dangling. The back cover featured Mrs. Henry Cannon, Nashville socialite, elegant hostess, and wealthy matron. Photographs illustrating the book depicted Minnie Pearl laughing with her *Grand Ole Opry* friends Roy Acuff and Grandpa Jones while an elegant and refined Sarah Cannon poured tea from a silver tea service given to her by her mother-in-law.

Sarah did not use Minnie solely for her own financial gain. She also used Minnie to promote her political views. Little evidence remains as to what those beliefs were specifically, but there is some evidence that Cannon was a states' rights supporter and she supported political candidates who opposed civil rights. Indeed, as Sarah accepted the whites-only world that was barn dance radio's mainstream culture (there were no blacks in Minnie's small Southern town, Grinder's Switch), she used Minnie offstage, in the tradition of Southern entertainers working for political campaigns, to police black behavior. Using Minnie to sustain segregation was especially important in the 1950s when segregation was under attack by the civil rights movement. Like those who supported states' rights, she most likely had a paternalistic attitude toward black men and women, believing, as many white Southerners did, that African Americans were childlike and in need of a white person's firm hand. Guidance and control was provided by Jim Crow segregation that simultaneously kept blacks in their place and managed their behavior. Moreover, as a Southern matron, she benefited (as her mother had) from working-class black labor: Mary Cannon (no relation, most articles pointed out quickly) was a black woman who worked for Sarah for approximately thirty years. Mary, who enjoyed some fame because she was Sarah's housekeeper, buttressed Sarah's status as a wealthy Nashville matron since one symbol of a well-to-do Southern woman was having black servants. Moreover, Mary also relieved Sarah of domestic duties so she could focus on making more money with Minnie Pearl.

Those beliefs fed into Sarah's contributions to the poster boy for states' rights, George Wallace, during his gubernatorial campaigns. Dressed as Minnie Pearl, Sarah introduced Wallace at 1958 rallies, saying "I'm as happy as a dead pig in the sunshine to introduce your next governor, George Wallace."[74] Minnie Pearl was also pictured next to political signs that said "Win With Wallace." Sarah, who was paid $3,000 for her appearances, was "political dynamite" for Wallace dressed as Minnie because the Alabama candidates were so similar in their positions on segregation (at least according to the New York–based *Wall Street Journal*) that an endorsement from her could be key to winning the election.[75] While Wallace lost his first gubernatorial election, Sarah was there once again in 1962 to promote his candidacy and probably heard him pledge to voters that "I shall refuse to abide by any such illegal federal court order even to the point of standing at the schoolhouse door."[76]

Finally, Sarah Cannon promoted charitable works in Nashville because Southern matrons were expected to raise money for good causes. Unlike other women, however, Sarah could use Minnie to raise money and awareness. She began working with the American Cancer Society after her sister Dixie died from breast cancer in 1967, and won praise for publicizing her own bout with breast cancer in 1984. She, of course, joked about her double mastectomy and reconstructive surgery, saying, "They gave me the breasts of an 18 year-old, so I'm 18 from the waist up."[77] She won national awards (one presented by President Ronald Reagan) for her charitable work, and administrators named a Nashville cancer institute for her after her death.[78]

Sarah's reaction to her multiple personalities was typical. When an interviewer questioned her in the 1980s about them, she laughingly said, "Well, a lot of people are two people. They just don't have a name for the other one!"[79] Sarah used Minnie to help the barn dance radio shift to meet the new challenges proffered by World War II to focus on Southern characters rather than on WLS's broad mix. Simultaneously, she showed the audience how to laugh at those challenges. Sarah was not sure at first that she wanted to be a woman with masculine characteristics or a woman who erased her sex appeal in order to be ugly, unmarried, old, and funny. She recognized, however, that the audience allowed her to play with the roles open to her and to construct characters that would assuage her need to be simultaneously feminine, funny, and financially successful.

"OH CARRY ME BACK TO THE MOUNTAINS"

Rose Lee Maphis and Laboring on the Air

Oh carry me back to the mountains
Beneath the Southern skies
Lay me to rest in the mountains
That's where my sweetheart lies.

—Rose Lee Maphis

Rose Lee Maphis loved working on Richmond, Virginia's *Old Dominion Barn Dance*. Why? "Because," she told me, "that's where I met my fella."[1] But marriage to Joe Maphis meant following him to California in 1951, where its barn dance radio scene promised new wealth. The move, their marriage, and their appearances on Los Angeles's *Town Hall Party*, a televised barn dance show, required the pair to transform their stage characters. Where once Rose was a cowgirl singer and Joe the skilled musician, together they were the singing hillbilly couple. Joe's guitar solos and witty repartee hogged the spotlight while Rose Lee, the supportive wife, played rhythm guitar and cued the bass player and drummer. California audiences loved their act so much that when the Maphises announced the birth of their son, one fan sent a handmade pair of tiny leather cowboy boots and another a handmade rocking horse. "When you're on television, they admired you and they wanted to give you something," Rose remembered.[2]

Once again, historical events caused barn dance stages to evolve, and female and male images like the hillbilly couple were used to make those changes. This time, it was the challenges posed by the postwar world and television. Now audiences looked forward to the suburbs, television shows, and juke boxes and abandoned the authentic Southern music they once relished and now considered an archaic oddity. Rose Lee Maphis (born in approximately 1924)[3] and her husband Joe weathered the changes, finding work on the *Town Hall Party* (until it, too, disappeared by the late 1950s), on California's honky-tonk circuit, and in recording sessions, becoming bit players in the new country and western music industry, the music scene that replaced barn dance radio once it died out in the 1960s.

How was Rose Lee Maphis able to remain a country music performer for nearly fifty years? Even with its changes, performance work was still a good job, one that had evolved to having specific work practices, a well-defined work culture, and labor rules since Linda Parker had first graced the stage in 1932. Maphis's work experiences demonstrate exactly what that work was for her and the women who preceded and followed her. This chapter is thus focused on her work, which she told me about in two oral interviews in 1998 and 1999. But industry proscriptions against women speaking on stage (it was all right for them to sing, just not speak) caused Rose significant discomfort during our interviews. She told me, "I wish Joe [her husband] was here. He had so much knowledge . . . I didn't have very much nerve. I have to talk now. I don't have Joe. Joe did all the talking in our family and I just tried to keep the band we worked with [going] . . . cue them. I never had the experience to really talk to the people. I was content doing what I was doing."[4] At some places in this chapter, then, other women's words and experiences will take center stage because Rose was uncomfortable speaking about some events, did not remember others, or had no experience with them.

❈ ❈ ❈

A native of Hagerstown, Maryland, Rose considered herself a hybrid, "a mixture . . . I grew up in Maryland; you know you have the Mason-Dixon line right up there," she said.[5] That hybrid quality helped her evolve over time and allowed her to forge her long career on country and western music stages. But her musical education by her family, as well as 1930s radio barn dance performers, also contributed to her development as an artist able to withstand historical changes.

Born Doris Schetrompf, Rose grew up on a farm where her parents kept a garden, produced eggs and butter, made and sold lime, sold Christmas trees off the family property, started the Hagerstown Racetrack, and rented homespun cabins to tourists. The family was also musical. "Daddy was a good singer," and her mother "knew so many hymns and she would sing them," Maphis recalled, "old Methodist-Baptist type hymns" such as "Old Rugged Cross" and "Bringing in the Sheaves."[6] Their farm income allowed for purchases of a few Jimmie Rodgers records that they played on a Victrola, and they bought their first radio sometime in the 1930s. From the first, the Schetrompfs eschewed the popular music of Bing Crosby and Frank Sinatra. "That was not my appeal," Rose Lee said, "I was just for listening to any hillbilly music."[7] She was passionate about the *Grand Ole Opry,* and to a lesser extent, the *National Barn Dance* (reception problems made it difficult to hear). Her favorite barn dance stars were Pee Wee King and the Golden West Cowboys ("That was my joy to hear them sing," she said), WLS stars Asher and Little Jimmie Sizemore, and the *Grand Ole Opry*'s Delmore Brothers. She also recalled hearing Linda Parker sing.[8]

Rose was an early consumer of barn dance music and bought the instruments and music sold by 1930s barn dance performers. She first bought a harmonica and she "blew on it some."[9] Then, she remembered, "I got a Martin, a real honest to goodness Martin guitar," and she sent off for WLS stars Asher and Little Jimmie Sizemore's guitar book.[10] She said, "I remember sending to them for a songbook that had the words and music plus guitar plus the guitar symbols [chord positions], you know . . . The first song I learned to sing was 'The Royal Telephone.' It was in the key of D. I remember that so well . . . when I got my first guitar it was too high for me to sing but that's where I had to sing it because that's where the chords were for it."[11]

Maphis learned to sing in the Sizemores' key, but from the first she knew her vocal range was adequate, not outstanding. "I never had a great voice. I didn't have much of a range," she recalled.[12] Those skills would limit her to a supporting role on stage instead of a starring one.

Barn dance radio programs had become so common by 1939 that Rose remembered that "just about every station had its own hillbillies," citing the four programs near Hagerstown alone.[13] But those programs needed musicians to perform for their audiences. There were a variety of ways women secured work, but in Rose's case, family connections secured her first audition on WJEJ Hagerstown in 1939. At her first performance, she remembered the producer asked her, "What are you going to use for your name and I said I don't know. So can't you just see Doris Schetrompf?"[14] The producer named her "Rose of the Mountains" for the rose she wore in her hair and for her theme song she played that night, "Oh Carry Me Back to the Mountains," a Patsy Montana standard she sang the first time I interviewed her.[15]

Family connections were only one way women found radio work. Letter writing was also common, appropriate for an industry that relied so heavily on fan letters. Indeed, many requests for work doubled as both fan letter and request for an audition. Letter writers typically sold their skills to a broadcaster by describing their Southern roots (if applicable), their musical ability, and their repertoire. Violet and Aline Flannery wrote John Lair for a job in February 1933, saying, "Just two more people wanting advice and information, as to how to secure an audition at W.L.S. Having the same mountain blood in our veins as the rest of you hill billies, we sure would like to make 'whoopee' with you."[16]

Performers also used amateur contests where proving one's originality, versatility, and expertise as a musician won you first prize and a spot on the air, at least in the 1930s. Amateur contests, especially fiddle contests, were "venerable" institutions, according to scholar Bill C. Malone, that dated from the 1730s and were considered a distinctly Southern, old-time phenomenon.[17] Contests were audience pleasers, and in the 1930s broadcasters regularly attended them, scouting new talent. Lily May Ledford was one performer who used those contests in the 1930s to showcase her talent. She recalled her standard contest act,

> I'd play my regular tunes, maybe "Mocking Bird" and "Cacklin Hen," then I'd go out—I kept a pair of new overalls for the occasion—I'd put them on over top my dress. Then I'd come back and play "Pop Goes the Weasel." Where you pluck the strings twice and don't have to use the bow, you can change the fiddle into different positions. Well, I'd play it through first the regular way, then I'd play it [the fiddle] in back of my head, then in back of my neck and behind my back and behind my knees. I'd put the fiddle bow between my knees and rub the fiddle up and down on it, and then on the "pluck-pluck," I'd take it back up into position. Then I'd sit on the floor, fall back, and play under one knee, and then the other, then under both of them, keeping my knees raised. Then I'd bow up a little and play under my back. When I'd hit the floor and finish my tune, of course they'd tear the house down. That way I'd win the contest.[18]

But what was once a venerable tradition that displayed rural musical skill became, by the 1940s, a marketing tool for large stations that did not reward musicians who were unique and different. Instead, locals won by mimicking famous barn dance stars, and talent contests tended to reinforce a star's popularity, although some winners could be recruited for the stage. WLS, for example, called its Home Talent Shows a "unique type of entertainment" that attracted 60,000 participants in 600 communities throughout the Midwest.[19] Judy Perkins (a future John Lair employee) and future Coon Creek Girl Evelyn Lange mimicked Patsy Montana on stage, and Perkins won her contest singing Montana's hit song, "I Wanna Be a Cowboy's Sweetheart."[20]

Like their counterparts in the 1920s, performers in the 1930s like Rose Lee worked for little or no money once they secured a radio job in order to garner experience as professional musicians. Called "wildcatting," this experience was crucial for first-time performers because, as radio professionalized and managers demanded performers adhere to a professional ethic, few wanted an amateur standing on their stages. Wildcatting was a tough job, however, because the work was haphazard and hard; women (as well as their male counterparts) had to work several jobs simultaneously to survive. Rose worked as a PBX telephone operator in a Hagerstown tannery while working on the air. Other future performers also worked two jobs. Judy Perkins ran an elevator for eleven dollars per week while wildcatting in Findley, Ohio, and future star Kitty Wells ironed shirts for nine dollars per week while she tried to break into radio.[21] When I asked Rose why she worked for free, she replied, "It was the love of it, really, and you just hoped that you'd get to do better."[22]

Although wildcatting was notorious for performers' tendency to starve, another element of wildcatting—control over one's career—allowed a few performers to be successful. Cynthia May Carver, who billed herself as "Cousin Emmy," was one of those successful wildcatters. A tough and astute businesswoman who proclaimed herself everyone's cousin, Emmy wielded barn dance radio's imagery like a weapon. In her self-published *Cousin Emmy Song Book,* she highlighted her motherly role, telling readers her "heart goes out especially to little children and old people."[23] She had "a voice like a locomotive whistle and a heart of gold," and in 1942, *Time* magazine told readers she could tame the "notoriously noxious air of St. Louis" with "the natural twang of real mountaineer goings on."[24] She used that imagery to control all components of her radio work, including where she performed, what songs she sang, even the kind of candy she sold at personal appearances. In her case, wildcatting was a successful enterprise from which she earned $300 some weeks in personal appearances and concession sales during the Great Depression.[25] John Lair may have warned Lily May Ledford about them, but the Cadillacs and diamonds as big as hickory nuts Emmy owned came from her successful, enterprising spirit.

Emmy the wildcatter also contracted with managers and stations when it suited her. She liked working with John Lair, but avoided other managers who exploited her or did not maximize her opportunities. She wrote Lair in 1941, "And I don't get any brakes from the program director . . . As he goes out with a act the Carlisle Brothers. I can tell he had ruther not have me here. But he can't very well fire me without some reason. He wanted two much of a cut." She closed her note to him saying, "the money is here if you will hury up and get the time."[26]

Few women (or men, for that matter) had Emmy's drive or talent, and it was their goal to find salaried work on large urban stations like WLS or WSM. Two factors made urban radio jobs good ones. First, those stations' reasonably secure sponsor base meant they guaranteed a weekly salary for an extended period of time. Second, musicians' unions such as the American Federation of Radio Artists (AFRA)[27] assured some performers a decent salary, especially in large cities where a union was active. Although unions could not guarantee that advertisers would sponsor a program indefinitely (mercurial advertisers tended to pull out of programs at a moment's notice), they did set a base pay for on-air appearances. In 1930, union base pay for all musicians on WLS was thirty-five dollars per week; by 1936, that salary had risen to sixty dollars per week. On stations with a smaller sponsor base, fifty dollars per week seems to have been the average. It was the expanding popularity of barn dance radio during World War II that secured Rose her first salaried job at a station in Maryland, probably in Baltimore.

Stations not only offered a weekly salary, they also offered opportunities to work side jobs. Recall that Sarah Cannon supplemented her salary on the Camel Caravan chaperoning the cigarette girls, a task that bumped her salary to $100 per week in 1941. By far, however, "personals," or local concerts, provided the most extra money for performers. Commonly, performers played at fairs, schoolhouses, theaters, and other smaller venues in their broadcast area, typically traveling as a troupe or show unit (comedienne Minnie Pearl traveled with Roy Acuff's Smoky Mountain Boys, for example). At each concert, they presented mini versions of their Saturday night barn dance, complete with music and comedy for their audiences.

Artists secured personals through a variety of means. City stations formed artist bureaus to book talent, which released artists from the time and tedium required to find personals. Artist bureaus typically responded to requests from school principals, PTA presidents, and civic organizations that desired an evening's entertainment or help with a fund-raiser. Library committee liaison Lillian W. Shumate wrote John Lair, "The Estill County [Kentucky] Library Lay Committee is planning to present an evening of entertainment in order to raise funds for the Library. Will you please inform us of the terms by which the Renfro Valley group would come here?"[28] City stations also used agents from talent agencies such as the Gus Sun Agency to book its talent on the road.

Like traveling vaudeville shows, personals were a year-round opportunity, but performers found that summers were especially busy because roads could be impassible during the winter, particularly in rural areas. Clear roads during the summers also allowed performers to travel farther, especially to the North where they found a broad base of customers. "You wouldn't believe how Northern people go for that country stuff," former Coon Creek Girl Betty Callahan remembered.[29] Knowing that, promoters publicized performers as novelty acts in the North and touted their performances as a chance to see primitive mountain folk in person, especially in the early 1930s before the barn dance genre appeared in Boston, New Hampshire, and Maine. When the Bowman Sisters traveled through Massachusetts in 1931, promoters advertised their appearances as a chance to see an archaic oddity in modern Boston: "Dramatizing the lives and customs of the primitive mountain folk of the Blue Ridge has long been a favorite subject of American novelists, but rarely is the public given to see them in person and observe their unique customs at close range."[30]

Personals were time-consuming and exhausting, however, because the time spent on the road could be extensive. The travel was so intense that many performers like Jenny Bowman kept tour diaries to track where they had been.[31] Bowman traveled and performed almost every day from January to May and then from August to December in 1931, when she wildcatted for a promoter in the Northeast.[32] Poor working conditions added to the exhaustive travel. Monotonous travel, greasy diners, unair-conditioned cars (which meant night driving to avoid the summer heat), and an endless grind characterized most touring experiences, according to Sarah Cannon. Days off were used to travel to another appearance.[33] Performers also played more shows when on the road; on Easter Sunday 1931, the Bowman Sisters played seven shows.[34]

Rose knew those concerts plus her daily duties at the radio station equaled hard work. Radio work on many barn dance stations by the late 1930s and early 1940s typically included an early morning show (usually between 4:30 A.M. and 7:00 A.M.) as well as an afternoon show, five days a week. Performers also worked the Saturday night barn dance from 7:00 P.M. until midnight. In between performances, they booked as many personals as possible, and then repeated their radio performance schedule the next day, no matter how late they returned the evening before. Maphis remembered the grind: "It became hard work like when you did an early morning program, you did an afternoon program and you go out [perform personals] that night and you do a show and you don't get back from that until wee hours of the morning. And then you gotta do that early morning program again. Now then's when it was work."[35]

It was hard work that paid well, but performers also bore the brunt of its high costs. To join the Chicago Musicians' Union in 1936, Lily May Ledford paid $105 plus monthly dues. No musician could play on the radio without a union card. Singers could sing without a union card because unions did not consider them musicians.[36] Expensive instruments (Rose's Martin guitar and Lily May's Vega White Lady banjo were not cheap) and managerial fees (John Lair expected 20 percent per week from his musicians) were also a performer's responsibility, and she was required to pay her own room and board when on the road.

Rose does not remember how sponsors or unions affected her salary, nor does she remember whether broadcasters paid her less than male performers, an important question to ask in a culture and time period that devalued women's work. Stars like Minnie Pearl and Lulu Belle Wiseman transcended assumptions that women worked for pin money (for frivolous baubles) rather than to feed and clothe themselves and their families because popularity with listeners, not gender, determined their salaries. Most women did not reach that upper echelon and seem to have been subject to salary inequities. Nor did star status necessarily protect women from unscrupulous managers. Patsy Montana was one performer who had firsthand knowledge of broadcasters' willingness to pay women less than men. Soon after her standard "I Wanna Be a Cowboy's Sweetheart" built a popular following in 1935, Montana renegotiated her contract with WLS. The station originally offered her forty dollars per week, though Montana knew men were paid sixty dollars. She told management no, and the station responded with the sixty dollar per week rate. She remembered, they "never tried to pull unequal pay on me again."[37] The Girls of the Golden West, on the other hand, demanded equal pay for their work and were fired from one station. Milly recalled,

The first time we left home was when we went to Abilene to sing on [border radio station] XER, and of course we didn't stay too long. The Hawaiian Boys told me they were making $300 and something a week and we went out there for $25 a week. And we were working harder than they were. So we were at that age where we believed everything somebody told us. So Mr. Brown would come out and take us to this restaurant in Milford to try and appease us and keep us happy, so I told him that I had heard that the Hawaiian Boys were making $300 a week and we wanted more money. They offered to double our salary. Well, there wasn't any place to spend it out there. But no it was during the holidays and everything, and I said, "You give us $100 a week at least, or give us our bus fare home." So we got our bus fare home.[38]

Milly learned that if she wanted to earn more, she needed to have a man negotiate pay, and later secured a manager (her husband) who negotiated for her.

There were other factors which circumscribed women's wages when they worked on the air. One factor was hiring policies, especially in the 1930s. Cast photos of the *Grand Ole Opry* feature two women (Sarie and Sally) in a cast of fifty; seventeen women and seventy-nine men played on the *National Barn Dance* in the same era. But by the 1940s, policies relaxed, and twelve women and fifteen men played on the *Renfro Valley Barn Dance*. There are several reasons for the difference in numbers. First, local prescriptions against women and work may have kept them from performing in the South. At the same time, stations kept more men in salaried on-air positions and hired women as infrequent guest stars, which earned them an equally infrequent paycheck.[39] Finally, broadcasters hired more men to play in backup bands. Fiddle players, bass players, and later, electric guitar and drum players were men's instruments, and few women played them on stage, even after Lily May Ledford and others proved their talent on the fiddle and bass. Only guitars and voice were commonly deemed appropriate for women.

Radio executives limited women in their work choices off the air, too, because Americans in the 1930s believed men worked technical, managerial, and entrepreneurial jobs while women worked in secretarial or service jobs. On barn dance radio, men were station engineers, announcers, or managers. Women answered fan mail, ran the music library, or did other kinds of secretarial work. Rose knew this firsthand because she worked as secretary on a station in Blytheville, Arkansas, when she was not on the air performing.[40]

Their gender may have circumscribed which jobs they worked, but radio's contradictions determined the length of time a performer, whether male or female, stayed on a station. While the audience searched for stability via authentic, old-time music, it also wanted new, exciting entertainers and modern entertainment. Broadcasters tried to balance listeners' daily exposure to established acts by searching for fresh talent. This meant that performers parted ways with a station once the area had been "worked out," or overplayed.[41] A bored listener, after all, tuned into other stations looking for exciting new performers. It was the rare performer (such as Minnie Pearl) who stayed at one station for her entire career. More typical was Rose Lee's experience; she worked at three different stations during World War II alone.[42]

Duration on a station was also limited by band disagreements with management. Rose worked with band leader Slim Steuart, a cowboy, she said, who spent "fifteen years a cowboy and never stepped in horse pucky." Together, they performed on a Norristown, Pennsylvania, station. But Steuart decided to leave for KMOX in St. Louis in late 1945 because of a disagreement with station management. Steaurt told management, as Rose Lee recalled, "When we go, the girls go because they came with me."[43] She did not dispute his claim and followed him to St. Louis, recalling, you "sorta go with the flow and where the world takes you."

Rose's experience with Steuart highlights another common experience on barn dance radio: managerial exploitation of performers. Managers required their performers to obey their commands, and Rose Lee, like many others, rarely challenged the decisions men made about her career. While Rose believed her passivity never harmed her, management exploitation was egregious in other cases, even from some managers who hired a substantial number of women (numbers did not circumscribe managerial intentions, particularly in a relationship where a large amount of money could be made). Some managers dangled the promise of a well-paying job to make performers behave. In one instance, Granny Harper angered John Lair, who wrote a colleague, "Granny, the old jitterbug, don't seem to want to come. I'll let her drop off here a little and she'll be anxious later on if we still want her."[44]

In another instance, WLS management signed Lulu Belle and her husband, Scotty Wiseman, to an illegal lifetime contract. It also did not tell the couple of a $20,000 offer to perform in a Hollywood movie. The exploitation was enough for Lulu Belle to tell an interviewer that WLS management was "mean as ratdirt."[45]

While management demanded acquiescence from women in exchange for stable work, women found subtle ways to mute that exploitation, devices so subtle that Rose did not remember using them. The first was a station's grapevine or rumor mill. Gossiping may have been Sarah Cannon's tool for national popularity onstage, but offstage, performers used gossip to keep fellow performers apprized of management practices. Some then used that information to protect their jobs. Granny Harper heard through the grapevine that the *Renfro Valley Barn Dance* was in financial trouble. She went to the ticket office and demanded her salary from ticket sales before she played another show.[46] The grapevine provided so much information that John Lair requested that his letters be hidden from employees who might see confidential information and spread the word.[47]

A performer's "drawing power" (popularity with listeners) also tempered management exploitation. Broadcasters wanted to keep those performers who were effective saleswomen and increased their salaries or promised lucrative bookings in order to retain their services. In turn, some women used their popularity against management. Ricca Hughes decided her drawing power warranted an increase in salary and wrote John Lair, "The hillbilly's [*sic*] . . . have always until this new set up [weekly wage], worked for nothing except the Personals so they all feel well taken care of under this arrangement . . . So how and why I should be expected to work for the same will perhaps always remain a mystery . . . Due to a smear of back biting rats the spot [radio station] has been and still is very very unpleasant—worth what I'm getting to keep them brushed off." Since Lair was not paying her what she was worth, Ricca promised that "under the circumstances I'm going to have to coax myself to work out a notice" if he did not increase her salary.[48]

Managers like Lair bristled when women like Ricca were not properly deferential. In part, it was a class issue: managers like John Lair were typically more educated and middle class, whereas Ricca's letter-writing abilities suggest she was more working class. But gender was a factor, too; management (which was almost exclusively male) expected women to defer. In response to Ricca's demands, Lair admitted her popularity, but he stiffened at her behavior. He wrote a colleague,

> I do feel that she is worth a little more money than she is getting now but I certainly don't like her attitude in the matter and if it was left entirely up to me I'm afraid I'd let her notice stand and see what she does about it. Chick, however, feels she is a terrific "draw" and is very anxious for us to keep her on . . . She counters with the idea that she is of tremendous value to the morning pro-

gram and is building up a big listening audience. A;l [*sic*] in all, she has the beginner's exaggerated conception of her value as a radio entertainer.[49]

He gave his go-ahead to his colleague, saying, "If Ricca will cut out the foolishness and two-bit politics and get down to work she'll be alright. On the other hand, if she gets the idea from this that she can step in about every two weeks, as she has been doing, and demand new terms the quicker she moves on the better for all concerned."[50]

Management exploitation (and women's ability to counter it) was only one of many common experiences Rose Lee Maphis had when she worked on barn dance radio. Another common experience was the breakup and subsequent reformation of duos, trios, and groups. There were multiple reasons for breakups. Men often left a duo or group because of illness (especially alcoholism), a better opportunity on another station, or dissatisfaction with band members. Women left for those reasons as well, but pregnancy and, to a lesser extent, marriage sometimes caused groups to break up. Rose Lee worked first as a solo artist, then joined the Saddle Sweethearts, played as a duo after two Saddle Sweethearts left to marry, and finally joined her husband's act after their marriage.[51] Marriage and pregnancy opened a revolving door for the Coon Creek Girls since one of its members was always pregnant or sick. Former Coon Creek Girl Betty Callahan said, "I swear everybody in Renfro Valley has been a Coon Creek Girl, I reckon. Even the boys."[52] But pregnancy and marriage did not necessarily cause women to leave the stage, especially if they married another performer. Moreover, as Lulu Belle found out in 1936, women were more popular after their children's births because the sentimental mother character, still a force on stage in the postwar era, needed children to make her more real.

Another common experience was the work culture that developed at barn dance radio stations spanning the nation. Historian Susan Porter Benson defined work culture as "the ideology and practice with which workers stake out a relatively autonomous sphere of action on the job . . . A realm of informal, customary values and rules mediates the formal authority structure of the workplace and distances workers from its impact . . . More than simply reactive, work culture embodies workers' own definition of a good day's work, their own sense of satisfying and useful labor."[53]

On barn dance radio, the work culture was a series of practices that reinforced the familial image sold on stage. As WLS manager Burridge D. Butler (known to *Stand By!* readers as "Daddy" Butler) told listeners, "All of our ideas center around the firesides of our listeners."[54] Rose remembered that on the *Old Dominion Barn Dance,* one worked as if a part of a family: "On the barn dance, we worked together . . . When you're on a show like that you work together. You just don't do your own stuff and that's it. You support and you work together."[55] Rose then described the specific work practices that workers decided portrayed a supportive, work culture: "On the Old Dominion Barn Dance that's when [I] really learned the thing. I really remember about working there whoever is working at the microphone to the audience you supported them with your attention. They had your attention. You didn't jabber, jabber [makes a hand motion mimicking a mouth speaking]. Talk to whoever you were sitting by or standing by. You reacted to the person at the microphone . . . You didn't do your number and go sit down."[56]

Appearing supportive had the added benefit of impressing the audience that the musicians had constructed an old-time community of faith and support. Because of its importance, there were significant repercussions for undermining this image. Maphis recalled,

> This was what was knocked into our heads on Monday mornings. You might be reprimanded for something—talking to so and so instead of paying attention to what was going on because you were supposed to be enjoying and listening and if the comedians were working or whatever you enjoyed that. You would clap for them. You didn't just sit there like a bump on the log either. If it was an up tempo you might be reacting in your own way whatever, pattin' your foot, clapping your hands a little. At least you had your attention on whoever was at the microphone.[57]

Barn dance radio's work culture came not just from standards decided on by workers, but from station management, too. Radio executives used a variety of business practices "to build good relationships with all the people," as John Lair told Lily May Ledford her first day at WLS.[58] They included knowing all station employees: Ledford remembered meeting all station employees, which numbered more than one hundred, on her first day. Station executives also demanded that performers treat each other well. Finally, WLS station rules also required performers to be at the station when not on the road and provided recreational rooms (a billiard room, for example) as well as rehearsal space for their use.

Barn dance radio programs may have broadcast wholesome family images over the ether, but offstage, sibling rivalry was as much a part of barn dance families as wholesome, supportive relationships were. Some stars' ability to draw large crowds and, therefore, enormous amounts of advertiser dollars made it necessary to show favoritism to some special children. Management paid them larger salaries, assured them greater job security, and featured them more prominently on stage. In some cases, management encouraged popular performers (who seemed to have willingly gone along) to behave more like squabbling than supportive siblings. For instance, broadcasters persuaded some performers to "crab," or intrude, on others when they were performing.[59] Patsy Montana remembered that while she was singing on stage, Lulu Belle used to peel grapes for audience members, behavior Montana considered rude and outrageous.[60] Authentic family relationships were thus as rife with tensions as they were with nurturing and care.

Lily May Ledford was a favored child on the *National Barn Dance,* and her peers responded with pointed attacks. Although she was not specific, she was hurt and angered by the jealousy: "Then too I began to hear talk in the dressing rooms and back stage that made me realize there was more than a little of professional jealousy among the talent. I was sorry to hear it and I didn't like that and didn't want to be jealous nor promote it. Jealousy is one of the most destructive things I've ever known among any group working together and enough of it can all but destroy a show or group and greatly hurt the performance of a sensitive person such as me."[61] She realized that it was the professional performers who saw her as a threat. She remembered there was

> some professional jealousy, which I hated and we were the butt of much of it for the more polished musicians felt bitter, as they were not in demand as much as we were. They imagined we were drawing big salaries because we were so rich in fans and their crowding around us. I understand their feelings, for they were hard working serious musicians. But they *were* in demand for the large commercial radio shows and us girls were more of the "drug trade" type, short commercials and was rarely placed on a net work show . . . We didn't mind this one bit.[62]

No one in the audience ever heard about jealousy or spiteful behavior because a code of silence formed a core part of barn dance radio's work culture. Moral and virtuous performers could only seem so if performers kept silent about jealous, spiteful behavior. That silence also hid other remarkably amoral behavior, especially among men, for whom alcoholism was an epidemic—not surprising for an industry that used to pay its performers with a swig from a jug. Rose Lee had personal experience because her husband Joe was an alcoholic. "I guess that was the thing to do [drink alcohol]. I don't know why," she said.[63]

Rarely, however, were men fired for drinking or other shenanigans, although some managers did think the allowance for men's behavior toward alcohol was a problem. John Lair recommended two fiddle players to a Boston radio station, describing them as "sober and level-headed."[64] The Rice Brothers and Gang wrote Lair for a job, selling themselves as a "clean cut bunch of boys, sober, reliable and dependable."[65] In some cases, Lair was willing to pay for popular male performers to dry out. He wrote Shorty Hobbs, of the comedy team Shorty and Eller, "I am now in a position to go to work on you and Eller as the feature act of the Barn Dance. As you know, I can do that only under one condition . . . I will make arrangements to let you have the money for the Louisville trip so that you can come back on the job and really get down to business. After you have taken this treatment I want to sign a contract with you and Eller which will allow for you both to get into better money."[66] "Treatment" for Hobbs was drying out in a sanitarium. It did not work, and Hobbs died at age thirty-seven from alcoholism.[67]

Many men dated women in their audiences, and some (even those who were married) had girlfriends in towns they visited regularly. At this point in our interview, Rose asked me to turn off the tape recorder, and she told me stories that she requested I not write about. But other performers were more than willing to tell tales a long time after the fact. Sarah Cannon remembered, "This always amused me, the way the boys could communicate with the girls on the front row during the show. They'd come off the stage and one of them would say, 'I have a date with the one in the pink sweater,' and then another one of them would say, 'I've got a date with the one in the short beige skirt.' They'd go out to eat between shows or take them back to the hotel."[68] Lulu Belle recalled, "These men on the show were always trying to get around you—you know, young girl, free, trying to get you somewhere in a bed."[69] Men's behavior taught female performers to be cynical about marriage, since male performers who supposedly valued the good family-man image onstage contradicted it offstage. Maphis remembered that marriage "really wasn't all that important to us girls . . . we were a little skeptical" after seeing the amorous behavior of married male performers.[70] Cannon said that she was "pretty disillusioned" by their behavior and held off marrying until she was thirty-four years old. "You have a hard time [in show business]," she said, "finding a man that you can be sure that will stay with you all the way."[71]

Only in rare circumstances did men face punishment for their behavior. The industry's double standard, however, decreed that women who mimicked men's amoral behavior be fired or sanctioned. Management may have turned a blind eye to men's sexual improprieties and alcoholism, but it was a different matter altogether when women drank, smoked, or even hinted at sexual promiscuity. Barn dance radio's intricate ties to feminine virtue were the prime reason. If women were immoral, the music they preserved could be deemed corruptible. Thus, when talent agents wrote broadcasters to sell them a new female performer, it was required that women behave within the moral parameters set by the sentimental mother or the wholesome cowgirl. In some cases, alcoholism and smoking cost women jobs. Talent agent William Ellsworth wrote Lair with several potential girl singers for hire, one of whom drank. He wrote, "Joe Brandt (of the old team of Joe & Jean) is with Whitey as his Cow-girl . . . She is nice looking but he is letting her go because she drinks too much and Lewis hates drinkers. For the same reason I doubt if you would care to employ her." In other cases, "moral" also meant avoiding the station's grapevine. One woman was appropriate for Lair's show because, as Ellsworth wrote, "Christine Campbell may be the Gal you want. She never takes a drink nor smokes and attends strictly to her own business."[72]

Managers enforced a rigid code of sexual conduct for women, although that was not always easy. In 1943, Lair's assistant, Gene Cobb, wrote him that several female performers "had been free on streets with boys" while they were out on the road. Those women acted too promiscuously for Cobb's taste, and he acted in Lair's stead to rein them in. He wrote in his poorly spelled and typed letter, "Have had a little trouble with [the Travers] Twins and Opal [Amburgey] showing up late and missing openings. Twins, missed opening twice last wk and I come D— near sending them home . . Opal only missed once, But have to watch her with the town cut ups . . I am sure that *you* do not appreciate are [*sic*] care to tolorate such, and I quoted *you* as such . . . So every thing in Georgia is peaches but CREAM."[73]

Rose changed her behavior to conform to the industry's double standard, to avoid what another performer, Wilma Lee Cooper, called "carry[ing] a bad name."[74] Maphis recalled, "I guess we all smoked but you didn't smoke in public. Didn't want people to see you smoke. It wasn't a very nice thing for a girl to do, to start."[75]

She remembered that the Saddle Sweethearts, her World War II band, were not drinkers, and whenever they needed to go out in public, "we would all go together."[76] Since they had husbands, they reassured their audiences (and colleagues) that women could preserve a moral past, and concerns about sexual promiscuity ceased to be a problem. When Rose Lee married Joe Maphis, she recalled, "Because I was married to Joe, I was no threat."[77]

Because historical circumstance dictated how performers, broadcasters, and the audience defined a genuine, authentic performer, Rose knew that her skills had to change as circumstances did. That her career survived through many eras meant she was remarkably flexible as well as proficient at many jobs. First, a skilled performer was a talented instrumentalist who could play and sing string band music. Rose was an adequate guitar player and singer, but others, such as Lily May Ledford and Cousin Emmy, were brilliant musicians. The irrepressible Cousin Emmy played fifteen instruments, musical and otherwise, including the banjo, fiddle, guitar, handsaw, rubber gloves, and "a tune I makes by just slopping against my cheeks with my hands," Emmy told an interviewer in 1943.[78]

Creating a character was also a kind of expert ability. In this case, skill was a woman's ability to act and sing a part in a way that was believable to her audience. She could portray a cowgirl or hillbilly singer as opposed to an opera singer who sang Bizet's *Carmen* or a popular singer who could croon the latest Bing Crosby tune. Women such as Jeanne Muenich or the Girls of the Golden West who were not born in the South or West had to manufacture backgrounds, dialects, and the appropriate singing style to be convincing on stage.

Bookers and producers searched for women who had skillfully created hillbilly or cowgirl personas. Booking agent William Ellsworth told John Lair of a "girl" singer from Michigan, Audrey Homberg. She had "an acquired hill-billy dialect and comedy style" and could perform multiple roles, including "do a dance step, and claims to be able to get a lot of laughs clowning. She reads music, and has a large library of western, and hill-billy songs."[79] The exceptional skilled worker could perform multiple roles, not all of them musical: for example, working as secretaries and librarians for the radio station where they also performed. Rose's secretarial job at the Blytheville, Arkansas, station where she also performed was evidence of this.[80]

Skill also meant entwining their act with the male troupe or announcer who acted as their stage chaperones. This meant not only finding men who fit the image female performers sought to sell but finding men who would not exploit them. Rose's World War II band, the Saddle Sweethearts, affiliated themselves with Bud and the Saddle Pals, a male barn dance troupe that needed "girl" singers. They worked with them on the air five days per week and appeared on personals with them. They also worked with cowboy singer Slim Steuart on the Norristown, Pennsylvania, barn dance.

The Sweethearts needed Bud and Slim as much as the men needed them. The announcer was in the public eye, and he directed other performers via voice cues, revealed to the audience which performers sang next, and read advertisements and reminders for other programs. In short, he was the front man for the show, the patriarchal figure who not only told the audience what performance came next but who reassured fans that performing women were under his moral guidance. Maphis remembered, "There was none of us of the four of us . . . speakers to speak for the group . . . We always had someone. 'Now here's the Saddle Sweethearts' and we would do our singing and that was it . . . There was always someone else speaking for us."[81]

Skilled performers like Rose altered their acts when personnel changes and contemporary events required it, using naming practices, costuming, instrumentation, and other tricks to make the needed changes. During World War II, for instance, Maphis morphed from hillbilly to cowgirl. She and Betty Gower (bass, guitar), Dotty Klick (accordion), and Mary Robinson (bass), formed the Saddle Sweethearts, in which they sang songs of the West and wore cowgirl clothing. "I was always fascinated with a cowboy," she said, "I always loved the Western dress. I loved the reading, the Western novels. The cowboy life just fascinated me . . . It was the fascination of the cowboy in love with the girl and I always liked to see the Western movies."[82] Because she was a second-tier act (meaning she was not a name act, but a performer who supported a "name act"), she needed to use her skills and talent to simulate more successful Western performers like Patsy Montana and the Girls of the Golden West. The Saddle Sweethearts had to imitate those more popular characters, right down to names and clothing. Maphis recalled, "We wore Western. We went to Rodeo Ben in Philadelphia and had costumes made. We had two costumes made. We had brown with yellow flowers and then we had a blue with a royal blue with a lighter blue yoke."[83]

They ordered cowboy boots through the mail, but they never wore other cowgirl trademarks like cowboy hats. The Saddle Sweethearts then built a repertoire that fit their clothing, name, and character. That repertoire had few, if any, original songs. Instead, they sang songs that catered to their listeners' desire for familiarity. Maphis remembered,

"We all liked Western. We did a lot of Western songs. We did Sons of the Pioneer stuff because we all had a pretty good ear for hearing the different parts."[84]

Rehearsals were how the Saddle Sweethearts and other performers gained skill in their profession. Rehearsals required a significant time commitment in order to achieve a level of comfort and to build a large repertoire of music. "We were *constantly* learning," WLS star Lulu Belle remembered. "You wouldn't have any idea how many songs we did."[85] Rehearsals also made the Saddle Sweethearts comfortable with each other, with the characters they assumed, and with the repertoire they constructed—what insiders like Minnie Pearl called "season[ing] an act."[86]

The Saddle Sweethearts used rehearsals to assess which woman's voice fit a given song. Maphis said, "I think Betty was the one mainly sang the lead and Mary did the tenor and I did the baritone. We would do a song three different ways. We'd do it with the lead in the middle, with the lead on top and that would put the tenor on the bottom and then also the lead on the bottom and the two above."[87]

During rehearsal, the Sweethearts learned to phrase and pronounce a song's words in similar fashion. Rose remembered, "You try to phrase alike and you blend, you work for a blend . . . you pronounce the same . . . you really have to work at that." She and her friends spent "quite a bit of time learning."[88] Family bands such as Lily May Ledford and the Coon Creek Girls (when sisters Rosie and Minnie were members) had nature and nurture on their side: genetically, their voices were more likely to sound similar, and they grew up in the same musical environment. But some family bands developed odd methods of rehearsal. Maphis recalled her friends the Dinning Sisters rehearsed lying on the floor with their heads touching each other.[89]

Adding or eliminating performers from groups required changes in acts—Rose faced yet another evolution in her onstage character when she met and married Joe—but skilled performers knew that history, too, affected how their characters would evolve. After World War II ended, a new consumer culture emerged, rooted in a modern set of images facilitated by television. Programs featured modern suburban couples like Ward and June Cleaver, and the closest thing to a Western motif on this and other family shows was the ranch-style house the Cleavers lived in. Television taught consumers to look forward in awed expectation of their future, not backward to find some stability and comfort in a Southern past. Westerns became popular on television, but they lacked the Southern characters that barn dance radio had had. Moreover, TV

Westerns were oriented toward fighting the emergent Cold War against the Russians, meaning they defined the good guys as Americans with the virtuous cowboy past and everyone else as the bad guys or "savages."

Barn dance programs tried to reinvent themselves for television viewing, and the hillbilly couple that Rose and Joe portrayed, a pair that embraced plain, simple values, were a staple part of these new programs. The *National Barn Dance,* the *Grand Ole Opry,* and the Los Angeles show the Maphises appeared on were woefully unsuccessful, however, and died by 1960 (with the exception of the Opry). The Maphises could not use radio to support themselves, either, because television caused radio programs to reinvent themselves. No longer were play parties and old-time tunes in the spotlight. Now, disc jockeys spun records from individual artists, and the spotlight was on the jockey selling specific tunes over the air rather than on a group of singers performing live for their fans.

Musical changes accompanied the postwar shifts. The Maphises modified their repertoire and stage act when they started playing the California Sound, the electrified country music that Southern migrants brought with them to central and southern California, a more working-class sound that featured drums, bass, and electric guitars. Rose recalled the difference this way: on barn dance shows, "You sang a lot of sad songs. 'Oh no, Mama, we'll never forget you and someday we'll meet you up there.' People can't dance to something like that. Out there [in California] if you're gonna sing a song, you're going to have to think about dancing."[90] That new music was played at new venues that caused the greatest discomfort for Rose Lee. She remembered, "Those days [while working on the *Old Dominion Barn Dance*] you didn't work in clubs . . . you weren't a very good person if you did . . . It just wasn't respectable."[91] The same restrictions did not exist in California, and the Maphises played personals in bars and honky-tonks such as the Blackboard Cafe in Bakersfield. The honky-tonks they played in were places where people drank hard, danced hard, and cheated on their spouses. Rose Lee said, "When you worked the clubs that's where the people . . . that's where you had your heartache and that's where you're smoking and you're drinking."[92]

The California Sound also required new instruments, and there was a beat to the music it had not had previously. The music's electrification also gave it a harsher, harder sound. This forced Rose to learn a new instrument, the electric guitar, and to perform with musicians who played the new instruments. "It was hard to get up there and sing and we'd never worked with drums before," Rose said.[93]

The song repertoires had to change, too, so they could speak directly to audience members' experiences. The pain they sought refuge from was no longer from hardships of the outside world devastated by the Great Depression or worldwide violence. It was from friends and loved ones (especially promiscuous women) in the honky-tonks themselves. Traitorous women who eschewed familial responsibilities in favor of spending time at a bar inspired Joe Maphis's most famous song, "Dim Lights, Thick Smoke (and Loud, Loud Music)":

Dim lights, thick smoke and loud, loud music
Is the only kind of life you'll ever understand.
Dim lights, thick smoke and loud, loud music
You'll never make a wife to a home-loving man.

A home and little children mean nothing to you
A house filled with love and a husband so true.
You'd rather have a drink with the first guy you meet
And the only home you know, the club down the street.[94]

The audience's behavior changed as well. In barn dance radio's heyday in the 1930s and 1940s, performers played for audiences who listened without any kind of overt movement except for applause at the end of a song. Families came to these events since they provided clean fun for the entire family. In honky-tonks, however, Maphis found that children were decidedly unwelcome and that "out there they're dancing . . . people gettin' up and dancing." Adults danced to songs about adult situations such as drinking, smoking, sexual promiscuity, and divorce. Dancing in honky-tonks was disconcerting for Rose Lee because "you didn't know if they liked you and what you were doing [if they danced]."[95] Lily May Ledford witnessed this at her personals. Only "men folks and mill workers that seemed pretty drunk," she said, came to her shows. She recalled, "I've stopped the show and asked them to be quiet as how that this was no burlesque show, only a simple hillbilly show as they should have known by the advertising, and we demanded respect or there might be some one that came to hear us not to yell and insult. That usually quieted them for a time."[96]

Rose featured the music she played in honky-tonks on the albums she and Joe recorded in the 1950s, which broadened their audience beyond Los Angeles and central California bars. It was also the only way to get their music on the radio, since disc jockeys now only played selections from albums. "Mr. and Mrs. Country Music," as they were called, recorded at least two albums (one a solo album by Rose Lee), and on both, mixed the California Sound with older barn dance radio favorites that both had grown up listening to.[97] "Whiskey Is the Devil in Liquid Form" spoke to fans who frequented the honky-tonks, while Linda Parker's standard, "Bury Me beneath the Willow," invoked Rose's days on barn dance radio.[98]

As the inclusion of "Bury Me beneath the Willow" suggests, barn dance radio's traditional themes lingered on in implicit, but still important, ways in a performer's act. The Maphises' album liner notes exhibited that legacy. On their album *Rose Lee and Joe Maphis,* country star Merle Travis wrote consumers, "It's always a treat to visit the Maphis family. Their beautiful walnut-shaded home is a cross-roads stopping place for Country musicians and entertainers. The Maphis house is never short of hospitality. In every nook and corner is charm that reflects their love of home. In every room you'll find remembrances of bygone days."[99] The Maphises' album was the right one to buy, Travis asserted, because they honored both family and the past, two consequential elements from barn dance radio's past.

Thus, by 1960, barn dance music had become regional fare once again for a few listeners, in this case, the California Sound for Southern migrants to Los Angeles (its eastern counterpart would have been the Nashville Sound). Barn dance radio's national popularity had so diminished that even the music's name changed—old-time music was now country and western music. Rose Maphis was able to make the transition from barn dance radio, aimed at a nation, to country and western music, sold once again to migrant Southerners, because she knew to change with the times and to remain flexible as the industry underwent substantial changes in the postwar era.

Coda

Barn Dance Radio's New Friend, Loretta Lynn

I am leaving Mississippi in the evening rain
Well these Delta towns wear satin gowns
in a high beamed frame
Loretta Lynn guides my hands through the radio
Where would I be in times like these
Without the songs Loretta wrote?

'Cause when you can't find a friend
You've still got the radio
And when you can't find a friend
You've still got the radio
The radio . . . listen to the radio.
The radio.

—Kathy Mattea, *Lonesome Standard Time*

When Loretta Lynn first sang on the radio, she did not croon like Linda Parker nor did she yodel like the Girls of the Golden West. Instead, she strutted off the airwaves. With hits like "Fist City," "Don't Come Home A-Drinkin' (with Lovin' on Your Mind)," and "Your Squaw Is on the Warpath," Lynn was a woman's woman in the 1960s and 1970s who sang about real life, not a fictional character whose idealized world bore little resemblance to her listeners' daily lives.[1] Country music scholars loved her as much as fans did, calling her an industry innovator. According to those scholars, she was one of the first women to grace country music's stages and her revolutionary style forged a commercial place for women on stages once reserved almost exclusively for men.[2]

Lynn's rags-to-feminist-riches story raises several important issues regarding the women who sang before her on barn dance radio stages. First, scholars called Lynn's forthright performances a feminist act because she tried to make women equal to men on stage, or so it seemed. Lynn and her contemporaries Kitty Wells and Patsy Cline were powerful, visible, heard in ways that women supposedly had not been before. It did not matter that Lynn consistently denied the feminist label, saying, "I'm not a big fan of Women's Liberation."[3] Second, calling Lynn and her peers "innovators" erased barn dance women from country and western music's past, since to be innovative in this case meant to be the first. Scholars claimed that few women had preceded Lynn and her peers, and those few had been bent on a political power play, similar to Lynn's. They were not there to work a good job or do something they loved. As Mary Bufwack and Robert Oermann wrote, "Our analysis of women's country music shows that working-class women do have a social awareness of their situation as women, of their subordination in male-female relationships, of their problems in the family context, and of their exploitation in the work force."[4]

What was the effect of this scholarly narrative on the seven women in this book once barn dance radio disappeared from the airwaves? Linda Parker, the Girls of the Golden West, and, to a lesser extent, Lulu Belle Wiseman, were erased, almost completely, from country and western music's history. Linda Parker was literally forgotten until scholar Dave Samuelson rediscovered her in the 1990s.[5] Recall how important Muenich's death was to the sentimental mother's popularity; her grave site in Pine Lake Cemetery in La Porte, Indiana, was rumored to be a popular destination for several years after her death. The marker itself captured Muenich's popularity as Linda Parker: it reads, "Linda Parker, Wife of Art Janes." Yet as her memory waned and the sentimental mother took a back seat to cowgirls and spinster comediennes, so, too, did visits to the grave site until Samuelson rediscovered it.[6] Parker's successor, Lulu Belle Wiseman, tried to survive the barn dance's demise, but she retired when the genre died out in the 1960s. She later became a North Carolina state legislator and voted against the Equal Rights Amendment when it was considered there.[7] She passed away in 1999 after suffering from Alzheimer's disease.

The Girls of the Golden West were similarly relegated to the margins of country music's history. They retired as a duo in 1949, and while Milly focused on raising her five children, Dolly remained "in show business full-time, becoming hostess of a kiddie program and doing pop hit parade material as a solo on other WLW shows," according to Bufwack and Oermann.[8] If not for their recordings and for Charles Wolfe's work documenting older stars, they, too, would have been erased. As it was, his interview with Milly Good McCluskey in 1978 (Dolly died in 1967 from heart problems) was printed in *Old Time Music* in 1986 and then rarely, if ever, used for scholarly purposes until Bufwack and Oermann wrote the encyclopedic *Finding Her Voice.*[9]

Neither the Girls nor Lulu Belle had the flexibility to move beyond what made them so successful in the 1930s, while Jeanne Muenich died before having to change her stage performance. Sarah Colley Cannon, Rose Lee Maphis, and Lily May Ledford, on the other hand, were able to survive barn dance radio's demise by reinventing themselves. In Cannon's case, her flexibility and ability to move between her multiple personalities meant future tastes, too, could be incorporated. That ability came in handy when she was featured on *Hee Haw,* a new way to present country music and a syndicated television hit in the late 1960s. Cannon also continued to use her dual personality to promote public causes, serving in one instance as chairwoman for the Ear Foundation at Baptist Hospital (Nashville), a foundation that sent deaf students to local schools. Its letterhead listed her as "Mrs. Henry Cannon (Minnie Pearl)."[10] In 1991, she suffered a stroke, and she lived in seclusion until she died in March 1996. At her passing, cartoonists published a poignant cartoon mourning the beloved Nashvillian's death: they drew a halo with a price tag that read "priceless."[11]

Along with her successes at reinventing herself as a performer, Rose Lee Maphis was able to reinvent herself as a hit songwriter in the 1970s. In 1972, she wrote "Love Is the Look You're Looking For" for Connie Smith, which hit number 9 on the *Billboard* record charts. It also won her an industry award for songwriting, something, she proudly stated in our interview, that Joe never did.[12] The Maphises continued to perform and write until Joe's death in 1986. Rose Lee quit and now supports herself sewing costumes for the performers with whom she once sang. When asked why she quit, she replied, "I know this [performing] was something that I did. See, Joe was the real attraction of the duet. He was the mainstay. I was the little added extra . . . We were a good opening act. When God called Joe my desire left right then. There was no way I was going out and sing by myself. I didn't want to. I didn't have the talent. I wasn't used to speaking to the audience. Joe did all that."[13]

Lily May Ledford, who grew up sixty miles east of Lynn's famed Butcher Holler in Kentucky, would not reinvent herself. Instead, she waited for history to catch up with her. Her performance for British royalty solidified her reputation as an authentic folk singer, and she played with luminaries such as Burl Ives, Woody Guthrie, and Pete Seeger in the 1940s and 1950s while still under John Lair's management. She stayed in his employ until 1957, when family responsibilities and his pay scale (he typically cut performers' salaries in down times to pay for the Renfro Valley complex) caused her to quit.[14] By the mid-1960s, college students, beatniks, and others were searching for an authentic cultural life beyond the examples Ward and June Cleaver presented them. They saw Southern folk music (and musicians) as pure, primitive relics from a simpler, more genuine past, just as their parents and grandparents had seen the barn dance stars in the 1930s. Folk festivals featuring folk musicians reappeared, and in 1966, folk festival organizer Ralph Rinzler came calling. He invited the Ledford sisters (Lily May, Rosie, and Black-Eyed Susie, their youngest sister) to the National Folk Festival in Newport, Rhode Island. Once again, Lily May stared wide-eyed at her audience, but this time, it was not British royalty she wished to impress but young people, "hair, beard and all and college bred."[15] "In our day," she wrote, "college kids would not have come across the road to see us, only older folks and farm boys and girls."[16] Now college students attended her nightly concerts as well as the banjo and fiddle workshops she held during the day. She became so popular that in 1979, the National Endowment for the Arts awarded her money for a five-month residency at Berea College where she gave banjo and fiddle workshops, convocations, and taught ballad and story classes.[17] She died in 1985 from the "dread cancer" and her gravestone, reading "Banjo Pickin' Girl," stands out in the Berea cemetery where she is buried.

There is no evidence that they ever met, but Loretta Lynn still framed her life story and character in ways remarkably similar to Ledford's and other barn dance women. Lynn was born to a poor coal-mining family in a Kentucky "holler" (hence her title, "The Coal Miner's Daughter"). Her isolated upbringing and strong family influence, like Linda Parker's mythology, promised fans she was the real thing. She paid her dues, working road shows just as Sarah Cannon and Rose Maphis did. And like Lulu Belle Wiseman, she used the birth of her twin daughters in August 1964 to promote herself as a newfangled sentimental mother. It worked.

Her twins were born just as she was named "Top Female Vocalist" in *Billboard* magazine's 1964 poll.[18]

There were certainly differences in Lynn's and barn dance women's careers. Barn dance shows had disappeared from the radio, and because country music did not play well on television (at least until *Hee Haw* found a successful format), those shows, too, had disappeared. Performers now recorded albums and then persuaded disc jockeys to spin them in order to boost record sales. Fans were also different, more willing to hear about the dark side of life in Kentucky hollers. They heard about Lynn's flour sack dresses whereas the same information would have appalled them when Lily May was on stage. There were times when real was still too real, of course. Stations across the country banned her song "The Pill" (1972), and Lynn remarked, "But then look at all the trouble I got into for singing 'The Pill.' So maybe people aren't ready for real life."[19] Perhaps a version of the sentimental mother still had a stranglehold on Lynn as she had had on Parker and others. Mothers might have sex to conceive children, but sex for its own sake was immoral and threatened the perception that country women were more virtuous than other women.

Even though there are differences, the similarities between Lynn and the seven women in this book remain strong and visible. Probably the most significant one was the use of Lynn as a symbol to mark an important commercial and musical change in country and western music. Broadcasters wielded her Coal Miner's Daughter image to sell the new cosmopolitan country and western music (called the Nashville Sound) emanating from a new center for that music, Nashville, in the 1960s. Lynn was now the good woman, a dynamic person who demanded proper treatment from her husband and industry executives alike. She was willing to tell women to "stand by their men," she wrote, but first her men, whether her husband or music industry executives, had to stand by her.[20]

Her supposed feminist character was thus both an incorporation of—and a reaction to—the ways women had been treated on and off stage before Lynn ever set foot there for the first time. And while Loretta never explicitly recognized their influence, the ways that Parker, Wiseman, the Goods, Cannon, Maphis, and Ledford negotiated various work practices, fit themselves into predetermined characters, and tangled with the modern music business affected Lynn's successful career as well. What is clear is that by the mid-1960s, the banjo pickin' girl had metamorphosed into the Coal Miner's Daughter and she was, once again, a national sensation.

Notes

Abbreviations

AFRA Armed Forces Radio Archives, Museum of Broadcast Communication, Chicago, Ill.

Banner collection
 Nashville Banner Collection, Nashville Public Library, Nashville, Tenn.

BCA Bayer Corporation Archives, Elkhart, Ind.

BKP Bradley Kincaid Papers, Southern Appalachian Collection, Berea College, Berea, Ky.

CMHOF Country Music Hall of Fame, Nashville, Tenn.

CPM Center for Popular Music, Middle Tennessee State University, Murfreesboro, Tenn.

FDR Franklin and Eleanor Roosevelt Papers, Roosevelt Institute, Hyde Park, N.Y.

GGW Girls of the Golden West Record Collection, Southern Appalachian Collection, Berea College, Berea, Ky.

JLP John Lair Papers, Southern Appalachian Collection, Berea College, Berea, Ky.

Ledford autobiography
 Lily May Ledford, unpublished autobiography, [ca. 1970s], Southern Appalachian Collection, Berea College, Berea, Ky.

Maphis I Rose Lee Maphis, oral interview with Kristine M. McCusker, Center for Popular Music, Middle Tennessee State University, Murfreesboro, Tenn., May 19, 1998.

Maphis II Rose Lee Maphis, oral interview with Kristine M. McCusker, Center for Popular Music, Middle Tennessee State University, Murfreesboro, Tenn., March 24, 1999.

MPF   Minnie Pearl File, Country Music Hall of Fame, Nashville, Tenn.

MSA   Marr Sound Archives, Miller-Nichols Library, University of Missouri-Kansas City, Kansas City, Mo.

Naff   Lula C. Naff Collection, Nashville Room, Nashville Public Library, Nashville, Tenn.

NBC   National Broadcasting Corporation Papers, State Historical Society of Wisconsin, Madison, Wisc.

SCC   Sarah Cannon Papers, Gaylord Entertainment, Nashville, Tenn.

SFC   Southern Folklife Collection, Wilson Library, University of North Carolina, Chapel Hill, N.C.

Introduction

1. Ledford autobiography, Aug. 1936, 23.

2. Ibid.

3. See, for example, Bill C. Malone, *Don't Get above Your Raisin': Country Music and the Southern Working Class,* ix.

4. Ann Schofield, *To Do and to Be: Portraits of Four Women Activists, 1893–1986.* See Bill C. Malone, *Country Music, U.S.A.,* and Jeffrey Lange, *Smile When You Call Me Hillbilly: Country Music's Struggle for Respectability, 1939–1954,* for examples of this kind of study.

5. See, for example, Mary Bufwack, "The Feminist Sensibility in Post-War Country Music."

6. Mary Bufwack and Robert K. Oermann, *Finding Her Voice: Women in Country Music.*

Chapter 1: "Family Songs of Surpassing Sweetness"

1. Susan A. Glenn, *Female Spectacle: The Theatrical Roots of Modern Feminism,* 13–17.

2. David McCullough, *Truman,* 71.

3. Minnie Pearl with Joan Dew, *Minnie Pearl: An Autobiography,* 63.

4. Bufwack and Oermann, *Finding Her Voice,* 69–70.

5. Ibid., 69–70.

6. "WLS Daily Programs," *Stand By!* 2, no. 52 (Feb. 6, 1937): 18–19, JLP.

7. M. Allison Kibler, *Rank Ladies: Gender and Cultural Hierarchy in American Vaudeville,* 9–10, 5, 7. The same process happened in cinema in the 1910s. See Shelley Stamp, *Movie-Struck Girls: Women and Motion Picture Culture after the Nickelodeon,* 6.

8. http://www.loc.gov/exhibits/bobhope.

9. Kibler, *Rank Ladies,* 13.

10. Malone, *Country Music U.S.A.,* 6; http://www.loc.gov/exhibits/bobhope/vaude .html.

11. Ibid.

12. Glenn, *Female Spectacle,* 19.

13. Ibid., 41.

14. Kibler, *Rank Ladies,* 66–67.

15. Malone, *Country Music, U.S.A.,* 110.

16. William Ellis, "The Sentimental Mother Song in American Country Music, 1923–1945," 23.

17. Malone, *Country Music, U.S.A.,* 10; Bufwack and Oermann, *Finding Her Voice,* 23.

18. Hattie Nevada, "The Letter Edged in Black," Center for Popular Music, http://musicman.mtsu.edu/broadsides/Binder14/JPEG/2744bro.jpg.

19. Richard Slotkin, *Gunfighter Nation: The Myth of the Frontier in Twentieth Century America,* 77.

20. "Otto Gray and his Oklahoma Cowboys," 2; Bufwack and Oermann, *Finding Her Voice,* 28–29.

21. Glenn, *Female Spectacle,* 47.

22. Ibid., 160, 158, 156.

23. Ibid., 171.

24. Announcement, Naff; program, "Mrs. Florenz Ziegfeld (Billie Burke) Presents the New Ziegfeld Follies," Nov. 3, 1937, Naff.

25. Program, "Earl Carroll Vanities," 8th edition, Naff.

26. Henry Shapiro, *Appalachia on Our Mind: The Southern Mountains and Mountaineers in the American Consciousness, 1890–1920,* ix.

27. Anthony Harkins, *Hillbilly: A Cultural History of an American Icon,* 35.

28. Dorothy Scarborough, *A Song Catcher in the Southern Mountains,* 4.

29. Jane S. Becker, *Selling Tradition: Appalachia and the Construction of an American Folk, 1930–1940,* 3–4; Shapiro, *Appalachia on Our Mind,* ix.

30. Becker, *Selling Tradition,* 2, 125–66.

31. Shapiro, *Appalachia on Our Mind,* 246.

32. Kay Baker Gaston, *Emma Bell Miles,* 10.

33. Ibid., 1–10, 11–15.

34. Ibid., 18.

35. Ibid., 34.

36. Ibid. Emphasis in original.

37. Ibid., 69. Emphasis in original.

38. Emma Bell Miles, *The Spirit of the Mountains,* 30.

39. Shapiro, *Appalachia on Our Mind,* 249.

40. Miles, *The Spirit of the Mountains,* 146; Harkins, *Hillbilly,* 42.

41. Credit for the book is generally given to Cecil Sharp, but he died before its completion and it seems that assistant Maud Karpeles finished the book for him. See Shapiro, *Appalachia on Our Mind,* 255, 257; Cecil Sharp and Maud Karpeles, *Eighty English Folk Songs from the Southern Appalachians.*

42. Shapiro, *Appalachia on Our Mind,* 259.

43. Susan J. Douglas, *Inventing American Broadcasting, 1899–1922;* Bernard G. Hagerty, "WNAX: Country Music on a Rural Radio Station, 1927–1955," 177.

44. Susan Smulyan, "The National Barn Dance, Early Broadcasting, and Radio Audiences," 2.

45. George C. Biggar, "The WLS National Barn Dance Story: The Early Years," 106.

46. James N. Gregory, *American Exodus: The Dust Bowl Migration and Okie Culture in California,* 6.

47. Chad C. Berry, "Social Highways: Southern White Migrants to the Midwest, 1910–1990."

48. Jack Temple Kirby, "The Southern Exodus, 1910–1960," 597.

49. Derek W. Vaillant, "Sounds of Whiteness: Local Radio, Racial Formation, and Public Culture in Chicago, 1921–1935," 32.

50. Lizabeth Cohen, *Making a New Deal: Industrial Workers in Chicago, 1919–1930.*

51. Emma Riley Akeman to Our Dear Bradley? Apr. 9, 1931, BKP.

52. Susan Smulyan, *Selling Radio: The Commercialization of American Broadcasting, 1920–1934,* 23–27.

53. "Materials Toward a Study of Early Country Music on Radio, IV. Dallas, Texas," 61–62.

54. Gene Wiggins, *Fiddlin' Georgia Crazy: Fiddlin' John Carson, His Real World, and the World of His Songs,* 69. No scripts or sound recordings from this era survive, if any existed in the first place.

55. Bufwack and Oermann, *Finding Her Voice,* 69.

56. Ibid., 70.

57. Mrs. Jean Warner to Listener's Mike, *Stand By!* 2, no. 29 (Aug. 29, 1936): 2.

58. Ibid.

59. Charles Wolfe, *A Good-Natured Riot: The Birth of the Grand Ole Opry,* 112.

60. Ibid., 118.

61. David C. Morton and Charles Wolfe, "DeFord Bailey: They Turned Me Loose to Root Hog or Die."

62. Jane Smith interview with McCusker.

63. Jacquelyn Dowd Hall, "Disorderly Women: Gender and Labor Militancy in the Appalachian South," 301; Wolfe, *A Good-Natured Riot,* 67–68.

64. Ibid.

65. Paul Kingsbury, ed., *The Encyclopedia of Country Music: The Ultimate Guide to the Music,* 282–83.

66. Biggar, "The WLS National Barn Dance Story," 107.

67. Loyal Jones, "Who Is Bradley Kincaid?" 122.

68. Photo, Edgar L. Bill, with signature, BKP; D. K. Wilgus and Nathan Hurvitz, "Bradley Kincaid," 86–94.

69. Bradley Kincaid, "Favorite Mountain Ballads and Old-Time Songs," Songbook #3, 1930, BKP.

70. Bradley Kincaid, "Favorite Mountain Ballads and Old-Time Songs," Songbook #1, 1928, 6, BKP.

71. Bradley Kincaid, radio address, "America's Debt to the Mountains," 3, 5–6, BKP.

72. Ibid., 5.

73. Ibid.

74. Bradley Kincaid, radio address, "The First Evening: A Close-Up of the Mountaineers," 3, BKP.

75. David Whisnant, *All That Is Native and Fine: The Politics of Culture in an Appalachian Region,* 184.

76. Kincaid, "Favorite Mountain Ballads and Old-Time Songs," Songbook #1, 1928, 6.

77. Bradley Kincaid to Mr. H. E. Taylor, Nov. 24, 1932, BKP.

78. Bradley Kincaid, "My Favorite Mountain Ballads and Old-Time Songs," Songbook #5, Pittsburgh, KDKA, 1932, listed in Loyal Jones, *Radio's "Kentucky Mountain Boy" Bradley Kincaid,* 34; Kristine M. McCusker, "Dear Radio Friend: Listener Mail and the National Barn Dance, 1931–1941," 190–91.

79. Ethel Ater to Bradley Kincaid, July 27, 1931, BKP.

80. Akeman to Our Dear Bradley? Apr. 9, 1931, BKP.

Chapter 2: "Bury Me beneath the Willow"

1. Karl and Harty, *Karl and Harty with the Cumberland Ridge Runners;* WLS *Family Album,* 1934, 21, JLP.

2. Ibid.; Bufwack and Oermann, *Finding Her Voice,* 47.

3. Mrs. James F. Victorin to Listeners' Mike, *Stand By!* 1, no. 28 (Aug. 24, 1935): 2, JLP.

4. O. W. to ibid.

5. Lois Almy to ibid.

6. John Lair, "Notes from the Music Library," *Stand By!* 1, no. 30 (Sept. 7, 1935): 12.

7. Radio script, "Bunk House and Cabin Songs," Jan. 18, 1936, JLP.

8. Dave Samuelson, "Linda Parker: The WLS Sunbonnet Girl," 16–17.

9. Benjamin Filene, *Romancing the Folk: Public Memory and American Roots Music,* 137.

10. Illinois, Indiana, Michigan, and Wisconsin were the four states.

11. Benedict Anderson, *Imagined Communities.*

12. Iris Marion Young, "The Ideal of Community and the Politics of Difference," 300. Vaillant, in "Sounds of Whiteness," examines issues similar to the ones discussed here although he is more focused on racial issues.

13. Program, "National Barn Dance," [ca. 1932–1935], JLP.

14. Kingsbury, *The Encyclopedia of Country Music*, 288.

15. Program, no title, no date [ca. 1930–1931], JLP.

16. Vaillant, "Sounds of Whiteness," 29.

17. David M. Kennedy, *Freedom from Fear: The American People in Depression and War, 1929–1945*, 85–88.

18. Patricia Cooper, "The Faces of Gender: Sex Segregation and Work Relations at Philco, 1928–1938."

19. Margaret T. McFadden, "'America's Boy Friend Who Can't Get a Date': Gender, Race, and the Cultural Work of the Jack Benny Program, 1932–1946," 119.

20. Cohen, *Making a New Deal*, 248.

21. John Lair, *Renfro Valley Then and Now*, 14, 16; Lisa Yarger, "Banjo Pickin' Girl: Representing Lily May Ledford," 104.

22. "Flashes: Renfro Valley Folk Going on Network Program in October," *Stand By!* 1, no. 31 (Sept. 14, 1935): 3.

23. Radio script, "Aladdin Barn Dance Frolic," Dec. 20, 1930, JLP.

24. Radio script, [untitled, ca. 1930–1931], JLP.

25. "WLS Play-Party Frolic," May 14, 1932.

26. Radio script, [untitled, ca. 1930–1931], JLP.

27. Ibid.

28. Ibid.

29. Ibid.

30. Ibid.

31. Biggar, "The WLS National Barn Dance Story," 110.

32. McFadden's "'America's Boy Friend Who Can't Get a Date'" makes a similar point regarding the *Jack Benny Show*.

33. Radio script, [untitled], Sept. 26, 1931, JLP.

34. Radio script, "Aladdin Barn Dance Frolic," Dec. 20, 1930, JLP. See also radio script, "Eleven oclock—Sat. night, Oct. 3rd., 1931 . . . WLS," JLP.

35. Hall, "Disorderly Women," 301.

36. Ibid., 28.

37. Karen Linn, *That Half-Barbaric Twang: The Banjo in American Popular Culture*, 130–35.

38. Typescript, WLS interview with John Lair, [broadcast 1930s], JLP.

39. Radio script, [untitled, ca. 1930–1931], JLP.

40. Ibid.

41. "Aladdin Barn Dance Frolic, no. 2," JLP.

42. Ann Lair Henderson, *On the Air with John Lair*, 33.

43. Ibid., 28–29.

44. Samuelson, "Linda Parker," 16–17.

45. John Lair interview with Powell.

46. Richard A. Peterson, *Creating Country Music: Fabricating Authenticity*, 107.

47. Kathy Peiss, *Hope in a Jar: The Making of America's Beauty Culture*, 48.

48. Biggar, "The WLS National Barn Dance Story," 110.

49. Clipping, Emory and Linda Lou Martin Materials, CMHOF.

50. Radio script, [untitled, ca. 1930–1931], JLP.

51. Faye Dudden, *Women in American Theater: Actresses and Audiences, 1790–1870,* 2–4, 175.

52. W. M. Ellsworth to Lair, June 14, 1942, JLP.

53. "Sally," *Stand By!* 2, no. 20 (June 27, 1936): 9.

54. "Trio Girl," *Stand By!* 2, no. 22 (July 11, 1936): 9.

55. Beth Cremer interview.

56. Radio script, "Monday Night in Renfro Valley," Oct. 14, 1940, JLP.

57. Hall, "Disorderly Women," 309.

58. Radio script, "Thursday Noon," Feb. 25, 1932, JLP.

59. Patsy Montana with Jane Frost, *The Cowboy's Sweetheart: Patsy Montana;* Maphis I.

60. Charles Arnett to Bob Shaw, Gus Sun Agency, Oct. 25, 1943, JLP.

61. Clayton McMichen to John Lair, Apr. 30, 1948, JLP.

62. Agreement between John Lair and Mantel Lamp Company, Dec. 29, 1930, JLP.

63. Maphis I.

64. Judy Perkins interview with Rice.

65. Ibid.

66. Repertoire Record for Linda Parker, "Solos," JLP.

67. Henderson, *On the Air with John Lair,* 30.

68. Karl and Harty, *Karl and Harty with the Cumberland Ridge Runners.*

69. John Lair, "Notes from the Music Library," *Stand By!* 3, no. 28 (Aug. 21, 1937): 11.

70. Peterson, *Creating Country Music,* pictures with captions after pages 155, 184.

71. Program, "WLS National Barn Dance," JLP.

72. "Thursday Noon Program," JLP.

73. Ibid.

74. Ibid.

75. Ibid.

76. Radio script, "Hamlin," Feb. 24, 1934, JLP.

77. Ibid.

78. Ibid.

79. Ibid.

80. Radio script, "Coon Creek Social," Jan. 3, 1935, JLP.

81. Ibid.

82. Ibid.

83. Radio script, "Play-Party Frolic, 7:45–8:15, May 7, 1932—8th St.," JLP.

84. W. Demont Wright to the Prairie Farmer Station, Feb. 18, 1934, JLP.

85. Ibid.

86. "A Well Wisher of WLS," Aug. 3, [ca. 1932–35], JLP.

87. Radio script, "Bunk House and Cabin Songs," Mar. 7, 1936, JLP.

88. Radio script, "Bunk House and Cabin Songs," Mar. 21, 1936, JLP.

89. Radio script,"Bunk House and Cabib [*sic*] Songs," Jan. 25, 1936, JLP.

90. Ibid.

91. Mrs. E. E. Muenich to John Lair, Feb. 18, 1936, JLP.

Chapter 3: "Hey, Hey, Hey, the Hayloft Gang Is Here"

1. C. L. Finley to Listeners' Mike, *Stand By!* 2, no. 47 (Jan. 2, 1937): 2; Mr. and Mrs. Ben Vall to ibid., 3, no. 1 (Feb. 13, 1937): 2, JLP.

2. Mrs. Earl Spaulding to ibid., 2, no. 21 (July 4, 1936): 2.

3. Hadley Cantril and Gordon W. Allport, *The Psychology of Radio,* 91–93.

4. William E. Lightfoot, "Belle of the Barn Dance: Reminiscing with Lulu Belle Wiseman Stamey," 4; Malone, *Country Music, U.S.A.,* 10.

5. Hall, "Disorderly Women," 298–321.

6. Wayne Daniel, "Lulu Belle and Scotty: 'Have I Told You Lately That I Love You?'" 71.

7. Lightfoot, "Belle of the Barn Dance," 8.

8. Daniel, "Lulu Belle and Scotty," 71.

9. "Girl on the Cover," *Stand By!* 1, no. 24 (July 27, 1935): 9; Lightfoot, "The Belle of the Barn Dance," 10.

10. Ibid.

11. Ibid.

12. "Hi Rinktum Inktum," *Alka-Seltzer Songbook,* CPM.

13. Ibid.

14. http://www.icdc.com/fmoore/carterfamily/single_girl.htm.

15. Loyal Jones, "Bascom Lamar Lunsford," and William E. Lightfoot, "Lulu Belle and Scotty," in Kingsbury, ed., *The Encyclopedia of Country Music,* 308, 309.

16. Daniel, "Lulu Belle and Scotty," 72.

17. Lightfoot, "Belle of the Barn Dance."

18. Marjorie Gibson, "Fanfare," *Stand By!* 1, no. 49 (Jan. 18, 1936): 6.

19. Lulu Belle, "The Royal Family: Lulu Belle, Winner of Queen Contest, Thanks Her Fans," *Stand By!* 2, no. 38 (Oct. 31, 1936): 3; Lightfoot, "From Radio Queen to Raleigh: Conversations with Lulu Belle," 4.

20. Lulu Belle, "The Royal Family."

21. Lightfoot, "Belle of the Barn Dance."

22. Vaillant, "Sounds of Whiteness," 26.

23. Biggar, "The WLS National Barn Dance Story," 109.

24. National Broadcast Corporation, Inc., "Let's Look at Radio Together," 1 (June 1935): 58, NBC.

25. Miles Laboratories annual report, 1934, BCA.

26. Miles Laboratories annual report, 1936, BCA.

27. Ibid.

28. Biggar, "The WLS National Barn Dance Story," 111.

29. Salary listing, BCA.

30. Biggar, "The WLS National Barn Dance Story," 110; Smulyan, "The National Barn Dance," 10.

31. Smulyan, "The National Barn Dance," 10; "WLS Daily Programs," *Stand By!* 2, no. 38 (Oct. 31, 1936): 16.

32. Souvenir program, WLS National Barn Dance, ca. 1936, JLP.

33. Ibid.

34. Souvenir program, WLS National Barn Dance, 1933–1934, BCA.

35. Agreement between the Mantle Lamp Company of America and John Lair, Dec. 29, 1930, JLP.

36. Sidney Strotz to John Royal, Mar. 14, 1934, NBC.

37. Pat Buttram, "Serious Side of Humor," *Stand By!* 3, no. 51 (Jan. 29, 1938): 2.

38. Continuity Changes, Program Department, Grand Ole Opry, Mar. 27, 1947; Feb. 27, 1947; Mar. 21, 1947; Feb. 13, 1947; Feb. 6, 1947, NBC.

39. Continuity Changes, Grand Ole Opry, Mar. 27, 1947, NBC.

40. Pamela Grundy, "We Always Tried to Be Good People: Respectability, Crazy Water Crystals, and Hillbilly Music on the Air, 1933–1935," 1601, 1610.

41. Daniel, "Lulu Belle and Scotty," 74.

42. Morton and Wolfe, "DeFord Bailey," 13–17.

43. Charles Wolfe, "Jamup and Honey," in Kingsbury, ed., *The Encyclopedia of Country Music,* 261.

44. Vaillant, "Sounds of Whiteness," 38.

45. Freeman Keyes to John Lair, Oct. 27, 1941, JLP.

46. Keyes to Lair, June 20, 1938, JLP.

47. Lair to Keyes, no date [probably 1938], JLP.

48. Recording, National Barn Dance, Dec. 5, 1942, AFRA.

49. Ibid.

50. "News and Gossip of the Studios," *New York Times,* Oct. 3, 1937, 180, and "News Acts Flash Down the Wave Lengths," *New York Times,* Sept. 11, 1938, 194, cited in Smulyan, "The National Barn Dance," 8, fn10.

51. Survey, 208–11, 1937, BCA.

52. Ibid., 19. Surveyors, for example, distinguished listeners by class using groups A, B, C, and D to designate differing class structures. Elite blacks, however, were not put in the top class ("A") but in the lowest class to denote not their economic ability, but their low place on the racial hierarchy.

53. Angel Kwolek-Folland, *Engendering Business: Men and Women in the Corporate Office, 1870–1930,* 17.

54. McCusker, "Dear Radio Friend," 191.

55. Mildred Madrinovich to Listeners' Mike, *Stand By!* 1, no. 24 (July 27, 1935): 2.

56. Mrs. R. M. Kirby to ibid., 2, no. 38 (Oct. 31, 1936): 2.

57. Maretta Terrill to ibid., 2, no. 47 (Jan. 2, 1937): 2.

58. Mrs. Myra Bowers to ibid., 3, no. 47 (Jan. 1, 1938): 2.

59. Edith Lamb to ibid., 2, no. 44 (Dec. 12, 1936): 2.

60. S. E. J. to ibid., 2, no. 49 (Jan. 16, 1937): 2.

61. Dorothy Sheldon to ibid., 3, no. 19 (June 19, 1937): 2.

62. "Radio—An Invited Guest," *Stand By!* 3, no. 47 (Jan. 1, 1938): 5.

63. Allan Mawby to Listeners' Mike, *Stand By!* 2, no. 25 (Aug. 1, 1936): 2.

64. Mrs. Ethel Price to ibid., 3, no. 23 (July 17, 1937): 2.

65. Kathleen Whiting to ibid., 3, no. 7 (Mar. 27, 1937): 2.

66. McCusker, "Dear Radio Friend," 184.

67. Mrs. John F. A. to Listeners' Mike, *Stand By!* 3, no. 19 (June 19, 1937): 2.

68. Marilyn June C. to ibid., 2, no. 49 (Jan. 16, 1937): 2.

69. Fed Up on L. B. to ibid.

70. Helene Kunkel to ibid., 2, no. 47 (Jan. 2, 1937): 2; B. Eck to ibid.

71. Mrs. Maybelle Harvey to ibid.

72. Betty Oxford to ibid.

73. Editors to ibid.

74. U. C. Y. to ibid.

Chapter 4: "Will There Be Any Yodelers in Heaven?"

1. GGW; radio transcription, "Pinex Mountain Merrymakers" [ca. 1937–1938], tape 14, program #1, JLP.

2. Ibid.

3. Ibid.

4. Marchand, *Advertising the American Dream,* 109.

5. Birth and death dates are from Richard Carlin, *Country Music: A Biographical Dictionary,* 153; "Golden West Girl," *Stand By!* 2, no. 48 (Jan. 9, 1937): 15–16, JLP; "Merry Maker," *Stand By!* 2, no. 49 (Jan. 16, 1937): 16.

6. Milly Good McCluskey interview with Wolfe, side 1, p. 1–4.

7. Border stations appeared in Del Rio, Mexico, and were mega stations that broadcast all over the United States using 500,000 watt towers. See Malone, *Country Music, U.S.A.,* 98–100.

8. Advertising card, JLP; Montana, *The Cowboy's Sweetheart,* 51–53.

9. Allison McCracken, "'God's Gift to Us Girls': Crooning, Gender, and the Re-Creation of American Popular Song, 1928–1933," 365.

10. Kingsbury, ed., *The Encyclopedia of Country Music,* 204.

11. Biggar, "The WLS National Barn Dance Story," 108.

12. Radio script, "Bunk House and Cabin Songs," Jan. 1, 1936, JLP.

13. Slotkin, *Gunfighter Nation,* 231–77.

14. Ibid., 247–48.

15. Ibid., 231.

16. Ibid., 234, 236–37.

17. "Golden West Girl," *Stand By!;* "Merrymaker," *Stand By!;* WLS *Family Album,* 1934, JLP.

18. "Golden West Girl," *Stand By!*

19. Radio transcription, "Plantation Party," [no date], JLP.

20. Radio script, "Bunk House and Cabin Songs," Dec. 29, 1936, JLP.

21. The Hired Man, "The Old Hayloft," *Stand By!* 2, no. 52 (Feb. 6, 1937): 6.

22. Tony Russell and Charles Wolfe, "Two Cowgirls on the Lone Prairie," 165.

23. Douglas B. Green, *Singing in the Saddle: The History of the Singing Cowboy,* 54, 63; Montana, *The Cowboy's Sweetheart,* 67; McCluskey to Wolfe, side 1, p. 10.

24. "Merrymaker," 16.

25. Radio script, "Bunk House and Cabin Songs," Feb. 15, 1936, JLP.

26. Richard Aquila, "A Blaze of Glory: The Mythic West in Pop and Rock Music," 192.

27. "Old Chisholm Trail," GGW.

28. "Oregon Trail," GGW.

29. Aquila, "A Blaze of Glory," 193, 195.

30. "Bunk House and Cabin Songs," Feb. 15, 1936, JLP.

31. "Take Me Back to My Boots and Saddle," GGW.

32. Radio script, "Bunk House and Cabin Songs," Mar. 8, 1936, JLP.

33. "Two Cowgirls on the Lone Prairie," GGW.

34. "I Wanna Be a Real Cowboy Girl," GGW.

35. "I'm Lonesome for You, Caroline," GGW.

36. Jocelyn Neal, "Why It Took a Man's Song to Make a Woman's Career: Dolly Parton and Artistic Independence."

37. Smith to McCusker; "Two Cowgirls on the Lone Prairie."

38. Green, *Singing in the Saddle,* 18–19.

39. Malone, *Country Music, U.S.A.,* 103.

40. McCluskey to Wolfe, side 2, p. 12.

41. "Golden West Girl," 16.

42. Russell and Wolfe, "Two Cowgirls on the Lone Prairie," 168.

43. Marjorie Gibson, "Fanfare," *Stand By!* 2, no. 41 (Nov. 21, 1935): 12.

44. Herman S. Hettinger, *A Decade of Radio Advertising,* iv; Smulyan, *Selling Radio,* 73–75.

45. Marchand, *Advertising the American Dream,* 109.

46. Radio script, "Monday Night in Renfro Valley," Dec. 16, 1940, JLP.

47. Hettinger, *A Decade of Radio Advertising,* 15.

48. Cantril and Allport, *The Psychology of Radio,* 136; T. J. Jackson Lears, "The Rise of American Advertising," 157.

49. Ibid., 157.

50. Radio script, "Pine Mountain Merrymakers" [ca. 1937–1939], JLP.

51. Ibid.

52. Radio script, "Audition," May 23, 1935, JLP.

53. Radio script, "Pine Mountain Merrymakers," Jan. 5, 1936, JLP; ad script, "Allis-Chalmers Commercials," May 21, 1938, JLP.

54. Bert S. Gittins Advertising, radio script, "First Commercial," June 1, 1940, JLP.

55. Roland Marchand, *Advertising the American Dream: Making Way for Modernity, 1920–1940,* 108–9.

56. Peterson, *Creating Country Music,* 106–7.

57. "Merrymakers," 10.

58. Smulyan, *Selling Radio,* 103–8.

59. Radio transcription, "Pinex Merrymakers" [ca. 1937–1938], tape 14, program #2, JLP; radio transcription, "Pinex Merrymakers" [ca. 1937–1938], tape 15, program #1, JLP.

60. Ibid.

61. "Pinex Merrymakers," tape 14, program #2.

62. Radio transcription, "Pinex Merrymakers" [ca. 1937–1938], tape 16, program #1, JLP.

63. Radio transcription, "Pinex Merrymakers" [ca. 1937–1938], tape 17, program #1, JLP.

64. Lillian Wakeland, Chicago, Illinois, to *Stand By!* 2, no. 37 (Oct. 24, 1936): 2, JLP.

65. Audition script, "Pine Mountain Merrymakers," Nov. 3, 1935, JLP.

Chapter 5: Banjo Pickin' Girl

1. Coon Creek Girls, *Early Radio Favorites;* Ledford autobiography, Aug. 1936, 47. There are two sections of Ledford's autobiography. The first section is paginated consecutively. A heading titled "Aug. 1936" begins the second section.

2. "A Program of American Music," June 8, 1939, FDR.

3. One version of the autobiography was published by the Seattle Folklore Society in the mid-1970s. Another longer version was published by Berea College in 1980.

4. Rosie Ledford Foley, Minnie Ledford, and Lily May Ledford Pennington (Ledford sisters) interview with Freeman and Faurot.

5. Ledford autobiography, 1–2; Cari Norris interview with author; Ellesa Clay High, *Past Titan Rock: Journeys into an Appalachian Valley,* 99.

6. Yarger, "Banjo Pickin' Girl," 32. See also Jacquelyn Dowd Hall et al., *Like a Family: The Making of a Southern Cotton Mill World.*

7. Ledford autobiography, Aug. 1936, 1.

8. High, *Past Titan Rock,* 76–77. Information is also from Ledford autobiography.

9. High, *Past Titan Rock,* 84.

10. Ibid., 5.

11. Ibid., 98.

12. Ibid., 59, 92, 98.

13. Ledford autobiography, 9.

14. Ibid., 11–12; Yarger, "Banjo Pickin' Girl," 41.

15. H. Lisle Krieghbaum to Howard Chamberlain, Nov. 21, 1935, JLP.

16. Ellesa Clay High, "The Coon Creek Girl from Red River Gorge: An Interview with Lily May Pennington," 59.

17. Ibid.

18. Ledford autobiography, Aug. 1936, 58.

19. Ledford autobiography, 19.

20. Ibid.

21. High, "The Coon Creek Girl from Red River Gorge," 70.

22. Ledford autobiography, Aug. 1936, 14.

23. Ibid., 13.

24. Ibid., 7.

25. Ibid.

26. Artist press release for the Renfro Valley Barn Dance, [ca. 1937–July 1939], JLP.

27. Ledford autobiography, Aug. 1936, 9.

28. Yarger, "Banjo Pickin' Girl," 68.

29. Ledford autobiography, Aug. 1936, 8.

30. John Lair to Miss Gertrude Knott, Apr. 11, 1938, JLP.

31. Ledford autobiography, Aug. 1936, 13–14, 10, 14.

32. Radio script, National Barn Dance, Sept. 19, 1936, JLP.

33. The Hired Man, "In the Old Hayloft: Lily May, The Mountain Gal," *Stand By!* 2, no. 46 (Dec. 26, 1936): 6, JLP.

34. Marjorie Gibson, "Fanfare," *Stand By!* 3, no. 1 (Feb. 13, 1937): 9.

35. Check Stafford, "The Latch String," *Stand By!* 2, no. 51 (Jan. 30, 1937): 10.

36. See, for example, "Lily May, The Mountain Gal: She *Will* Have Music," *Stand By!* 2, no. 35 (Oct. 10, 1936): 7.

37. "Lily May: The Mountain Gal," *Stand By!* 2, no. 51 (Jan. 30, 1937): 7.

38. Ibid.

39. Harkins, *Hillbilly,* 84–85.

40. Yarger, "Banjo Pickin' Girl," 41.

41. Ledford autobiography, Aug. 1936, 17.

42. Ibid., Aug. 1936, 15.

43. Ibid.

44. Ibid.

45. Lair interview.

46. For the term *cultural regression,* see Whisnant, *All That Is Native and Fine.*

47. John Lair to Freeman [Keyes], Monday Morning, [no date, ca. late 1930s, early 1940s], JLP.

48. Harry Rice, "Renfro Valley on the Radio, 1937–1941," 17.

49. Ibid.

50. John Lair, *The Renfro Valley Barn Dance,* [ca. 1939], JLP.

51. News Service, "Barn Dance Programs to Come from Renfro Valley Itself," Oct. 27, 1939, JLP.

52. Ad, *Variety Radio Directory,* 1938–1939, 1308, JLP.

53. Ester Koehler was from Wilton, Wisconsin, and Evelyn Lange was from Greenville, Ohio.

54. Malone, *Country Music, U.S.A.,* 10.

55. High, *Past Titan Rock,* 171.

56. Ibid.

57. Ledford sisters interview.

58. G. Malcolm Laws Jr., *Native American Balladry: A Descriptive Study and a Bibliographic Syllabus,* 193.

59. Yarger, "Banjo Pickin' Girl," 65.

60. Ledford sisters interview.

61. Coon Creek Girls, *Early Radio Favorites.*

62. Yarger, "Banjo Pickin' Girl," 105.

63. Ibid., 102, 105.

64. Ibid., 106.

65. Whisnant, *All That Is Native and Fine,* 184.

66. Sarah Gertrude Knott to Eleanor Roosevelt, Feb. 24, 1939, FDR; Bulletin, "General Plan," "National Committee," FDR.

67. Knott to Roosevelt, Feb. 24, 1939, FDR.

68. Kennedy, *Freedom from Fear,* 120, 250–56.

69. http://www.arthurdaleheritage.org.

70. Ibid.

71. Filene, *Romancing the Folk,* 133.

72. Emily S. Rosenberg, *Spreading the American Dream: American Economic and Cultural Expansion, 1890–1945,* 166; Warren F. Kimball, *Forged in War: Roosevelt, Churchill, and the Second World War,* 7, 16, 27, 56–57.

73. R.A.C. Parker, *Chamberlain and Appeasement: British Policy and the Coming of the Second World War,* 106. Emphasis in original.

74. Douglas, *Listening In,* 208.

75. Grete M. Franke to Malvina Thompson, May 27, 1939, FDR.

76. Notes of welcome speech for king, speech #1228, FDR; clipping, "White House Musical Program for Royal Pair Is All-American," FDR. Supreme Court justices, cabinet secretaries, and congressional officials were the only American dignitaries invited. Franklin intended the evening for top government officials only, but used newspaper reports and Eleanor's "My Day" column to publicize the details of the visit to Americans. List of invitees, "Musical at the White House," FDR; Rochelle Chadakoff, ed., *Eleanor Roosevelt's My Day: Her Acclaimed Columns, 1936–1945,* 126.

77. Clipping, "White House Musical Program for Royal Pair Is All-American," FDR. See also Robert H. Allen, "Coon Creek Girls from the Kentucky Hills," *New York Times,* June 4, 1939, 6.

78. "Program of American Music," 3, FDR.

79. Ibid.

80. Ibid.

81. Vaillant, "Sounds of Whiteness," 38.

82. Clipping, "Last Shall Be First: Marian Anderson to Be Presented to King and Queen at White House," FDR; Clipping, "D.A.R. Head Will Mill with 1300 at Garden Party," FDR; Chadakoff, ed., *Eleanor Roosevelt's My Day,* 112.

83. Eleanor Roosevelt to Adrian Dornbush, Mar. 5, 1939, FDR.

84. Telegram, Frank S. Griffin to Mrs. Franklin D. Roosevelt, May 24, 1939, FDR. Letters against Anderson's appearance include one letter from a Ku Klux Klan member.

85. Oliver Huckel to friends, June 22, 1939, FDR.

86. Editorial, "The Roosevelts' Hospitality," *Youngstown Vindicator,* June 12, 1939, clipping in FDR.

Chapter 6: "Howdee! I'm Jes So Proud T'Be Here"

1. Clipping, "Pearls of Wisdom," *Tennessean,* Mar. 5, 1996, 4A. Choosing which name to use in this chapter is difficult since this woman had multiple names and performed multiple characters. Therefore, "Sarah" is the human being building these multiple roles, "Sarah Colley Cannon" is the offstage character, and "Minnie Pearl" is the onstage character. "Sarah Colley" is the offstage character before her marriage in 1947 to Henry Cannon.

2. "Eight Thousand Enlisted Men Pack Fort Sam Houston Service Club," *Military Service News,* Dec. 12, 1941, SCC.

3. Cannon interview tapes, #7, SCC; Sarah Cannon, "First Heckler Brought Tears, Sage Advice," "Minnie's Memories," *Nashville Banner,* June 9, 1986, Banner collection.

4. Cannon interview tapes, #7.

5. Ibid.

6. Pearl, *Minnie Pearl,* 11, 13, 16.

7. Ibid., 13.

8. Clipping, "Rites Conducted for Mrs. T. K. Colley, 88," *Hickman County Chronicle* 25, no. 2 (Aug. 29, 1963), SCC.

9. Pearl, *Minnie Pearl,* 42. Emphasis in original.

10. Lynn Spigel, *Make Room for T.V.: Television and the Family Ideal in Postwar America,* 15.

11. Pearl, *Minnie Pearl.*

12. Ibid., 43, 66, 44–45, 61.

13. Ibid., 42, 73, 96.

14. Ibid., 119.

15. Sarah Cannon, "An Alabama Country Woman Was the Model for 'Minnie,'" "Minnie's Memories," *Nashville Banner,* [no date], Banner collection; Pearl, *Minnie Pearl,* 122.

16. Ibid.

17. Sarah Cannon, "Minnie of the Early Opry Days Had a Softer, More Gentle Voice;" "Minnie's Memories," *Nashville Banner* [n.d.], Banner collection.

18. Cannon interview tapes, #7 and #8.

19. Pearl, *Minnie Pearl,* 145.

20. Cannon interview tapes, #4; Pearl, *Minnie Pearl,* 120–30.

21. Pearl, *Minnie Pearl,* 128 (emphasis in original), 129–30.

22. Thomas Colley died in 1937, and because her sisters were married with families, Sarah had to support her mother.

23. *Minnie Pearl: Old Times.*

24. Ibid.; Cannon interview tapes, #6.

25. Pearl, *Minnie Pearl,* 148.

26. Tom Roland, "Her Friends Remember Minnie's Love, Laughter," *Tennessean,* Mar. 5, 1996, 4.

27. Sarah Cannon, "Firing by Roy Acuff a Painful Memory," "Minnie's Memories," *Nashville Banner,* May 19, 1986, Banner collection; Cannon interview tapes, #6 and #7; Sarah Cannon, "Laughs Came Hard During Early Road Days," "Minnie's Memories," *Nashville Banner,* Apr. 14, 1986, no page, Banner collection.

28. Kennedy, *Freedom from Fear,* 469–70, 476–77.

29. Robert Hunt interview with McCusker.

30. Kennedy, *Freedom from Fear,* 712.

31. Tom Brokaw, *The Greatest Generation,* 288, 323. Troops were still segregated based on race, however, and to a lesser extent, on class.

32. Lange, *Smile When You Call Me Hillbilly,* 81–82.

33. *Minnie Pearl: Old Times;* Sarah Cannon, "Popularity Came Easy at Military Bases," "Minnie's Memories," *Nashville Banner,* June 2, 1986, no page, Banner collection; Cannon interview tapes, #6.

34. James Kovach to Mr. Harry T. Floyd, Jan. 17, 1949; NBC Network Order, Dec. 9, 1949; NBC Network Order, Nov. 30, 1948, NBC.

35. Tom Stewart to Mr. Tom McCray, Mar. 11, 1949; Telegram, Walter D. Scott to Mr. T. C. Shays, July 26, 1950, NBC.

36. Cannon interview tapes, #7.

37. Ibid.

38. *Minnie Pearl: Old Times.*

39. George D. Hay, "The Girl Reporter of Grinder's Switch," *Grinder's Switch Gazette,* 1, no. 1 (Sept. 1944): 1, SCC.

40. Sally Yerkovich, "Gossiping as a Way of Speaking," 192.

41. Alexander Rysman, "How the 'Gossip' Became a Woman," 179; Yerkovich, "Gossiping as a Way of Speaking," 196.

42. Ibid.

43. Wolfe, *A Good-Natured Riot,* 233, 225.

44. Ibid., 236.

45. Clipping, "Pearls of Wisdom," *Tennessean,* Mar. 5, 1996.

46. Remer Tyson and Billy Bowles, "She Didn't Always Say 'How-DEE!'" *St. Louis Globe-Democrat,* Mar. 13, 1978, B1, MPF.

47. Radio script, Prince Albert Tobacco's Grand Ole Opry, Feb. 25, 1950, SCC.

48. Radio script, ibid., Feb. 8, 1947.

49. Radio script, ibid., Jan. 4, 1947.

50. *Minnie Pearl: Old Times.*

51. Ibid.

52. Minnie Pearl Joke Collection, SCC.

53. Sarah Cannon, "Opry Folks' Results Mixed in NY Show," "Minnie's Memories," *Nashville Banner,* Dec. 29, 1986, Banner collection.

54. Radio script, Prince Albert Tobacco's Grand Ole Opry, Feb. 1, 1947, SCC.

55. Radio script, ibid., Jan. 14, 1950.

56. Radio script, ibid., May 6, 1950.

57. Radio script, ibid., June 17, 1950.

58. Minnie Pearl, "Howdy!" *Grinder's Switch Gazette* 2, no. 2 (Oct. 1945): 2, SCC.

59. Pearl, "Howdy!" *Grinder's Switch Gazette* 1, no. 7 (Mar. 1945): 2. Emphasis in original.

60. Pearl, "Howdy!" *Grinder's Switch Gazette* 2, no. 3 (Nov. 1945): 2.

61. McFadden, "'America's Boy Friend Who Can't Get a Date,'" 113–34.

62. Pearl, *Minnie Pearl,* 16.

63. *Minnie Pearl: Old Times.*

64. Clipping, "Minnie Pearl: The Girl with the Big Future," *Radio Varieties* (Jan. 1941): 19, SCC.

65. Ibid.

66. Clipping, "College Graduate Scores on 'Opry' as Girl Hillbilly," *Record Roundup* (1947), MPF.

67. Clipping, society page engagements, *Tennessean,* Feb. 16, 1947.

68. Minnie Pearl, "Up in the Air with Minnie," *Country Song Roundup* 1, no. 7 (Aug. 1950): 12, SCC.

69. Paul Bryant, "The Belle of Grinder's Switch," *Mountain Broadcast and Prairie Recorder* (Oct. 1946): 8, SCC.

70. *Minnie Pearl,* Everest Records T90475, MSA.

71. "For Sale!—'Minnie Pearl,'" *Grinder's Switch Gazette* 2, no. 1 (Sept. 1945): 1–2, SCC.

72. Sarah Ophelia Cannon, *Minnie Pearl's Diary,* introduction page; clipping, "One of 11 Closed Chicken Shops" (July 20, 1970), CMHOF.

73. Minnie Pearl, *Minnie Pearl Cooks.*

74. Eleanor Nance Hamilton, "That Minnie Pearl Is Political Dynamite," SCC.

75. Ed Cony, "Alabama Hoedown: Few Issues Split Them so Governor Candidates Lean on Hillbilly Music," *Wall Street Journal,* May 6, 1958, SCC.

76. Five photographs, SCC; Dan T. Carter, *The Politics of Rage: George Wallace, the Origins of the New Conservatism, and the Transformation of American Politics,* 90, 105.

77. "Pearls of Wisdom."

78. http://www.minniepearl.org.

79. Bob Allen, "The Two Faces of Sarah Cannon," *Nashville! Magazine* 8, no. 7 (Oct. 1980): MPF.

Chapter 7: *"Oh Carry Me Back to the Mountains"*

1. Maphis I; Maphis II.

2. Maphis II.

3. Rose refused to say how old she was. This is the best guess based on clues she gave me.

4. Maphis I.

5. Maphis II.

6. Ibid.

7. Maphis I.

8. Ibid.

9. Ibid.

10. Ibid.

11. Maphis II.

12. Ibid.

13. Maphis I.

14. Ibid.

15. Ibid.

16. Violet and Aline Flannery to John Lair, Feb. 12, 1933, JLP.

17. Malone, *Country Music, U.S.A.,* 18.

18. High, *Past Titan Rock,* 94.

19. WLS *Family Album,* 1934, 42, JLP; Clipping, Evelyn Lange Perry Scrapbook, CMHOF.

20. Perkins interview; clipping, Perry Scrapbook.

21. Perkins interview; Green, "Kitty Wells: The Queen Still Reigns," 41–44.

22. Maphis I.

23. *Cousin Emmy Song Book,* 1939, JLP.

24. "Cousin Emmy," *Time,* December 6, 1943, 62.

25. Cousin Emmy to Mr. Lair, Aug. 1937, JLP.

26. Cousin Emmy to John Lair, Feb. 11, 1941, JLP.

27. This union is now the American Federation of Theater and Radio Artists, or AFTRA.

28. Mrs. Thomas Shumate to Mr. John Lair, Feb. 9, 1941, JLP.

29. Betty Callahan Baker interview with Rice.

30. Charles Wolfe, "Up North with the Blue Ridge Ramblers: Jennie Bowman's 1931 Tour Diary," 138.

31. Ibid.

32. Ibid., 136–45.

33. Minnie Pearl with Susan G., "In the Good Old Days (When Times Were Bad)," 6.

34. Wolfe, "Up North with the Blue Ridge Ramblers," 136–45.

35. Maphis II.

36. Ledford autobiography, Aug. 1936, 9.

37. Montana, *The Cowboy's Sweetheart*, 73.

38. Russell and Wolfe, "Two Cowgirls on the Lone Prairie."

39. Photo Collection, CMHOF; Keystone Fence, "Meet the Radio Folks," [ca. early 1940s], JLP.

40. Maphis II.

41. Ledford sisters interview.

42. Maphis I.

43. Maphis II.

44. Lair to Glenn Hughes, Feb. 5, 1941, JLP.

45. Lightfoot, "From Radio Queen to Raleigh," 6.

46. Jo and Wayne Midkiff interview with Rice.

47. John Lair to Leonard, Apr. 3, 1941, JLP.

48. Ricca to Mr. Lair, Apr. 18, 1941, JLP.

49. Lair to Leonard, Apr. 3, 1941, JLP.

50. Lair to Leonard, Apr. 16, 1941, JLP.

51. Maphis I.

52. Baker interview.

53. Susan Porter Benson, *Counter Cultures: Saleswomen, Managers, and Customers in American Department Stores, 1890–1940*, 228.

54. Marjorie Gibson, "Fanfare," *Stand By!* 3, no. 3 (Feb. 13, 1937): 7.

55. Ibid.

56. Maphis II.

57. Ibid.

58. Ledford autobiography, Aug. 1936, 3–5.

59. Lightfoot, "From Radio Queen to Raleigh," 6.

60. Clipping, Jack Hurst, "Barn Dance Days," *Chicago Tribune Magazine* (Aug. 5, 1984): 8–13, 15, CMHOF.

61. Ledford autobiography, Aug. 1936, 13.

62. Ibid., 40.

63. Maphis I.

64. John Lair to Miss Juanita Dooley, Feb. 6, 1941, JLP.

65. Hoke Rice to John Lair, Mar. 18, 1941, JLP.

66. John Lair to Shorty Hobbs, June 4, 1942, JLP.

67. Cremer interview.

68. Pearl, "In the Good Old Days," 6.

69. Lightfoot, "Belle of the Barn Dance," 15.

70. Maphis I.

71. *Minnie Pearl: Old Times.*

72. W. M. Ellsworth to Lair, June 15, 1942, JLP.
73. Gene Cobb to John Lair, Nov. 2, 1943, JLP.
74. Video, *Women in Country Music,* CBS, Jan. 1992.
75. Maphis I.
76. Maphis II.
77. Maphis I.
78. "Cousin Emmy."
79. W. M. Ellsworth to John Lair, Feb. 13, 1941, JLP.
80. Maphis I.
81. Ibid.
82. Maphis II.
83. Maphis I.
84. Ibid.
85. Lightfoot, "From Radio Queen to Raleigh," 7. Emphasis in original.
86. Pearl, *Minnie Pearl,* 156.
87. Maphis II.
88. Ibid.
89. Maphis I.
90. Ibid.
91. Ibid.
92. Ibid.
93. Maphis II.
94. *Heroes of Country Music: Legends of the West Coast.*
95. Maphis II.
96. Ledford autobiography, Aug. 1936, 80.
97. Peter La Chapelle, "'Spade Doesn't Look Exactly Starved': Country Music and the Negotiation of Women's Domesticity in Cold War Los Angeles," 32–33.
98. Rose Lee and Joe Maphis, *Rose Lee and Joe Maphis with the Blue Ridge Boys;* Rose Lee Maphis, *Rose Lee Maphis.*
99. Rose Lee and Joe Maphis, *Rose Lee and Joe Maphis with the Blue Ridge Boys.*

Coda

1. Kathy Mattea, *Lonesome Standard Time;* Loretta Lynn, *Loretta Lynn: Country Music Hall of Fame Series.*
2. Bufwack and Oermann, *Finding Her Voice,* 262–69.
3. Loretta Lynn with George Vecsey, *Loretta Lynn: Coal Miner's Daughter,* 56.
4. Bufwack and Oermann, "Songs of Self-Assertion," 3, CMHOF.
5. Samuelson, "Linda Parker."
6. Ibid. Cemetery records listed Muenich under her married name (Jeanne Muenich Janes), not her stage name, hence the difficulty finding the grave site.
7. Lightfoot, "From Radio Queen to Raleigh," 3–9.

8. Bufwack and Oermann, *Finding Her Voice,* 97.

9. Russell and Wolfe, "Two Cowgirls on the Lone Prairie."

10. Jamie Gerth to Ronnie Pugh, MPF.

11. Editorial cartoon, *Tennessean,* Mar. 6, 1996, MPF.

12. Maphis I.

13. Ibid.

14. Ledford autobiography, Aug. 1936, 78.

15. Ibid., 88–89.

16. Ibid.

17. Cari Norris, "Lily May Ledford as 'Traditional Artist.'"

18. Lynn, *Loretta Lynn,* 115.

19. Ibid., 77.

20. Ibid., 55.

BIBLIOGRAPHY

Published Sources

Anderson, Benedict. *Imagined Communities.* London: Verso, 1991.

Aquila, Richard. "A Blaze of Glory: The Mythic West in Pop and Rock Music." In *Wanted Dead or Alive: The American West in Popular Culture.* Ed. Richard Aquila. 191–215. Urbana: University of Illinois Press.

Becker, Jane S. *Selling Tradition: Appalachia and the Construction of an American Folk, 1930–1940.* Chapel Hill: University of North Carolina Press, 1998.

Benson, Susan Porter. *Counter Cultures: Saleswomen, Managers, and Customers in American Department Stores, 1890–1940.* Urbana: University of Illinois Press, 1986.

Berry, Chad C. "Social Highways: Southern White Migrants to the Midwest, 1910–1990." Ph.D. diss., Indiana University, 1995.

Biggar, George C. "The WLS National Barn Dance Story: The Early Years." *John Edwards Memorial Foundation Quarterly* 7, no. 3 (Autumn 1971): 105–12.

Brokaw, Tom. *The Greatest Generation.* New York: Random House, 1998.

Bufwack, Mary. "The Feminist Sensibility in Post-War Country Music." *Southern Quarterly* 22, no. 3 (Spring 1984): 135–44.

Bufwack, Mary, and Robert K. Oermann. *Finding Her Voice: Women in Country Music.* Nashville: Vanderbilt University Press and the Country Music Foundation, 1993, 2003.

Cannon, Sarah Ophelia. *Minnie Pearl's Diary.* New York: Greenberg Press, 1953.

Cantril, Hadley, and Gordon W. Allport. *The Psychology of Radio.* 1935. Reprint, New York: Arno Press, 1971.

Carlin, Richard. *Country Music: A Biographical Dictionary.* New York: Routledge, 1995.

Carter, Dan T. *The Politics of Rage: George Wallace, the Origins of the New Conservatism, and the Transformation of American Politics.* 2nd ed. Baton Rouge: Louisiana State University, 2000.

Chadakoff, Rochelle, ed. *Eleanor Roosevelt's My Day: Her Acclaimed Columns, 1936–1945.* New York: Pharos Books, 1989.

Cohen, Lizabeth. *Making a New Deal: Industrial Workers in Chicago, 1919–1930.* Cambridge: Cambridge University Press, 1990.

Coon Creek Girls. *Early Radio Favorites.* Old Homestead Records.

Cooper, Patricia. "The Faces of Gender: Sex Segregation and Work Relations at Philco, 1928–1938." In *Work Engendered: Toward a New History of American Labor.* Ed. Ava Baron. 320–50. Ithaca, N.Y.: Cornell University Press, 1991.

Daniel, Wayne. "Lulu Belle and Scotty: 'Have I Told You Lately That I Love You?'" *Bluegrass Unlimited* 20, no. 9 (March 1986): 70–76.

Douglas, Susan J. *Inventing American Broadcasting, 1899–1922.* Baltimore, M.D.: Johns Hopkins University Press, 1987.

———. *Listening In: Radio and the American Imagination.* New York: Times Books, 1999.

Dudden, Faye. *Women in American Theater: Actresses and Audiences, 1790–1870.* New Haven, Conn.: Yale University Press, 1994.

Ellis, William. "The Sentimental Mother Song in American Country Music, 1923–1945." Ph.D. diss., Ohio State University, 1978.

Filene, Benjamin. *Romancing the Folk: Public Memory and American Roots Music.* Chapel Hill: University of North Carolina Press, 2000.

Gaston, Kay Baker. *Emma Bell Miles.* Signal Mountain, Tenn.: Walden's Ridge Historical Association, 1985.

Glenn, Susan A. *Female Spectacle: The Theatrical Roots of Modern Feminism.* Cambridge, Mass.: Harvard University Press, 2000.

Green, Archie. "Hillbilly Music: Source and Symbol." *Journal of American Folklore* 78, no. 309 (July-September 1965): 205–28.

Green, Douglas B. "Kitty Wells: The Queen Still Reigns." *Journal of Country Music* 8, no. 9 (June 1980): 41–44.

———. *Singing in the Saddle: The History of the Singing Cowboy.* Nashville: Vanderbilt University Press and the Country Music Foundation, 2002.

Gregory, James N. *American Exodus: The Dust Bowl Migration and Okie Culture in California.* New York: Oxford University Press, 1989.

Grundy, Pamela. "We Always Tried to Be Good People: Respectability, Crazy Water Crystals, and Hillbilly Music on the Air, 1933–1935." *Journal of American History* 81, no. 4 (March 1995): 1591–1620.

Hagerty, Bernard G. "WNAX: Country Music on a Rural Radio Station, 1927–1955." *John Edwards Memorial Foundation Quarterly* 11, no. 4 (Winter 1975): 177–82.

Hall, Jacquelyn Dowd. "Disorderly Women: Gender and Labor Militancy in the Appalachian South." In *Unequal Sisters: A Multicultural Reader in U.S. Women's History.* Ed. Ellen Carol DuBois and Vicki L. Ruiz. 298–321. New York: Routledge, 1990.

Hall, Jacquelyn Dowd, James Leloudis, Robert Korstad, Mary Murphy, Christopher B. Daly, and Lu Ann Jones. *Like a Family: The Making of a Southern Cotton Mill World.* Chapel Hill: University of North Carolina Press, 1987.

Harkins, Anthony. *Hillbilly: A Cultural History of an American Icon.* New York: Oxford University Press, 2004.

Henderson, Ann Lair. *On the Air with John Lair.* Mt. Vernon, Ky.: Polly House Productions, 1998.

Henderson, Jerry Eugene. "A History of the Ryman Auditorium in Nashville, Tennessee: 1892–1920." Ph.D. diss., Louisiana State University, 1962.

Heroes of Country Music: Legends of the West Coast, vol. 4, Rhino, R2 72443/S1X 18273, 1996.

Hettinger, Herman S. *A Decade of Radio Advertising.* 1933. Reprint, New York: Arno Press, 1971.

High, Ellesa Clay. "The Coon Creek Girl from Red River Gorge: An Interview with Lily May Pennington." *Adena* 2, no. 1 (Spring 1977): 44–74.

———. *Past Titan Rock: Journeys into an Appalachian Valley.* Lexington: University Press of Kentucky, 1984.

Jones, Loyal. *Radio's "Kentucky Mountain Boy" Bradley Kincaid.* Berea, Ky.: Appalachian Center/Berea College, 1980.

———. "Who Is Bradley Kincaid?" *John Edwards Memorial Foundation Quarterly* 12, no. 43 (Autumn 1976): 122–37.

Karl and Harty. *Karl and Harty with the Cumberland Ridge Runners.* Old Homestead Records.

Kennedy, David M. *Freedom from Fear: The American People in Depression and War, 1929–1945.* New York: Oxford University Press, 1999.

Kibler, M. Allison. *Rank Ladies: Gender and Cultural Hierarchy in American Vaudeville.* Chapel Hill: University of North Carolina Press, 1999.

Kimball, Warren F. *Forged in War: Roosevelt, Churchill, and the Second World War.* New York: William Morrow, 1997.

Kingsbury, Paul, ed. *The Encyclopedia of Country Music: The Ultimate Guide to the Music.* New York: Oxford University Press, 1998.

Kirby, Jack Temple. "The Southern Exodus, 1910–1960." *Journal of Southern History* 49 (November 1983): 585–600.

Kwolek-Folland, Angel. *Engendering Business: Men and Women in the Corporate Office, 1870–1930.* Baltimore, M.D.: Johns Hopkins University Press, 1994.

La Chapelle, Peter. "'Spade Doesn't Look Exactly Starved': Country Music and the Negotiation of Women's Domesticity in Cold War Los Angeles." In *A Boy Named Sue: Gender and Country.* Ed. Kristine M. McCusker and Diane Pecknold. 24–43. Jackson: University Press of Mississippi, 2004.

Lair, John. *Renfro Valley Then and Now.* 1957. Reprint, Mt. Vernon, Ky.: Polly House Productions, 1992.

Lane, Geoff. "The Queen of Country Music." *Country Music* 3, no. 3 (December 1974): 40–45.

Lange, Jeffrey. *Smile When You Call Me Hillbilly: Country Music's Struggle for Respectability, 1939–1954.* Athens: University of Georgia Press, 2004.

Laws, G. Malcom, Jr. *Native American Balladry: A Descriptive Study and a Bibliographic Syllabus.* Philadelphia: American Folklore Society, 1964.

Lears, T. J. Jackson. "The Rise of American Advertising." *Wilson Quarterly* 7 (Winter 1983): 157.

Lightfoot, William E. "The Belle of the Barn Dance: Reminiscing with Lulu Belle Wiseman Stamey." *Journal of Country Music* 12, no. 1 (1987): 2–15.

———. "From Radio Queen to Raleigh: Conversations with Lulu Belle." *Old Time Country Music* 6, no. 2 (1989): 4–10.

———. "From Radio Queen to Raleigh: Conversations with Lulu Belle, Part 2." *Old Time Country Music* 6, no. 3 (1989): 3–9.

Linn, Karen. *That Half-Barbaric Twang: The Banjo in American Popular Culture.* Urbana: University of Illinois Press, 1991.

Lynn, Loretta. *Loretta Lynn: Country Music Hall of Fame Series.* MCA, MCAD-10083, 1991.

Lynn, Loretta, with George Vecsey. *Loretta Lynn: Coal Miner's Daughter.* Chicago: Henry Regnery, 1976.

Malone, Bill C. *Country Music, U.S.A.* Austin: University of Texas Press, 1985, 2003.

———. *Don't Get above Your Raisin': Country Music and the Southern Working Class.* Urbana: University of Illinois Press, 2002.

Maphis, Rose Lee. *Rose Lee Maphis.* Columbia Records, CL1598, 1961.

Maphis, Rose Lee, and Joe Maphis. *Rose Lee and Joe Maphis with the Blue Ridge Boys.* Capitol Records, T1778, 1962.

Marchand, Roland. *Advertising the American Dream: Making Way for Modernity, 1920–1940.* Berkeley: University of California Press, 1988.

"Materials toward a Study of Early Country Music on Radio, IV. Dallas, Texas." *John Edwards Memorial Foundation Quarterly* 5, no. 14, pt. 2 (Summer 1969): 61–62.

Mattea, Kathy. *Lonesome Standard Time.* Polygram Records, P2–12567, 1992.

McCracken, Allison. "'God's Gift to Us Girls': Crooning, Gender, and the Re-Creation of American Popular Song, 1928–1933." *American Music* 17, no. 4 (Winter 1999): 365–95.

McCullough, David. *Truman.* New York: Simon and Schuster, 1992.

McCusker, Kristine M. "'Bury Me beneath the Willow': Linda Parker and Definitions of Tradition on the National Barn Dance." *Southern Folklore* 56, no. 3 (1999): 223–44.

———. "Dear Radio Friend: Listener Mail and the National Barn Dance, 1931–1941." *American Studies* 39, no. 2 (Summer 1998): 173–95.

———. "Rose Maphis and Working on Barn Dance Radio, 1930–1960." In *The Women of Country Music: A Reader.* Ed. Charles K. Wolfe and James E. Akenson. 61–74. Lexington: University Press of Kentucky, 2003.

McFadden, Margaret T. "'America's Boy Friend Who Can't Get a Date': Gender,

Race, and the Cultural Work of the Jack Benny Program, 1932–1946." *Journal of American History* 80, no. 1 (June 1993): 113–34.

Miles, Emma Bell. *Spirit of the Mountains.* 1905. Reprint, Knoxville: University of Tennessee Press, 1975.

Minnie Pearl. Everest Records T90475, MSA.

Minnie Pearl: Old Times. Video produced by Opryland USA, 1988.

Montana, Patsy, with Jane Frost. *The Cowboy's Sweetheart: Patsy Montana.* Jefferson, N.C.: McFarland Press, 2002.

Morton, David C., and Charles Wolfe. "DeFord Bailey: They Turned Me Loose to Root Hog or Die." *Journal of Country Music* 14, no. 2 (1992): 13–17.

Neal, Jocelyn. "Why It Took a Man's Song to Make a Woman's Career: Dolly Parton and Artistic Independence." Paper presented at the annual meeting of the Organization of American Historians, Memphis, Tennessee, April 6, 2003.

Norris, Cari. "Lily May Ledford as 'Traditional Artist,'" Kentucky Folkweb, http://www.wku.edu/kentuckyfolkweb/KYFolklife/KYFolklife_Ledford.html (accessed April 27, 2005).

"Otto Gray and his Oklahoma Cowboys." *John Edwards Memorial Foundation Quarterly.* 1, no. 2 (Summer 1971): 2.

Parker, R. A. C. *Chamberlain and Appeasement: British Policy and the Coming of the Second World War.* New York: St. Martin's Press, 1993.

Pearl, Minnie. *Minnie Pearl Cooks.* 1970. Rev. ed., Nashville: Aurora Publishers, 1971.

Pearl, Minnie, with Joan Dew. *Minnie Pearl: An Autobiography.* New York: Simon and Schuster, 1980.

Pearl, Minnie, with Susan G. "In the Good Old Days (When Times Were Bad)." *Journal of Country Music* 13, no. 3 (1990): 4–6.

Peiss, Kathy. *Hope in a Jar: The Making of America's Beauty Culture.* New York: Metropolitan, 1998.

Peterson, Richard A. *Creating Country Music: Fabricating Authenticity.* Chicago: University of Chicago Press, 1997.

Rice, Harry. "Renfro Valley on the Radio, 1937–1941." *Journal of Country Music* 19, no. 2 (1997): 16–25.

Rosenberg, Emily S. *Spreading the American Dream: American Economic and Cultural Expansion, 1890–1945.* New York: Hill and Wang, 1982.

Russell, Tony, and Charles Wolfe. "Two Cowgirls on the Lone Prairie." *Old Time Music* 43 (Winter 1986/87): 161–68.

Rysman, Alexander. "How the 'Gossip' Became a Woman." *Journal of Communication* 27, no. 1 (Winter 1977): 176–80.

Samuelson, Dave. "Linda Parker: The WLS Sunbonnet Girl." *Journal of the American Academy for the Preservation of Old-Time Country Music* 30 (December 1995): 16–17.

Scarborough, Dorothy. *A Song Catcher in the Southern Mountains.* New York: Columbia University Press, 1937.

Schofield, Ann. *To Do and to Be: Portraits of Four Women Activists, 1893–1986.* Boston: Northeastern University Press, 1997.

Shapiro, Henry. *Appalachia on Our Mind: The Southern Mountains and Mountaineers in the American Consciousness, 1890–1920.* Chapel Hill: University of North Carolina Press, 1978.

Sharp, Cecil, and Maud Karpeles. *Eighty English Folk Songs from the Southern Appalachians.* Cambridge, Mass.: MIT Press, 1968.

Slotkin, Richard. *Gunfighter Nation: The Myth of the Frontier in Twentieth Century America.* New York: Harper Perennial, 1993.

Smulyan, Susan. "The National Barn Dance, Early Broadcasting, and Radio Audiences." In *The Hayloft Gang.* Ed. Chad Berry. 1–20. Urbana: University of Illinois Press, forthcoming.

———. *Selling Radio: The Commercialization of American Broadcasting, 1920–1934.* Washington, D.C.: Smithsonian Institution Press, 1995.

Sochen, June. "Mildred Pierce and Women in Film." *American Quarterly* 30, no. 1 (Spring 1978): 3–78.

Spigel, Lynn. *Make Room for T.V.: Television and the Family Ideal in Postwar America.* Chicago: University of Chicago Press, 1992.

Stamp, Shelley. *Movie-Struck Girls: Women and Motion Picture Culture after the Nickelodeon.* Princeton, N.J.: Princeton University Press, 2000.

Vaillant, Derek W. "Sounds of Whiteness: Local Radio, Racial Formation, and Public Culture in Chicago, 1921–1935." *American Quarterly* 54, no. 1 (2002): 25–66.

Whisnant, David. *All That Is Native and Fine: The Politics of Culture in an American Region.* Chapel Hill: University of North Carolina Press, 1983.

Wiggins, Gene. *Fiddlin' Georgia Crazy: Fiddlin' John Carson, His Real World, and the World of His Songs.* Urbana: University of Illinois Press, 1987.

Wilgus, D. K., and Nathan Hurvitz. "Bradley Kincaid." In *Stars of Country Music.* Ed. Bill C. Malone and Judith C. McCulloh. 86–94. Urbana: University of Illinois Press, 1975.

Wolfe, Charles. *A Good-Natured Riot: The Birth of the Grand Ole Opry.* Nashville: Vanderbilt University Press and the Country Music Foundation, 1999.

———. "Up North with the Blue Ridge Ramblers: Jennie Bowman's 1931 Tour Diary." *Journal of Country Music* 6, no. 3 (Fall 1975): 136–45.

Women in Country Music. Television special, CBS, January 1992.

Yarger, Lisa. "Banjo Pickin' Girl: Representing Lily May Ledford." M.A. thesis, University of North Carolina, Chapel Hill, 1997.

Yerkovich, Sally. "Gossiping as a Way of Speaking." *Journal of Communication* 27, no. 1 (Winter 1977): 192–96.

Young, Iris Marion. "The Ideal of Community and the Politics of Difference." In *Feminism/Postmodern.* Ed. Linda J. Nicholson. 300–324. New York: Routledge, 1989.

Oral Interviews

Baker, Betty Callahan, to Harry Rice. Taped interview, April 12, 1995. Southern Appalachian Collection.

Cremer, Beth, to unknown interviewer. Taped interview, January 16, 1969. Southern Appalachian Collection.

Foley, Rosie Ledford, Minnie Ledford, and Lily May Ledford Pennington (Ledford sisters) to Dave Freeman and Charles Faurot. Transcribed interview, September 1966. Southern Folklife Collection, Manuscripts Department, Wilson Library, University of North Carolina, Chapel Hill, North Carolina.

Henderson, Ann Lair, to Kristine M. McCusker. Telephone interview, January 4, 1999.

Hunt, Robert, to Kristine M. McCusker. Oral interview, May 26, 2005.

Lair, John, to Reuben Powell. Transcribed interview, October 26, 1967. Southern Appalachian Collection.

Maphis, Rose Lee, to Kristine M. McCusker. Taped interview, May 19, 1998. Center for Popular Music, Middle Tennessee State University, Murfreesboro, Tenn.

Maphis, Rose Lee, to Kristine M. McCusker. Taped interview, March 24, 1999. Center for Popular Music, Middle Tennessee State University, Murfreesboro, Tenn.

McCluskey, Milly Good, to Charles Wolfe. Transcribed interview, April 20, 1978.

Midkiff, Jo and Wayne, to Harry Rice. Taped interview, August 2, 1996. Southern Appalachian Collection.

Norris, Cari, to Kristine M. McCusker. Telephone interview, November 9, 1998.

Perkins, Judy, to Harry Rice. Taped interview, September 10, 1996. Southern Appalachian Collection.

Smith, Jane, to Kristine M. McCusker. Oral interview, July 20, 2005.

Web Sites

Arthurdale Heritage, Inc., http://www.arthurdaleheritage.org (accessed June 23, 2006).

http://www.icdc.com/~fmoore/carterfamily/single_girl.htm (accessed December 27, 2006).

"Bob Hope and American Variety," Library of Congress Exhibitions, http://www.loc.gov/exhibits/bobhope (accessed March 15, 2006).

Minnie Pearl Cancer Foundation, http://www.minniepearl.org (accessed June 23, 2006).

INDEX

120; southerners and, 106–7; technology and, 118–19
Pearl Harbor, Hawaii, 103, 111
Peer, Ralph, 60
Peiss, Kathy, 39
Perkins, Judy, 42, 128
personal pitch, 80. *See also* crooning, 80
personals, 129–31, 144. *See also* work culture
pianos, 106
"Pill, The," 151
"Pinchemtite Holler" (fictional location), 91, 100
Pine Mountain Merrymakers, 80–81
Pinex Cough Syrup, 58; mountain life and, 92; Pine Mountain Merrymakers and, 80–81; westerners and, 68, 78–80
pioneers, 35, 36; Ledford and, 90; mountain life and, 94
Play Party Frolic, The (radio program), 45, 47
"Pop Goes the Weasel," 127
poverty, 97–98; rural life and, 35; Wiseman and, 54. *See also* Great Depression
Prairie Farmer (magazine), 56; audience and, 62
Prairie Ramblers, 31, 60; Atchinson and, 77
pregnancy, 135
Prince Albert's Tobacco, 112, 119
print media, 57
promiscuity, 139–40, 144
Protestant work ethic, 72
public service, 66

race, 17, 64–65; folk music and, 100; *Grand Ole Opry* and, 21; national identity and, 84, 100–102. *See also* African Americans
Racherbaumer, Rocky, 65
Radio Digest: Wiseman and, 55
"Radio Queen" title: Wiseman and, 55
Radio Varieties (magazine), 120
Randolph Field (San Antonio, Tex.), 103
Reagan, Ronald, 122
Record Roundup (magazine), 120
Red River Gorge, Ky.: Ledford and, 82, 84; mountain life and, 87, 92, 95
Red River Ramblers, 87–88
reform, 27. *See also* New Deal

Renfro Valley, Ky., 130; automobiles and, 93; country music and, 150; folk music and, 100
Renfro Valley Barn Dance, 11, 40–42, 45; advertisers and, 61; Girls of the Golden West and, 71; Ledford and, 98; mountain life and, 87, 93–94; working culture and, 132, 134
Renfro Valley Boys, 59
Rice Brothers and Gang, 138
R. J. Reynolds, 110
Robinson, Mary, 141–42
Rochester, Indiana, 87
Rodgers, Jimmie, 76–77, 126; mountain life and, 92; national identity and, 85; yodeling and, 71
Roosevelt, Eleanor, 82–84, 97–98; national identity and, 100–102
Roosevelt, Franklin Delano, 3, 36, 82–84, 97–99, 111; national identity and, 100–102
Rosie the Riveter, 105
"Royal Telephone, The," 126
rural life, 3, 35, 117–18, 120; Alka Seltzer and, 59; audience and, 9; Girls of the Golden West and, 69; migrants and, 19, 38, 41–42; musical skill and, 128; national identity and, 85; nature and, 118; urban life and, 113; vaudeville and, 11
Rural Radio (magazine), 114
Rush, Ford, 104
Russians, 143
Rutledge, Charlie, 34
Ryman Theater, 9, 13

Saddle Sweethearts, 135, 139–42
Samuelson, Dave, 148
San Antonio, Tex., 103
San Antonio Rose (stage performer), 112
Sarie and Sally, 114–15
savages, 35–36, 143
Schetrompf, Doris. *See* Maphis, Rose Lee
Schmeling, Max, 99
scientific advertising, 69–70, 78–81. *See also* advertising
Scotland, 17, 23; ballads of, 37
Scruggs, Earl, 89
Sears, Roebuck Company, 18
Seattle, Wash., 113
secularism, 36

Kristine M. McCusker is an associate professor of history at Middle Tennessee State University. She is coeditor of *A Boy Named Sue: Gender and Country Music* and has published articles in *Southern Folklore* and *Journal of American Studies.*

Music in American Life

Only a Miner: Studies in Recorded Coal-Mining Songs   *Archie Green*
Great Day Coming: Folk Music and the American Left   *R. Serge Denisoff*
John Philip Sousa: A Descriptive Catalog of His Works   *Paul E. Bierley*
The Hell-Bound Train: A Cowboy Songbook   *Glenn Ohrlin*
Oh, Didn't He Ramble: The Life Story of Lee Collins, as Told to Mary Collins
    Edited by Frank J. Gillis and John W. Miner
American Labor Songs of the Nineteenth Century   *Philip S. Foner*
Stars of Country Music: Uncle Dave Macon to Johnny Rodriguez   *Edited by*
    Bill C. Malone and Judith McCulloh
Git Along, Little Dogies: Songs and Songmakers of the American West
    John I. White
A Texas-Mexican *Cancionero:* Folksongs of the Lower Border   *Américo Paredes*
San Antonio Rose: The Life and Music of Bob Wills   *Charles R. Townsend*
Early Downhome Blues: A Musical and Cultural Analysis   *Jeff Todd Titon*
An Ives Celebration: Papers and Panels of the Charles Ives Centennial Festival-
    Conference   *Edited by H. Wiley Hitchcock and Vivian Perlis*
Sinful Tunes and Spirituals: Black Folk Music to the Civil War   *Dena J. Epstein*
Joe Scott, the Woodsman-Songmaker   *Edward D. Ives*
Jimmie Rodgers: The Life and Times of America's Blue Yodeler
    Nolan Porterfield
Early American Music Engraving and Printing: A History of Music
    Publishing in America from 1787 to 1825, with Commentary on Earlier
    and Later Practices   *Richard J. Wolfe*
Sing a Sad Song: The Life of Hank Williams   *Roger M. Williams*
Long Steel Rail: The Railroad in American Folksong   *Norm Cohen*
Resources of American Music History: A Directory of Source Materials from
    Colonial Times to World War II   *D. W. Krummel, Jean Geil, Doris J. Dyen,*
    and Deane L. Root
Tenement Songs: The Popular Music of the Jewish Immigrants   *Mark Slobin*
Ozark Folksongs   *Vance Randolph; edited and abridged by Norm Cohen*
Oscar Sonneck and American Music   *Edited by William Lichtenwanger*
Bluegrass Breakdown: The Making of the Old Southern Sound   *Robert Cantwell*
Bluegrass: A History   *Neil V. Rosenberg*
Music at the White House: A History of the American Spirit   *Elise K. Kirk*
Red River Blues: The Blues Tradition in the Southeast   *Bruce Bastin*
Good Friends and Bad Enemies: Robert Winslow Gordon and the Study of
    American Folksong   *Debora Kodish*
Fiddlin' Georgia Crazy: Fiddlin' John Carson, His Real World, and the World of
    His Songs   *Gene Wiggins*

The University of Illinois Press
is a founding member of the
Association of American University Presses.

_____

Composed in 9.7/13 ITC Cheltenham
with Ultra Condensed display
by Jim Proefrock
at the University of Illinois Press
Designed by Dennis Roberts
Manufactured by Cushing-Malloy, Inc.

University of Illinois Press
1325 South Oak Street
Champaign, IL 61820-6903
www.press.uillinois.edu